Around the World
in a
Green Goddess

by
MURIEL L. KILVERT

BOLTON & PRICE
2004

First Edition 2004

ISBN 0 9527364 1 1

BOLTON & PRICE
"OakHaven" Sproughton
Ipswich, Suffolk IP8 3BA

Printed by Print Wright, Boss Hall, Ipswich

Contents

World Route Map

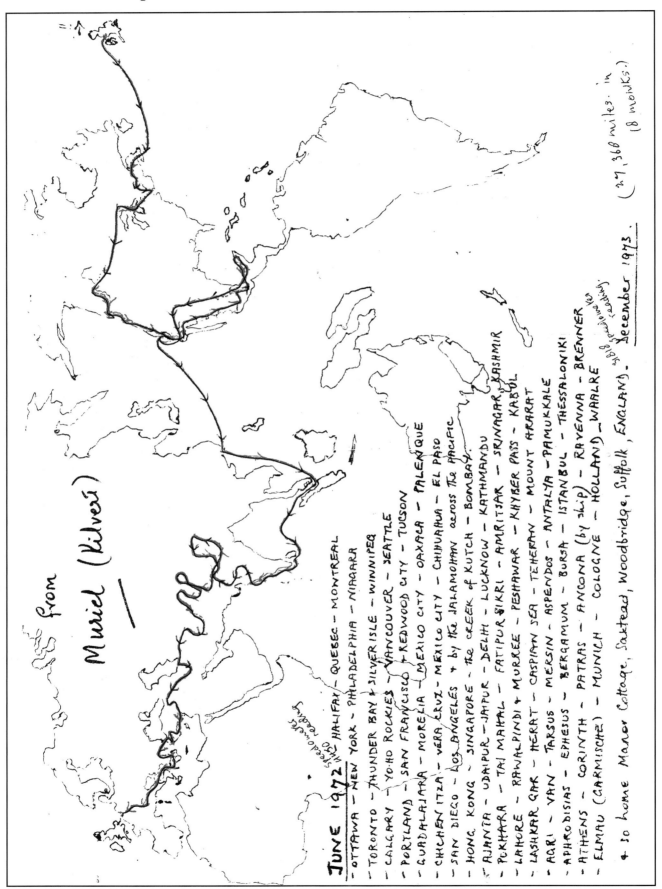

from

Muriel (Kilvert)
—————

JUNE 1972 HALIFAX – QUEBEC – MONTREAL
– OTTAWA – NEW YORK – PHILADELPHIA – NIAGARA
– TORONTO – THUNDER BAY & SILVER ISLE – WINNIPEG
– CALGARY – YOHO ROCKIES – VANCOUVER – SEATTLE
– PORTLAND – SAN FRANCISCO & REDWOOD CITY – TUSON
– GUADALAJARA – MORELIA – MEXICO CITY – OAXACA – PALENQUE
– CHICHEN ITZA – VERA CRUZ – MEXICO CITY – CHIHUAHUA – EL PASO
– SAN DIEGO – LOS ANGELES ✦ by the JALAMOHAN across the PACIFIC
– HONG KONG – SINGAPORE – the CREEK of KUTCH – BOMBAY.
– AJANTA – UDAIPUR – JAIPUR – DELHI – LUCKNOW – KATHMANDU
– POKHARA – TAJ MAHAL – FATIPUR SIKRI – AMRITSAR – SRINAGAR, KASHMIR
– LAHORE – RAWALPINDI & MURREE – PESHAWAR – KHYBER PASS – KABUL
– LASHKAR GAH – HERAT – CASPIAN SEA – TEHERAN – MOUNT ARARAT
– AGRI – VAN – TARSUS – MERSIN – ASPENDOS – ANTALYA – PAMUKKALE
– APHRODISIAS – EPHESUS – BERGAMUM – BURSA – ISTANBUL – THESSALONIKI
– ATHENS – CORINTH – PATRAS – ANCONA (by ship) – RAVENNA – BRENNER
– ELMAU (GARMISCHE) – MUNICH – COLOGNE – HOLLAND) WAALRE

✦ so home Manor Cottage, Saxtead, Woodbridge, Suffolk, England.

December 1973.

(27,360 miles. in
(8 months.)

Dedication

My dear Great Uncle Frank, Soon it will be 100 years since you made the last entry in your diary. I sometimes wonder, if you wrote it as a record or just for yourself. I wonder what you would think if you knew that hundreds of people now own copies of an edited version; that parts of it are read over the wireless, to the world at large; and that John Betjeman, when Poet Laureate, appeared on television in an appreciation and appraisal of you and your writing. You wrote with such immediacy that you made it possible for us to walk with you on your daily round, and for us to appreciate what you saw and what you felt. I feel that I have shared with you something of your joy of the country in the early morning light or on cold winter nights, when frosts have clung to the hedgerows, and appeared as lace under the sharp clear light of a full moon. I feel that I know more of my relations, and that I have been introduced to your friends and acquaintances when for example, you played croquet or went out to dinner and made your "... *homeward journeys under the stars, glittering frosty and keen*"; or that I have drunk claret and eaten grapes with you and your friends on a picnic and have stood with you and the old soldier as you and he dug his potatoes. Your writing is so vivid, vital and vibrant that had you lived to old age, I believe you never could have become a boring old man! Like you, I love being alone with nature.　　I would love to have seen what you would have written about Yellowstone Park, in the USA had you been there as I was one August. After a hot dry and dusty summer, the first snows fell. The great colourful gorge was washed and sparkling in the sunlight and the sandstone rocks gleamed pink, grey, gold and purple. A heron's nest was just visible perched upon the top of a rough and jagged rock thrust up from the bottom of the gorge. A great waterfall gushed down into the fast moving Yellowstone River on its way to join the Missouri, while thousands of red pole pines were generously sprinkled like sugar with glistening, shimmering pure white snow. Or by contrast what you would have written about the vast, silent Arizona Sonora desert? En route to Mexico it was as dry and as arid as could be. A month later I was returning to California, rain had fallen, the ground was covered with purple, crimson and yellow flowers, providing a vivid carpet against which the stiff, still cactus trees displayed their white waxy flowers, while the ocotillos waved their red flowered tips in the wind.

Some 30 years ago I drove around the world, and encountered many 'strangers' and was looked after by many kind people. I have had so much pleasure, that I would like to write to tell you about many of these experiences. First, though, I will tell you something of myself. This will enable the eighteen months of travel to fit into a framework.

As you know Perch had two children, Thermuthis Marion and Robert Edgar, my father. Robert married Stephanie Maton, and they had three children: my brother, Robert Wynne, myself, Muriel Leigh, and my sister, Lesley Frances. My brother Bob married Marguerite Wright and they had two children: John Robert Francis and Susan Mary. John, in turn, has married Alison Colclough, and they have two children, Matthew and Robert, so through them, the Kilvert name and motto, "Peregrinamur" should continue. I have never married. Lesley has three children and six grandchildren.

My very first recollection is that of sitting in a warm puddle of water left on the asphalt road after a thunderstorm, outside the Brigade Major's quarters at Eastney barracks, on some sunny Summer day in 1920. I was two and a half years old and dressed in a smocked white frock with a lace-trimmed white petticoat which, like most of my petticoats, had a way of showing below my frock. I was wearing white cotton knickers that did up with a button. They had frilly lace around the legs and were awkward to manage. I had been dressed to go out to tea, and had wandered off while the finishing touches were being given to my baby sister. When discovered I was not popular, but sitting in that warm puddle with the warm dark asphalt had given me great satisfaction. Those were spacious days.

I had a lovely large nursery. I was able to put my feet into wooden wagons that had been designed to be pulled behind a wooden 'car' on a piece of string, but I used them as roller skates. I loved the sensation of speed and of balance; but I had to be careful not to bump the wainscoting too hard, for this brought the grown-ups into my domain with a reprimand, and possibly the confiscation of my improvised roller skates!

My Father was in the Royal Marine Artillery, not, in those days, to be confused with the Royal Marine Light Infantry, with whom they later amalgamated. The R.M.A. felt themselves to be so superior to the RMLI that a Naval Chaplain, John Daugleish, who later became the Bishop of Nassau, preached a sermon in Eastney Barrack's Church likening the RMA to the Pharisee and the RMLI to the Publican in the parable of the Pharisee and the Publican! My Father was Brigade Major when I first became conscious of him. He was over 6ft tall, athletic, shy, gentle and beloved. He believed in command through example and put it into practice. In the First World War he won the DSO (Distinguished Service Order), was twice mentioned in despatches and was recommended for advanced promotion for his services in HMS Neptune at the Battle of Jutland. After the war he won the Officers' Bayonet Cup. He rode in the winning Officers' jumping competition at Olympia, played both rugger and hockey for the Navy in foreign stations, and won the Browndown Cup for shooting.

My father had very little small talk. Well I remember being sent for to get the conversation going between my father and the Naval Chaplain, already mentioned. I was thrust into the drawing room by my mother, who had withdrawn to look after my sister. I looked the stranger up and down and came out with, "H'm, not much hair, have you?" This was just what was needed to break the barrier of shyness between the two men who then became firm friends, the Chaplain, known to me as 'Ish' later acting as 'adoptive' father to me after my father died.

I used to love seeing my father, riding his horse, Rodney, to church on Sundays at the head of the brigade. After the service there was a time of relaxation on the Officers' lawn while the band played popular tunes. The Officers and their families strolled about chatting to each other, or teasing and playing with the children.

My father and I used to go for long walks alone together. We must have looked very strange as at two and a half I was short and tubby, nearly square! I could only just reach his strong sensitive hand but was so happy to be out with him that I never complained of the strain of holding one hand up so high for so long. We used to talk of the tides, the moon and the stars and identified the ships that were afloat in the Solent. To me this was really living. We encouraged the RMA tug o'war teams, or men who were putting the weight, and bayonet fighters in masks and padded tunics, who were to be found attacking straw bodies that hung from a sort of gibbet. We visited the stables and I was put astride my father's grey. We walked along the gunners' walk, with its unmistakable smell of wallflowers mingled with disinfectant. Those were halcyon days: the sun shone and everything was secure. When my father went to sea we moved out of barracks to a nearby terraced house which seemed cramped after the spaciousness of 'Teapot Row', as the quarters in barracks were called.

My parents adored each other. Once my mother took my sister and me to Weymouth where we stayed in furnished rooms in order that my mother would be there when my father's ship came in. In this way they could enjoy an extra twelve hours of each other's company. My brother being four years older than I often seemed to be away at school, but I clearly remember one incident when I was about 4. He and a friend from his school came home to tea. They borrowed my beach ball, a much prized possession, and, alas, accidentally kicked it down the moat to be lost for ever.

My mother was rather short but good looking, with a bright, cheerful face and a warm personality. She was both artistic and musical and could play the piano by ear. Each year she sang in The Messiah and nightly I would go to bed to hear her strike a note on the piano and then launch into the soprano part of one of Handel's choruses. She read aloud most beautifully. She had not learnt to cook until the war, when she excelled as a well organised 'good plain cook', and a sponge cake and marmalade maker. She had a great sense of fun which was particularly appreciated by small children with whom she always had an instant rapport. For a number of years she and I did not understand each other, but after my father had died, and I had become ill, we became mutually dependent and grew to be very fond of each other.

My mother had relied absolutely upon my father, so when at 35 she was widowed and left with three children of 9, 5 and two and a half years, life became very different. We left Southsea and moved to Salisbury, so that my sister and I could be educated as day girls at the Godolphin School and we would not be too far from Marlborough, where my brother was destined to follow my father. Bravely she husbanded her small income. We had no car nor wireless set and a visit to a theatre or the cinema was a real event. We were nearly two miles from the City and over two miles from the school, but we walked these distances in all weathers, only sometimes taking a bus part of the way on the return journey from the City if we had much to carry.

It was wonderful to be young in the City of New Sarum, as Salisbury was still called by some. It really was the market town for the area and little had changed for generations. The market square was cobbled and on each Tuesday a cattle market was held there, with stalls displaying fruit, vegetables, fish and meat flanking one side of the square. On Saturdays there were no cattle, but more stalls and many a bargain in furniture, cutlery, books, china and glass were to be had. In September of each year, the Mop Fair was held. It was a great occasion and not so very different from the earlier Mop Fairs when farmhands were taken on for the year. Blue Boar Row, which flanked the market and was the main street, was closed to traffic, and stalls were erected offering many games of skill and chance. Balloons were much in evidence, and red-faced men who were visitors to the district called out to us in unknown accents to try to win a goldfish.

The shops in Salisbury in 1923 were for the most part in private hands. I well remember Mr Sly's jewellers shop on the corner of Blue Boar Row and Endless Street. It had such character with its plush carpet, very likely an old and genuine Wilton, and its long-legged Bentwood chairs with small round seats. I had to be helped on to them, I remember, but this indignity was rewarded by the view of the treasures in the lighted glass countertop case. There were diamond brooches, repeater watches, and old fob watches that were wound up with a key that was separate from the watch. There were bracelets of fine gold and rings with delicate claw settings. There were mourning rings and bejewelled rings, earrings and necklaces of jade or of emerald which, lit by the electric light bulbs, glistened and gleamed under one end of the counter on their dark blue velvet cushion. Mr Sly used an eyeglass that fascinated me, and so as not to leave fingerprints, always had a fine chamois leather with which to handle the jewellery. Generally we went into his shop only to have a clock or a watch repaired, and yet we were always treated with much courtesy. He was surrounded by glass fronted cupboards, within which were such things as old Sheffield candlesticks, Georgian gravy boats, silver teapots and milk jugs, and often beautifully shaped salt cellars and mustard pots. This little corner shop was a veritable treasure house, that had dignity and an atmosphere of its own.

Further along Blue Boar Row there was Style and Gerrish, the linen drapers as my grandfather called them. Mr Gerrish had a little pointed beard and pince-nez glasses and wore striped trousers and a tail coat, and was usually to be seen in his shop. The Misses Sheppard used to sell dresses to my mother, and Mrs and Miss Larkham sold us knitting wool, buttons and ribbon. Bread was baked locally in several bakers' shops; pre-packed mass produced bread was yet to come to Salisbury. Another shop I used to like to visit was Mr Till's saddlery. In his shop there was always a satisfying smell of leather and Mr Till made the goods that he had for sale, ranging from superb saddles to dog leads and wrist watch straps. He also made the book sacks for the Godolphin School from brown canvas with real leather edging and handles. They stood up to hard wear for many years — I still have mine. One other early recollection is of a visit which we paid to a large seed and supply stores where a tall man in a long grey cotton coat served us. We were to buy a tool for the gardener who spoke broad Wiltshire. He had asked my mother to get him a 'ribbook', but my mother could not work out what he wanted! She approached the sympathetic looking salesman and, fixing her eyes on him, took a deep breath and asked for a 'ribbook'. He smiled in a friendly fashion, went to the back of the shop and returned with a reap hook in his hand. We walked home and our gardener was well satisfied with it.

How I loved Salisbury Close; there is a rightness about it. The great Cathedral towers above all the surrounding houses, seeming to reach up with its glorious spire soaring gracefully 404 feet from the ground, a little out of true but reliable, nonetheless, reputedly carrying a casket within which, it was believed, is a piece of Our Lady's robe.

I went to school both at the Godolphin and later to St Michael's in Bognor Regis before meeting my cousin Charmian Wyndowe, Will's daughter, and granddaughter of your sister, Emily Jardine. During the Second World War I was in the WRNS first as a Motor Transport Driver, and later as an Administrative Officer. After the war, like you, I went up to Oxford, to Lady Margaret Hall, and then ran a school in the Sudan and helped to run another in Ceylon (now called Sri Lanka). Later I was principal for fourteen years at Runton Hill in North Norfolk and in 1965 took four girls from there on a lovely camping holiday to Petra via Turkey, and Syria to Jordan; and back via Crete, Italy, Switzerland, Germany and Holland. This was good preparation for my prolonged World Trip in *Peregrine*, of which I now write. I hope that you would not put me amongst the '*noxious tourist*' of whom you wrote, as the following itinerary demonstrates the many and varied topics which I have been led to reflect and lecture upon both during and after my return, while enjoying Nature's wonderful scenery and man's archaeological splendours in some of the remotest parts of the world. What a privilege and an eye opener it was to have visited and experienced, however superficially, such places as Harappa on the Indus River, Alexandria, Cairo, Abu Simbel and the Valley of the Kings on the Nile; and to have seen artefacts and sculptures of the Sumerians from Babylon, and the river valleys of the Tigris and Euphrates: and later to have visited Persepolis, the centre c.500 BC of the Persian Empire under Cyrus, later to be part of Alexander the Great's Empire, which in turn gave way to the spread of Greek culture to be seen today in the remains of theatres and city centres in Turkey, Istanbul and throughout Greece, from the Parthenon in Athens to the splendours of the Peloponnese, with their reflections in later buildings to be enjoyed in Italy and Europe; as well as discovering something of the little known prehistoric Mexico.

So, Uncle Frank, I dedicate this account of my eighteen month journey around the world some thirty years ago, to you: and I hope that you and my discerning readers will agree that it reflects ideas of a 'traveller' rather than a 'tourist'.

Chapter 1

Introduction

"It was a glorious afternoon, unclouded, and the meadows shone dazzling like a sea in the glory of the sheets of buttercups. The deep, dark river, still and glassy, seemed to be asleep and motionless except when leaf or blossom floated by. The cattle by the mill plashed and trampled among the rushes and river flags and water lilies in the shallow places, and the miller Godwin came down with a bucket to draw water from the pool."

"So wrote my Great Uncle Frank, my grandfather's elder brother, in his diary on Saturday 16th May 1874. Uncle Frank is known to many as the Reverend Robert Francis Kilvert (1840-1879), who kept a daily diary during the nine years that lead up to his untimely death in 1879. His first curacy was to the Reverend Richard Venables at Clyro, a village near Hay-on-Wye in a lovely part of England that borders on Wales, with the Welsh mountains constantly in view. Then for four years he was curate to his father, the Reverend Robert Kilvert, at Langley Burrell near Chippenham in Wiltshire. His next post was as Rector in the Parish of St Harmon in Herefordshire. He was then appointed Vicar of Bredwardine in Radnorshire where within two years of his appointment and just five weeks after his marriage to Elizabeth Rowland he died at the age of 38. He was beloved wherever he went, and the local press recorded the sadness of his early death. His funeral procession must have been a sad and moving sight, for the road from the vicarage to the church had previously been garlanded with flowers by his parishioners to welcome him with his wife home from their honeymoon. Now, just one month later the same route was lined with mourning parishioners and the remains of flowers.

Perhaps Professor A.L. Rowse, in his book *English Spirit* (1944, *Macmillan*), gives us a clue that explains the love and trust that people had for him, for he writes: *"Kilvert was that very rare creature, a diarist who was not in the least egoistic nor even introspective. What he shares with us is his own apprehension of life, completely and without any reserves; but life viewed always in its aesthetic aspect, qua beauty, as one who was essentially an artist saw it. There remains something about the inner man that escapes us, to which we have not the key."*

I remember my Aunt telling me that as a small child she greatly enjoyed sitting on his knee, where she felt secure, for he was so understanding and kind. He told her of birds and animals and their habits; of places which he knew ... he hated senseless conversation, and he loved walking alone in the country *"...alone among the quiet peaceful meadows, tracing out the ancient footpaths, and walking in the footsteps of generations that have gone before."* He knew and loved the country, and the people who lived there. He gave us an unique picture of life in Victorian England, for all doors were open to him. He visited the people regularly, taught in the local school, sat with the dying, read to some parishioners, and even helped to dig potatoes for another. He joined in family tea parties, and listened to folklore, or to stories told him by farmers or by the old soldier who had fought in the Napoleonic Wars. He knew of Parish tragedies and of the past. These accounts are most revealing, for they give a faithful picture of parish life between 1870 and 1879. They take account of relationships of the 'well to do' and of those families who worked the land.

Uncle Frank was a welcome guest in the nearby country houses and writes of archery and of croquet on the lawn, of picnics with grapes and claret, and of pleasant dinner parties and homeward journeys under the *"...stars glittering frosty and keen,"* when they *"...came home at a rattling pace."* The diary gives a picture of village life centred on the Church with a sense of space, and of time to read, to walk and to reflect. He records the village whole, and in colour with the seasons.

Uncle Frank had an acute and independent mind and his diary reflects his awareness of the human element in any situation. We can notice this from his remarks about the Franco-Prussian War or from his observations on the occasion of the collision of the Royal Yacht with a sailing dinghy in the Solent. Uncle Frank was a caring person, with an understanding of and respect for individuals which caused him to profess egalitarian views, uncommon in the Victorian days of the 1870s.

His sensitive love of the countryside was outraged when he saw the bleak barren mining areas of Cornwall *"...with their tall chimney shafts,"* and the effluence *"...defiling and poisoning streams with the white tin washing."* He hated the loud unthinking tourist, and on 5th April 1870 wrote, *"Of all noxious animals... the most noxious is a tourist."* But he enjoyed the *"...delicious feeling in stripping in the open air and running down naked to the sea with the red early morning sunshine glowing on the naked limbs of the bathers."*

He was a wide reader of both prose and poetry and knew, and loved, among other writers, William and Dorothy Wordsworth. . He was a lover of music and found the elementary efforts on a violin by his friend the schoolmaster most amusing. When he could he went to concerts; and he also went as often as he could to Dulwich Art Gallery and to the annual Art Exhibitions at Burlington House. He was stirred by the best and was sensitive to beauty, and had a real apprehension of character; he was susceptible to the charm of women, and the beauty of children, especially girls, and in his loves: Daisy Thomas, Kathleen Mavourneen and Etty Brown. His entries on these subjects are both delicate and intense.

In his latter years my uncle suffered from 'poor eyes', and noticeable ill health. In his entry on 20th June 1878 he records, *"Palmer took me aside as soon as I came in and offered me, from Canon Walsham How, the permanent Chaplaincy at Cannes. He thought it might be desirable for me to accept it on account of my health."* Yet throughout the diaries, my uncle shares with us his love of living. He is mystified by the life of Monks, though he appreciates the qualities of Father Ignatius. He gives us a lovely savour of his University, Oxford, when he introduces some friends to 'eights' week, and reminiscences with them on his memories of Wadham in his undergraduate days.

Preparations

"Ex-Government surplus fire tenders for sale, £450 – Low mileage." So read the advertisement that prompted me to action, and seemed to be an answer to prayer. For two years I had been looking for a suitable vehicle in which to drive around the world. I wanted a strong mobile home, and what better than an ex-Government fire-tender, with but 1,160 miles on the clock?

Furthermore, when I went to Great Bentley to look at her, I was introduced to a professional car body expert who envisaged no undue problems in substituting desert signals 'cabins' taken from Army vehicles for the original 450 gallon water tank. We were in business. On the spot I sold the water pipes, pump and ladders for £250, and the fire tender was mine for £200. I called her *Peregrine*, for 'Peregrinamur' is our family motto. Scale drawings of the machine were sent to me, and I designed the layout of my mobile home. An old kneehole table was taken apart to provide a writing/dining/chart table behind the passenger's seat; a galley with hot and cold water taps, a two-burner gas stove and grill, and a gas operated fridge and storage space came next, with a shower (hot and cold) and a flushing loo which would need to be emptied from time to time.

Aft of this through a door was a two-berth night cabin with lights and shelves over bunks, and storage and hanging space. Three outside lockers provided storage respectively for a tent and camping equipment, for car spares and tools, and for stores and food. A 50 gallon water tank, and 35 gallon petrol tank ensured that we could with impunity stray from the beaten track.

During the six weeks between my retirement at 55 and my departure I worked hard putting the finishing touches to the earlier preparations, and with the help of several unsuspecting friends who dropped in to see me, *Peregrine* was painted outside in grey tractor paint, while inside the galley and shower area were painted white, and the ceilings and night cabin were in eau de nil (duck egg) to prevent too much glare. I had made counterpanes, curtains and covers, and put up shelves and 'fiddles' so that equipment would stay in place as we travelled. Finally I packed in stores and the many useful and practical presents which well-wishers had given to me – one of which was a moped that just fitted under the dining table! Anglia TV and a representative from Women's Hour came to record a programme.

We were moving, but all was not plain sailing, for *Peregrine's* measurements of 21ft long, 7¾ft wide and 10ft high made her too tall for container ships. Finally after ringing about 20 shipping companies, the ACL (Atlantic Crossing Line) agreed to ship her from Liverpool on 5th June to arrive at Halifax, Nova Scotia, on 13th June.

My first travelling companion was my 18-year-old niece, Susan, a former pupil at Runton Hill, who had three months to spare before going to her training college. We had agreed to meet near to number 1 car park at London Airport at 1.00pm on 13th June 1972. I had caught the bus down from the air terminal in Buckingham Palace Road and was now standing on an island near to the entry to number 1 car park, on what I deemed was a vantage point. I was feeling unprotected and rather forlorn as I waited there, much as a hermit crab without its shell might feel. There seemed to be no other passengers in a like predicament. My luggage was beside me: a smart blue and black zipped suitcase, that was all right, but then there was a bulging basket and, worse still, a large white plastic bag with silly shapes on it. Other people's baggage looked so much more compact than mine and I began to wish I could dispense with all but the blue and black suitcase, for I felt conspicuous with the basket and the bag.

There was no sign of my brother and his wife, who should have been bringing Susan to join me. Perhaps there was another entry to number 1 car park? People looked pityingly at me as they drove by, secure in their metal shells. At last I saw the pale blue car, whose occupants spotted me, and now I just had to wait for the parking procedure before being joined by the family.

The usual bustle of the air terminal was apparent as we entered the foyer. Girls in various uniforms with quaint little hats at differing angles were standing below airline signs, behind shiny aluminium counters and beside scales that would weigh our luggage before it was put on the conveyor belts and withdrawn from sight. Now I was without my suitcase I was more conscious of my awkward luggage. Susan had a smart little white dressing case and looked very chic in a well cut black coat over a pale blue frock with black ornamental stitching. We all went to the departure lounge and sat in line on the square seats, upholstered in bright colours and balancing on their thin metal legs. The carpet deadened the noise of pacing feet, and one felt it deadened the thoughts of the passengers and their companions.

This was a big moment for Susan – a new experience. She looked so young and vulnerable, yet relaxed and ready for adventure. A voice announced our flight to Halifax and the party divided, Bob and Marguerite standing back while Susan and I passed through the barrier, passports and tickets in hand. With many others we were directed through gate number 3 and formed a small part of the raw material that was being processed into the waiting DC7. Many of our travelling companions, including a lady in our row, were Canadians returning from a holiday in Europe, and the plane was so full that her daughter was sitting a few rows in front of her. Eventually all the seats were filled, the doors were closed, the ramp removed, the engines started, words of welcome were spoken by the Captain, the signal was given and we were airborne.

During the flight Susan and I reviewed our plans for the next three months. We intended to drive across the great American continent, for the most part keeping to Canada but dipping down into the States in order to visit New York City and Plymouth Meeting, near to Philadelphia in Pennsylvania.

We also looked back over the last two years of planning for the trip. I had just handed over Runton Hill School, which I had been running for 14 years, to a headmaster. I was ready for a prolonged holiday, away from the sound of bells that had punctuated my life for so long.

Many people had asked me how I intended to finance such a trip, and to the end seemed sure that I had been left money by some rich relation, but this was not the case. I was financing myself, and this is one of the reasons why I bought sturdy *Peregrine*, which had done duty during the war at Biggin Hill Airfield. She was first licensed in 1954 but, according to her speedometer, had only done 1,160 miles. I sometimes thought of her clocking up this mileage over a period of 18 years – emerging from her place in a hangar, and being driven around the perimeter of the airfield, and then returning to be plugged in to the local electricity supply to keep her batteries well charged and her engine warm, so that she could be alerted at a moment's notice. She started life green in colour, with AFS on her side, with the chubby nose of the Bedford and a lovely bell on her roof, alongside a powerful roving spotlight. The new inside layout gave the impression of a small boat, and the windows, a great feature, were fitted with glass, mosquito netting and solid metal shutters, so that the whole was a veritable fortress on wheels. The whole vehicle, with equipment, weighed about 3¾ tons. She ran on petrol, averaging about 8 miles to the gallon, and had back axle drive through the double back wheels.

Schematic Drawing for *'Peregrine'*

The Night Cabin

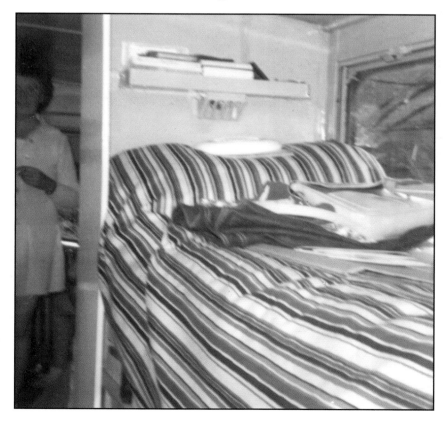

Canada —Route Map

Chapter 2

CANADA

Near to the shores of Newfoundland we saw the tip of an iceberg and then the deeply serrated coastline of Nova Scotia, the myriads of glistening lakes and the many fir trees. We had crossed the Atlantic, put our watches back and were ready to land. It was mid-afternoon in Canada and once through the formalities we boarded a bus and were driven through the city of Halifax, and found our way to the docks. Halifax is a venerable port and has a fine castle built on a hill, above its green and spacious city. We saw young people playing organised games in the parks, and large cars with tinted glass were speeding about the roads. We had arrived and now, we thought, we will claim *Peregrine* and drive to a good spot for the first night of our holiday, the dream of the last two years. Life is seldom that simple.

We lost no time in spotting *Peregrine* on the quay, grey, large but unobtrusive – but strangely, a red cup that had been locked inside was in evidence upon a railway truck. I was sure it was my red cup, for it had some tell-tale splashes of white paint upon it. My heart sank, for I had packed all my equipment into *Peregrine*: the moped, a tape recorder, a camera, field glasses, a compass, a transistor radio, as well as clothes, blankets, kitchen equipment and food. On closer inspection we were dismayed to find that not only had *Peregrine* been broken into, but that she had been dented and damaged in transit. The authorities were extremely good to us and most apologetic; a delightful port official handed me the keys and gave us permission to sleep in *Peregrine* on the quay. Customs officials and the shipping agents were most helpful, but nothing could alter the fact that she had been ransacked and everything was in chaos.

Susan and I looked at each other in despair, it seemed hopeless. We were weary, worried and exhausted from the long journey in a crowded plane, and it was already midnight by our time, though only 9.00 pm by Canadian time. There was nothing for it but to gain some order from the chaos before we could turn in. We found that the moped and the tape recorder were still there, and mercifully only one pair of new sandals and a windscreen fan seemed to have been stolen, as far as we could tell. Finally by about 2.00am there was just enough order for us to produce a meal, and our bunks were clear, so after a welcome supper we thankfully retired for the night.

We were awoken, immediately it seemed, by a dock train, to find that it was 6.00am on 14th June. A tall and good-looking member of the Royal Canadian Mounted Police donned overalls and examined *Peregrine* thoroughly and insurance agents came around. We offered coffee and found we had many new friends but no-one, apparently, could repair the damage to *Peregrine* in Halifax; this could only be done in Montreal. Somewhat reassured, we drove out of Halifax in the late afternoon, and headed south-west along the coast en route for Kejimakujik Park.

The inland area all around Halifax was covered with acre upon acre of coniferous trees. We had seen these from the aeroplane all the way from Newfoundland, looking down upon the deep blue Atlantic, with its fringe of white foam near to the shore. We had seen many, many lakes, and the serrated coastline, broken by several rivers that end in bays or creeks or tree-clad gorges.

Now we were surrounded with these rather stumpy fir and pine trees that grow in the thin layer of earth that covers the great grey boulders that emerge and show their smooth washed surfaces between the trunks of the trees. We saw names on the signposts that told of the earlier days of this now sparsely populated area of Canada – Halifax, Frenchvil, Timber Lea and Upper Pantallon, rub shoulders with each other and spill over into Peggy's Cove and Fox Point, where we spent the first night of our travels. Hubbards, Mahone Bay and Luneburg were not far away, while Lake Mushamush, Whale Lake, Shell Lake and Kejimakujik spoke eloquently of the earlier inhabitants, the Indians who had sent messages to each other by their petrographs on the stones we were later to see.

These petrographs, to be found by the water's edge, were inscribed perhaps two thousand years ago or more and they depict, for instance, a dug out canoe, a wild animal or a man with a spear. These messages were carried from man to man when, as far as is known, no written language was used. They are primitive in execution and remind one of the graffiti incised by Norfolk choir boys to beguile away the sermon hours in Salthouse or Cley Churches, for instance! They carry too something of the aura of the paintings of Lascaux, or similar petrographs to be found in the Dordogne valley or in caves in Northern Spain.

Timber Lake is large, of a scale that we were soon to accept as the norm, and the constant movement of the water has washed these stones quite smooth. Many of the tall graceful trees were new to us. They shone out in their new pale lime green in contrast to the firs that we had met along our way. Somewhat hidden in a clearing we found an 18th century Christian cemetery, fenced off with a wooden paling, and containing about twenty headstones. There was no obvious sign of ruins of any kind to go with them; however, one felt that this must have been an earlier settlement, a chosen site, for there was a bay, and not too far away there was an island that would have provided security from those who might have been hostile.

After our first night camping at Fox Point we made for Annapolis Royal and the Bay of Fundy, and there we pulled up for petrol – or gas as we soon learned to call it – and were met by a jovial Scotsman who had settled in Canada after the war, but had lost nothing of his Glaswegian accent in the intervening years. "This is a good rig," he said, "what is it?" "A British fire tender which did duty on the airfield at Biggin Hill," I replied. He wrote his name and address in our book, and said how much he enjoyed life in Canada, adding that he and his wife and children were planning to visit Scotland next year. Then, "Have a good trip," he called. This was to be the farewell that we came to expect as we drove west across this great and beautiful country.

The Bleakneys of Wolfville, who are members of the Kilvert Society, were our first hosts. They live in a lovely `old, house built in 1867 overlooking Fundy Bay where the sea, on the incoming tide, rises faster and higher than anywhere else in the world. Mr Bleakney, a professor of Biology at the University of Wolfville, and Nancy his wife love England and had read about *Peregrine* in the In Britain article. Mr Bleakney kindly organised the water for our tank while Mike, Sue, Caroline and children, some of whom came on bicycles from a wide area, swarmed over *Peregrine* and told us, among other things, that we were very sensible to have mosquito netting.

Leaving Nova Scotia for New Brunswick Susan and I were enchanted by the vast expanse of countryside to be seen from near Fredericton where we seemed to be atop the world. We gazed in wonderment all around us upon great areas of forests and arable land, and upon the St John River that wound its way slowly along a wide valley where it gave life to several farms, to the cattle and to the trees that hugged its shores. In the far distance there were ranges of tree-clad hills which seemed to be a dark purple, then hazy blue with various shades of green. The new shoots of different varieties of fir and pine trees shone out in their bright pale greens, jostling together against the more sombre hues of the older growth.

We made our way up to Grand Falls and saw the fast falling water, gambolling and playing in the sunshine with the spray rising into the clear air, free and expendable, before falling with its great weight upon the well-washed boulders, giving rise to sounds of light spray contrasting with the booming noise of the main waterfall.

Reaching Rivière du Loup on the southern banks of the St Lawrence Seaway we turned *Peregrine's* nose to the south. As we drove along we saw evidence of the early European settlers along these shores. The little houses, many of them over two hundred years old, were built of wood with a verandah, and steps up to the front door. The occupants we learned were both farmers and skilled woodcarvers, as had been their fathers and grandfathers before them. Properties were divided from each other with old wooden fences running in straight lines from the river's edge so that each farmer should have access to the vital waterway providing both water and means of communication.. Further south the villages were clustered round a church or chapel, and the general pattern usually included a school with a flag pole and perhaps a meeting hall.

Quebec city had a real feeling of a French town with its venerable wall encircling part of it, the only city wall in the North American continent, we learned. It enclosed a park that commanded a vantage point on the banks of the St Lawrence River, from where it was easy to imagine the French and British soldiers in their blue and red tunics scrambling up the hillsides with their cumbersome guns and fluttering standards. An ancient fort with several fortified concentric circles was a living reminder of those uneasy days of the past. The Plains of Abraham, that now surround a sturdy Museum set in a large park, also contributed to the sense of size and space into which Wolfe led his men nearly 200 years ago. On this day the sun was shining and lighting up amusing black and white jaunty 'mushroom' umbrellas on the quay. Two young men were expertly playing with a frisbee – the local craze of the time.

We were allowed to park for the night in the Museum car park, one of the many unusual spots we were to experience, for *Peregrine* in her grey paint looked much more like a Brinks Security van than a caravan! An especially interesting modern piece of sculpture stands near to the Museum. Unlike any European piece of sculpture it has a feeling of the pillars of the Hypostyle Hall, (from the Valley of the Kings in Egypt), combined with cubism and the local totems, which gives it its Canadian flavour. Carved in wood it both blends with its surroundings and forms a link from the past with the present. We had a great time in Quebec and got out the moped for the first time, Sue as usual riding pillion because the insurance for her to drive was too high.

Back over the St Lawrence River again we headed for Montreal, a crowded city with modern high rise blocks, some pushing 40 or 50 storeys into the sky, dwarfing the older buildings. We asked a mounted policeman at traffic lights how to find the way to ACL who are to make arrangements for *Peregrine* to be repaired. With his consent, we left *Peregrine* on a steep hill with a sandbag under one wheel, and walked to Cunard House via a circuitous route because the Canadian Highway was being built through Montreal and the excavations were tremendous. We made all our telephone calls from ACL, before returning to *Peregrine* and then on to join our hosts for the night, the first of two separate families of friends who had invited us to visit them.

This middle-aged couple with grown-up children had emigrated from England about 30 years ago and were currently living in an established residential area. They made us most welcome for our short stay in their well-appointed home. The next morning we drove *Peregrine* to a shipyard where 'The Work' was in the hands of a most colourful middle-aged man, with ear-length curly hair, dressed in lilac- coloured herringbone trousers, an extravagantly striped shirt, a large flowery tie and an accentuated square-shouldered jacket. He interpreted some remark from the insurance company as an order to him, and played merry hell with them on the telephone. He gave certain orders to a delightful, deaf, elderly skilled craftsman, who was assigned the job of righting *Peregrine*. This man became a great friend, and knew exactly how to deal with both his boss and with *Peregrine*. He went his own way about things and did an excellent job in spite of a heavy downpour of rain which turned the yard to mud. The shipyard job completed, we retouched *Peregrine* with the grey paint we had brought with us, and away we went in time to join the rush hour traffic that was leaving the city! That was an experience: never fewer than three lanes and sometimes six in each direction, and constantly dividing onto the network of motorways. Everything is on such a large scale. We passed a two-engined train pulling 87 trucks with cars treble banked on them!

We had been so kindly received by everyone and now we were made welcome by the Buckmans, a young couple who had arrived in Canada about six years ago. They were still living in one of the new immigrant 'cantons' Canada has provided. These small garden towns on the outskirts of the major cities are self-supporting, having their own shopping centres, clubs and swimming pools. Sue joined David and the children for a dip, while I took in water for *Peregrine* and then met a newspaper reporter. The houses are well planned: there are some tall blocks of flats or apartments, and some single or two-storeyed houses, generally open plan in design, for families of two, four or six people. These houses often have basement garages and rooms for washing machines, as well as children's play/TV rooms. On the ground floor there is generally a good sized room divided into three with kitchen, dining and sitting room areas. Often there are large glass French windows letting on to a patio. Gardens are small and unfenced, and communal play areas are at hand for children of differing ages. Most families have two cars, and the children a great number of toys such as bicycles, toy cars, scooters and kites, and the older children have swimming tackle, flippers, goggles, or wet suits where surfing is offered. All houses have large refrigerators and ice boxes or freezers. Food is elegantly and hygienically packaged and displayed in vast supermarkets which flank car parks large enough to accommodate a first class football pitch!

Montreal is a beautiful city and seen to best advantage from Northern Hill at night when the St Lawrence seaway itself is lit up, as well as the liners riding at anchor or being guided through the man-made channel. The high rise blocks with lights ablaze from their many windows are given a horizontal anchoring by several well lit bridges and overpasses fanning out from the Jacques Cartier bridge that straddles the St Lawrence River from the mainland to St Helena Island, the site of the World Fair Expo '67. Strange little French-style houses flank the docks, occupied by people who only speak French and wish to cut themselves off from the British. Replies are only made to questions asked in French, however bad!

The Canadians were interested in *Peregrine*, and a delightful man, a polio sufferer, wrote her story in the local paper. Canadian TV did a live programme; the man in charge of this, a maestro of generous proportions, wore a wide-brimmed felt hat, and a bronco check shirt. He was most professional and had as an assistant an artistic photographer. The latter was an outspoken separatist and argued his case with much feeling. After the interview undertaken in a one-way street between two main streets, a 'live drive, was recorded. This was a real test as *Peregrine* had to be within ten yards of the camera car, keep to a prearranged route, and obey the usual traffic regulations in very crowded conditions! When we were stopped at red traffic lights two Mounties looked at us in amazement and, overcoming their initial shock, were intrigued at what they saw. A bus driver came alongside, took off his cap and said, "Congratulations!" before driving on. When we had been filmed going round the block the maestro and his team signed our visitors' book, and we signed our payment form and earned our second TV fee.

These fees were to buy our petrol as we went along. I had started with less than £300, plus the money for sea passages, and intended to do the journey of about 28,000 miles without drawing more. *Peregrine* at best only went eight to ten miles to a British gallon. This was a challenge with plenty of scope!

We arrived in Ottawa on the eve of St John the Baptist's Day. The police were expecting trouble from the French element. We had barely pulled up near to the Parliament buildings when a real James Bond figure appeared. He was wearing the inevitable gabardine, produced a silver embossed identity card from his inner pocket, showing that he was a policeman of the Special Branch, and asked what we were carrying. He suspected bombs! Incredulous but relieved when he realised *Peregrine* was but a mobile home, he mingled with the crowd and was gone. We parked in Champlain Park, within sight and sound of the Parliament building and the carillon that gives a quavering concert on Saturday nights. Somehow in spite of the 'No Parking' notices, we were allowed to stay in this car park for five days and nights! The authorities must have thought that we were connected with a display of old Army vehicles and equipment on show at the Army Museum close by! When we visited the exhibition we saw Lord Dorchester's carriage and also the 5-ton Crerar field car.

Ottawa for a time had been called Bytown, after Colonel By who engineered the lock system on the canal, a tremendous feat of engineering by which vessels may be raised within 100 yards from the St Lawrence river to the Rideau canal. Colonel By was reprimanded for his pains as the costs – measured only in thousands – were considered by the British Government to have been too high! The Bytown Museum is housed in a charming little square house which had been the lock keeper's house. It is run by elderly ladies in a delightfully amateurish way, which produces a charm of its own. It displays the goods and chattels of early settlers, and it has an especially good and varied set of lamps and candlesticks. The bare boards and plain wooden furniture indicated the hard conditions of the early days in Canada, but despite the primitiveness and the consequent privations, one got an impression of the splendour of the life of the wealthier immigrants. The large size of the stoves and cooking vessels brought home to us the size of families and the cold climate they endured. Bytown was renamed Ottawa in 1855 — and then in 1857 was chosen by Queen Victoria as the capital of Canada! This was in order to mark a peace agreed between Great Britain and the Iroquois and Algonquin Indians. While we were looking around a black squirrel ran along a wire and disappeared through a hole into the roof space of this old house. He was quite at home and seemingly undisturbed by humans.

. We continued our sight-seeing, and found that many students are engaged on various jobs during the long Summer vacations. A delightful girl student showed us around part of the Governor General's house, which was guarded by Canadian Mounties in their scarlet tunics. One room, the ballroom, is surprising, it has a pink and cream striped ceiling, like a tent, over a black and white floor covering. Christmas parties with many balloons are an annual feature in this large room, our guide told us.

From the top of the Parliament Tower the winding river dominates the view with its floating logs making patterns near the pulping factories, which speak of the wealth of this country, much as the woolsack spoke of the wealth of England in former years. Remic Rapids and the Rideau Falls play around projecting promontories, and are a constant reminder of the dangers and importance, even now, of the waterways of which Canadians rightly are very proud.

Canada's capital city Ottawa has a lovely new cultural centre. It has been most imaginatively designed and has a staircase spiralling round a sparkling glass sculpture, which gives it a feeling of space and light. Local artists have had fun with murals. Within a comparatively small area yet with a feeling of space, an opera house, a theatre, a concert hall and a music room for intimate chamber concerts, as well as a refreshment centre, are grouped together. This building is surrounded by a wide verandah. On the last weekend of each of the Summer months craftsmen and women display examples of their work. There was a puppet theatre show, both made and activated by the artist Oudier. Two ladies had driven across the prairies with examples of their Peruvian style weaving; one of whom showed us how she had made double-sided belts and other small items on a portable 'H' loom as they drove the long distance from their home. Several woodworkers came bringing varied and beautiful naturalistic carvings of fishermen and farmers, and animals and fish, and also modern style sculptures. They came from the traditional woodcarving area through which we had already driven. There was a glassblower who blew Roman style glass. All the craftsmen and women were ready to talk about their lives; there was a feeling of contentment, and a sense of achievement which always seems to be engendered by people who are fulfilled by their skills and way of life.

We drove on through farming and nursery-garden land to Ogdensberg, where a long and beautiful bridge spans the St Lawrence River marking the border with the USA at that point. The US Customs men looked suspiciously at *Peregrine* and said to us, "We will have to take that rig apart." The man looked fierce enough, and we waited, having heard that wheels were sometimes removed and holes pierced in cars. Our big wheels, six in number, were too heavy for either of us to lift. At last our turn came. The Customs man climbed aboard *Peregrine*, looked baffled, opened an odd drawer here and there, dallied, then turned, and smiling said, "You're through – have a good trip."

We ran into a savage thunderstorm, the rain bouncing high on the roads which soon flooded bringing the traffic to a halt. Even storms are on a large and powerful scale here. As the sun began to set we found ourselves in a small town called Longlake. There beside a small cafe right on the shores of the lake was a little pull-in. A friendly middle-aged couple ran this intimate country cafe. They invited us to park *Peregrine* alongside them for the night. It was an idyllic spot – quiet, with a fisherman in his punt just off shore, and a footbridge reaching across to a small island where silver-stemmed birch trees bearing shivering pale green leaves contrasted with the steady dark green of the firs. All were reflected in the still water of the aptly named Long Lake, and the whole was tinged with the pink of the setting sun.

As we drove through Albany and Schenectady to Wappinger Falls en route for New York City, the increasing density of the population forced itself upon us – advertisements, signboards, flashing neon lights, and garish coloured lighting replaced the stars and the wide open spaces of Nova Scotia, New Brunswick and Quebec provinces through which we had driven. A hurried pace and feeling of competition pervaded the air and nowhere could we see the sort of parking spot we had so far enjoyed. We followed a sign into Le Mesier Park, given we read, by the Le Mesier family for the enjoyment of local residents: and there we were away from the bustle and hurry of the freeways. We spotted a small single storey Police HQ, where we asked if we might spend the night. A policeman came out and inspected *Peregrine*, then pointed to a lamppost from which hung a notice, 'Parking 20 minutes only' and said, "Park by that lamp-post and you'll be all right." Squirrels came down from the trees as night fell. All was quiet. We were in the States not far from New York City, our destination for the next day.

The police visited us in the morning, and after friendly exchanges on both sides off we went to New York City. We read a large notice forbidding trucks in Central Park, but we told ourselves that we did not come into that category, so drove into the park and found a parking spot by a boating lake. Police were patrolling, and we asked if they would keep an eye on *Peregrine* while we went to the Metropolitan Museum. They willingly agreed to do this and off we went, secure in the knowledge that we were being well looked after.

On our return from the Museum, we went to our friends, the police, to learn where we might safely park for the night, as we had been invited to dine with our cousins in 84th Street. We told the police of our most satisfactory night in Le Mesier Park, and they told us how to find Station 5 Central Park. Accordingly we drove round and boldly entered the Police Station. The faces of the duty constables visibly fell, imagining that we were going to report rape or bag-snatching, but they waited patiently and listened incredulously to our request to be allowed to spend the night outside their station. They came to look at *Peregrine*, and graciously said that we might leave her where she was. They said that they could not be responsible for her, but that they would be in and out constantly throughout the night. Our cousin, a freelance journalist, and his wife, could not believe our story and were only convinced after they had driven us back that evening and accepted coffee in our home. They are still dining out on the story!

New York City in the rush hour on a Friday night is an experience on its own. We thought we should visit the United Nations building, and somehow got mixed up in the one-way system. A tremendous thunderstorm broke, the rain poured down with splashes like half-crowns on the road, and lightning forked wildly across the sky, while thunder clapped and roared overhead. The traffic was largely at a standstill, and as frustrated drivers became frantic, all rules of the road were broken as cars surged forward to catch the lights. We pulled in to a space at the side of the road, made a proverbial British pot of tea, activated our sound recorder, then sat back to observe the human race fighting its own rules and each other. The police had elected to tow away a parked car and as they and their 'victim' struggled east-west across the intersection they effectively blocked all north-south traffic for twenty minutes, including an ambulance. Horns blared, thunder roared, rain pattered, and pandemonium reigned. We made a tape recording of these monstrous sounds!

Somehow, gradually, there was some movement, the rules of the road prevailed, the crowds subsided, and the commuters left the city. We finished our pot of tea and drove out to Elizabeth, New Jersey. The roads to the south-west of New York City looked as unpromising as those to the north-west. It was still pouring with rain. We decided to make straight for the Police Station this time, which was not easy to find as it was tucked away among residential houses. We found it, however, and walked up the steps, draped as they were with a number of young men and women. We boldly asked if we might park *Peregrine* among the ambulances and black marias, all neatly drawn up behind wire netting. Several police conferred with each other, and eventually, since they could think of no real reason why we should not be safely looked after there, they ushered us in. They evidently found our whole set up unusual, for they alerted the local press. An apologetic nice young man called upon us in the morning. He wrote his report after asking many questions, but said that there was no fee for us. We complained, in fun, that we kept entertaining the great American public 'for free' —we had already done a free TV show in Central Park! His conscience was pricked and he returned, shortly before we left, bringing us a present of delicious red wine.

On an impulse we next drove up to Green Brook National Park. This stands high on a ridge to the north of the New York to Philadelphia road. It is well wooded yet commands a fine view of the plain below. A notice proclaims that Rock Park was one of George Washington's vantage points in the American War of Independence. Another notice forbade unauthorised cars in the park after 9.00pm which was unfortunate as it was an ideal camping spot. There was peace and quiet and room to breathe, and we were away from the swiftly moving cars and flashing lights on the freeway. The Ranger came along, obviously an old soldier, and we told him we would so much like to stay. He was noncommittal and disappeared, but returned shortly to say that his wife would like us to park in their garden. We were all friends at once.

On the morrow, a Sunday, the Ranger's wife kindly took us to her Church, a fairly modern, immensely ugly, chapel where we sat in the gallery and tried to make out what was being said and sung against the noise of the new air conditioning plant, that sucked and blew air like a dragon dressed in too tight a collar! After the service we were given sweet pink lemonade and introduced to members of the congregation. The Ranger and his wife were extremely kind. They showed us over their house and arranged a supper party for us. Also they introduced us to members of the park community, one of whom was a radio ham. He invited us to his 'shack' and spoke to Australia and Scandinavia while we were there. He gave us his code so that we could call him should we need to get an urgent message home at any time. The 'shack' had to be seen to be believed: a great mast stood in the garden beside the house and a semi-basement room was full of mysterious electrical 'junk'. Ham cards had been received from other operators around the world, from well-known voices of people whom he had never met nor was ever likely to meet. He had inherited the craze from his father, who had been an early operator. He was fascinated by the story of the English radio ham who had intercepted calls between members of a gang of bank robbers, and who then alerted the police, who had caught the robbers in the act; and he explained to us how this had happened.

Our next port of call was Plymouth Meeting, Pennsylvania where we had been invited to stay with friends. It was obvious that we were driving into 'older' country, for we were among houses of the English country house style, and the land was well 'larded' with golf courses. Whilst we had appreciated the spontaneous kindness and consideration shown to us on our way, it was as nothing to the welcome and hospitality we received from our host and hostess at Plymouth Meeting. We were there for Independence Day, 4th July, and were taken to a nearby club where many members had British connections and were wearing red, white and blue. We were warmly welcomed and asked to give conducted tours of *Peregrine*. Sports were arranged for the children and tennis and swimming for the adults, while drinks and lunches were served in the shade outside the clubhouse. The scene reminded me of a kaleidoscopic view of England embodying Ascot, the long 'picnic' interval at Glyndebourne, a county cricket match, and a school sports day all rolled into one! Only the chatter with the restrained Eastern American accent, and the hot relentless sun, established that this was not a British gathering of friends in England.

We were taken to visit the old city of Philadelphia, with its elegant 18th and 19th century buildings. From the recently established Independence Mall we saw Independence Hall which was built in 1732 as the State House of Pennsylvania. It is of mellowed red brick and supports a small red dome raised on six white stone columns. Although Philadelphia was founded by the English Quaker William Penn it nevertheless surprised us to see these dignified and distinguished buildings there. The imposing Independence Hall is flanked by Congress Hall and Old City Hall built in the 1790s, and inside furniture from the time of the signing of the Declaration of Independence in 1776 has been set out with quill pens and sand, just as would have been the practice at the time, so it is easy to imagine the scene. Within these walls the USA Constitution was framed by Washington, Jefferson, Hamilton and Lord Justice Marshall. The Great Liberty Bell is on show on the ground floor. It cracked, legend has it, when it was being tolled for the passing of Lord Justice Marshall in 1835.

Jefferson was the first President to use Washington as the capital city of the United States, once it had been drained and especially built for the purpose. Since that time Philadelphia has reverted to being the State Capital of Pennsylvania. However it retains the dignity of its historic past. It also boasts the oldest national learned society, the Philosophical Society founded in 1743 and housed in its Hall, of 1789, adjacent to the Old City Hall. Philadelphia also has the second Bank of the USA: it occupies a Palladian building which was started in 1819 and was undergoing extensive renovations when we were there.

Philadelphia itself bore the marks of the recent severe flooding which followed the tornado Agnes. Trees that lined the River Delaware had mud marks and bric-a-brac 15 to 20 feet up their trunks – but this was to be as nothing by comparison with the Susquehanna River valley. It is impossible to imagine the power of water when it is in spate. To have experienced Agnes must have been most alarming; the trail she left behind her demonstrated this all too clearly. Uprooted trees were carried across fields demolishing any bridges in their path. Railway lines were upended, cars, caravans and small sheds had been bowled along like toys, and when the storm subsided, marooned where they had landed. Villagers were desperately trying to get their carpets dry. A Church which was built on a platform up a flight of six steps had the pews out in the sun to dry while parishioners were trying to clean off the mud. Notices were posted on many bridges putting a limit on the speed and weight of vehicles.

After seeing so much devastation, it was pleasant to turn off the main road and a relief to drive up a farm track into the shade of some tall beech trees. It restored and refreshed us to find a small contained pond, still and calm, and full of wild life. The dragonflies were of particular beauty. There were three main varieties, distinguishable each from the other by their colour, their size and their flight. The largest ones were black, few in number, and constantly flew about in pairs, making short and purposeful flights as though they wished to get somewhere for some special reason. The next examples were black-bodied with gossamer-fine blue wings. They swooped most gracefully, flying, it seemed, for the sheer joy of movement. They stopped momentarily to examine a bulrush frond or a kingcup, and then they flew on again, weaving casual random patterns as they skimmed the water, rose and dived again. The third sort were all blue and very small, delicate, shy and hesitant. They moved their wings so fast that no colour could be seen as they fluttered about. Music was provided for these concurrent dances by the incessant croaking of frogs hidden in the mud at the edge of the pond.

This was a lovely interlude *en route* for perhaps the most famous waterfall in the world, Niagara Falls. We approached these falls with mixed feelings, for inhabitants of this great continent had warned us that they were just a tourist attraction, very crowded and very gimmicky. On the USA side a large park full of trees and reminiscent of Hyde Park flanks the river for perhaps half a mile. There is a natural island just off shore, and from here it is possible to be alone with the rapids, the spray and the hollow booming noise of the water as it cascades hundreds of feet over the Horseshoe Falls to the river below. An amusing bright red train plies around the park, and is a great help for the aged and parents with tired children. The functional graceful rainbow bridge takes one from the United States back to Canada, and from the Canadian side one looks into the concavity of the horseshoe.

It is true that thousands of sightseers come in coaches and cars, and click their cameras and suck their candy floss, but none had arisen at 6.30am on the morning we were there to see the sun rise over the American Falls. The horizontal light gave the water a pale translucent quality, the spray was gold and silver, seemingly, at the same time. The great Horseshoe Falls gathered its water from the swirling tide, dodging the rocks and selecting its spot for the overspill. On the turn the water becomes pale, then reaches out with long fingers and frothy white spray, before concentrating its force in the long downward fall to the olive green, apparently still, waters beneath. The quantity and force of the water is so great that it arches away from the rocks, so that small craft can safely go behind the curtain of water. Leonardo da Vinci drew those wonderful water fountain pictures of the carefree bubbles making patterns below the surface as they fell and then broke the surface again on their way up. What paintings Leonardo da Vinci could have produced from a study of the waters of Niagara ...

Peregrine so far had given us little mechanical trouble. It is true that several of the 30 bolts that hold the sump to the engine had had to be replaced, and all had had to be tightened in Montreal, and that the top of the carburettor had worked loose which had temporarily brought us to a standstill – but we had not been seriously held up until we entered Toronto at about 10.00pm, when an electrical fault developed, and this defeated both us and one of the mechanics, an impetuous fellow, at a nearby garage. This caused the ever polite police to visit us to discover why we never moved forward when the lights changed to green. At midnight we agreed to be towed across the road into the garage forecourt. The impetuous boy got the garage car, looking like a racing stock car, and he drove it at *Peregrine* as a bulldozer might attack the wall of a house destined to be demolished. We complained, but he was deaf to our entreaties. We reached the garage forecourt, but at a price – we had a battered wing and a bent bumper. Mercifully this youth was then off duty and a pleasant European student got to work with the aid of the Bedford handbook, and by about 12.45am we were mobile again. Now all we had to do was to find our way to our cousin's flat. We had a car searchlight athwart our roof, and Susan deftly swung it from side to side to enable us to check on street names and house numbers. We found the house, but no-one was at home so we pulled off the road and slept.

Most fortunately, Tam, our cousin, arrived early in the morning, as we were pondering our next move. We were soon en route for their farm at Tottenham. This Tottenham is in a remote part of Ontario with a directional address No.2 which means near to Railroad No.2. Was 'our' Tottenham ever remote like this?

We left Toronto, the second largest city in Canada, on a six-stream freeway, with cars cascading along much as the waters of Niagara are divided by rocks and surge forward. Gradually the road narrowed and the traffic lessened, and the speed of cars dropped. Once again we were among trees, cultivated fields, and pastures with Charollais cattle, and we were breathing real fresh country air. We drove through the lowland market gardens of the recent Dutch settlers and the older farming communities of settlers from Ireland. We then turned onto a dirt road in hilly country with properties bounded by old 'serpentine' fencing, three bars to an upright arranged in a zig-zag line to withstand the winds and snows of the Winter. The old oak or cedar wood fences have become mellowed to a lovely grey-green. The old farmsteads are wooden frame houses infilled with clapboard, and some of them have had modern mosquito screening added, sometimes enclosing the verandah. There may be roses and flowering shrubs in the gardens, but attempts at 'real' gardening are not made, for there is a long dry Summer season when water is a scarce commodity. Winters are cold when farms are snowbound. Many farmsteads are characteristically surrounded by old barns and maple woods.

We spent twelve days with Tam and Betty his wife, and their two children, which gave us time to meet a number of their friends and the people among whom they live. John, a smallholder of Tottenham, was typical of the independent approach of the small farmer to be found off the beaten track. He lived alone with his faithful, well-trained black and white sheepdog. They both came to greet Tam and me as we went by his farm. He had a splendid clear-cut face, spare high cheek-boned and rugged; he looked at each of us with a steady twinkling gaze, his farseeing blue eyes missing nothing, yet displaying a quiet contentment with his way of life. He was simply dressed in grey trousers and an open-neck checked shirt. He was always ready for the job in hand, this he undertook with a quiet confidence and a certain spring. He was never hurried. Always accompanied by his dog, he joked readily, and taking leave of us he took off his fine trilby-shaped black-banded straw hat and waved us goodbye. A satisfying and satisfactory meeting.

Mr B. was another person who imparted a flavour of this gathering of farms known as Tottenham. He rattled up the hill to his farm in a ramshackle old car which served him well, but would be unlikely to pass the MOT over here. He had a good memory for names and places and could recall circumstances of several years back with ease and precision. A slow and deliberate worker, though not skilled in any particular craft, he had been helping Tam to bound his farm with old pinewood fences. He drove the uprights into the soil and then fixed the three horizontal bars to them, often finally securing them by twisting narrow wire around them. This scarcely showed and it is much quicker than tenon and mortising. In the Winter he pottered in the woodshed, making good use of the wood fire to heat the shed while he repaired implements and sawed logs for the sitting room fire. He had a great capacity for keeping the old machinery on the move which may not have been super-efficient, but it did the job.

We visited Maple Farm, where some elderly Canadians of Irish extraction lived. They were happily sitting on their old verandah chairs and rocking to and fro. They had some primitive electric lighting which attracted the mosquitoes. They had not indulged in anti-mosquito netting, and we were bitten alive. However, although uncomfortable, these bites are not injurious. Their farmhouse drive and equipment looked as if they needed several young and active men to bring the holding up to standard again. They did not appear to notice that their maintenance was not keeping pace with the dilapidations! We had a splendid chat on the history of the area and of the old customs, some of which are "... *yielding place to new*" (from Tennyson's "Morte d'Arthur": "... *The old order changeth, yielding place to new, And God fulfils himself in many ways, Lest one good custom should corrupt the world*"). They were most hospitable and welcoming. We were no longer aware of any slackening of standards as we accepted theirs. Their hospitality more than overcame any suggestion of critical appraisal with which we might have started.

There was very little farm equipment in this area, and any there was, was shared by those who needed it. The farms were mostly run by one to three men and men came with equipment to help others when needed. Reciprocally, the borrowers helped the owners on their fields when the equipment was 'at home'. There was no central focal point in this collection of farms, but there was great understanding among the inhabitants of the area. Like all farmers, they worked hard in the season of harvest, but life in the Winter months was restricted by the heavy falls of drifting snow which confined farmers to their farms. In the July sunshine with temperatures in the 80s and 90sF this seemed difficult to imagine.

Each farm had its own water supply, its own deep freeze with rations for three to five weeks and, until recently, its own electricity supply. Milk was produced locally on the farm and eggs were available. Each household was therefore self-supporting. In some areas, snowmobiles in Winter were the substitutes for cars, while snow-shoeing and cross-country skiing were also ways of getting about.

Many of us think that there is a sterility of Canadian art. Some have heard of Grandma Moses, some have seen her lively, viridian green portrayals of early settlers: their trails across the great continent, their patches of land cleared for building their wooden frame log cabins; their tobogganing at Christmas time. Grandma Moses started to paint when she was over 60, and she has left for us an unique history in diagrammatic picture form with the unsophisticated presentation of a child. Grandma Moses was not striving for effect, she was contributing to the history of the settlers in an immediate and vivid way, while relating her own personal experiences. She used viridian green straight from the box, and drew Lowry-like figures scampering all over the canvas, busy about their individual chores.

While she was making such splendid use of her retirement in Winnipeg, a group of artists were blazing another trail in Ontario. Each of the seven had studied in Paris, and has made bold use of colour giving a flavour of the French Impressionists. Each of the seven has contributed his or her very especial flavour of the character of Canada. There are landscape paintings depicting vast tracts of trees, the fall, colours of Eastern Canada, the force and grandeur of the great Rockies, the farmlands and limitless space, the coastlines, and the great clear sky-scapes in the brilliant light of the prairies, while the portraits show the rugged character of the individuals of the continent, be they Indian or settler.

The seven artists are Johnston, Jackson, Varley, Frank, Carmichael, Lismer McDonald and Lauren Harris. Casson and Le Moine Fitzgerald may almost be numbered among them. An especial gallery has been built near to Toronto in a private garden, and here a great selection of the work of these artists has been well hung and lit in a two-storey log cabin. The whole enterprise is truly Canadian; the flavour of the country permeates the exhibition.

The Royal Ontario Museum alone would give Toronto the right to a very special place in Canada. This Museum is wonderfully rich in Chinese exhibits, perhaps, outside China, one of the richest in the world. It has more than one complete funeral procession of Ming/Tang pottery. These are most impressive, comprising about 50–80 mounted and walking mourners, each an individual, each superbly executed. There are Ching dynasty (AD 1644-1712) carved ivory figures of infinite beauty revealing naturalistic charm in stylised stances. There is a wonderful collection of jade, deep green, pale green, cream and brown jade, red jade and yellow jade. This jade is used for bowls, carved animals, ornaments and a great number of phials and beautiful small bottles of many and various shapes. Then there are the Chinese frescoes ... and this in no way exhausts the collection. It is also a well represented museum, with classical treasures from Egypt, Greece and the Roman Empire, as well as some fascinating geological exhibits, including fossilised trilobites, some 450 million years old from the North American Shield. This Pre-Cambrian Shield which extends around Hudson Bay also provides a wealth of information on the Indian exhibits. The one which I liked best was an initiation boat in which Indian boys spend three days alone in the forests before being accepted as adults of their band or tribe. The boat was carved with weird traditional beasts of the armadillo type, and with birds and a sort of grasshopper. Once used, the boat was generally burned.

The road system that leads one to and from Toronto was the first eight-lane highway that I had seen. It seemed a millennium of years away from the space and time enjoyed by those earlier local world occupants, whose art and culture we had been celebrating in the Museum. Freeway driving on the network of concrete flyovers and underpasses has to be seen and experienced to be believed. Possibly *Peregrine's* size and bulk kept us free from 'assault' or collision – for we returned unscathed! But how is progress measured?

Back at Tam and Betty's, Susan with Hughie, who was her contemporary, put together an Unidentified Flying Object – two great circles of strong white paper with a central circular hole decorated with great red rounds of tissue paper. Then they lit a wood fire in the workshop, clambered on the roof, held the UFO over the chimney and filled it with hot air before letting it go to climb higher and higher...only to come down in the garden! A further attempt was made at filling the UFO with hot air, cameras were brought out and the donor and his wife joined in the preparations for a successful flight. We were all agog and ready to ring the authorities to report a flying saucer from outer space, expecting that others would do the same when they saw our UFO. Up it went higher and higher into the bluest of skies tinged with the pink rays of the setting sun. It looked very fine as it bravely crossed a field and we wished we had put a tag inside so that we might be notified of the extent of its flight, but then it got into a pocket of air and faltered, coming down within two hundred yards of the woodshed.

Tam very kindly arranged for Betty to accompany us to Canada's Shakespeare Theatre in Stratford Park, Ontario, to see 'King Lear' and 'Much Ado about Nothing'. The Festival Hall, which holds 3,000, is built in the shape of a bell tent with a blue crown with white 'ear' points on top, the Canadian flag surmounting all. Through the park flows a river – the Avon, naturally – complete with both black and white swans. The theatre was a hundred yards away and we established ourselves in this park for three nights. Whilst there we were visited by several folk, including 'Oliver' from "As You Like It", who came across after their afternoon rehearsal, as wagers had been laid in the Green Room about *Peregrine*! Oliver seemed to have won as he plumped for a Bedford! Everyone was in festive mood, young couples strolled around and families played or rested on the extensive lawns. We returned to Toronto via Guelph, so obviously a city of German origins.

Eventually we had to leave Tam and Betty and their haven, and we continued our journey north to Georgian Bay, skirting the east side of Lake Huron, and reached the Trans-Canadian highway at Sudbury. We found a boat launching jetty and drove *Peregrine* alongside the many empty cars parked on the quayside while their owners were afloat. We explored a lagoon with the sun setting in a red ball and lighting the water and the silver birch stems with a red-gold glow. A loon flew overhead making its plaintive call. A local fisherman joined us and welcomed us, regaling us with local news and stories. He told us that the name 'loon' in Canada was given to divers, including the colymbus. In England, we learnt that the name can also apply to grebes. Our bird was solitary and the fisherman seemed a loner too.

It was late July 1972 and we had driven up the beautiful east side of the Great Lakes, in brilliant sunshine or beneath fast-moving billowy clouds, and joined the magnificent Trans Canadian Highway at Sudbury. Sudbury is a smelly mining area, its National Park is surrounded by giant-sized nickels and dimes. Sudbury is in the centre of a bleak and barren excavated area that man has exploited and where nothing grows. It was here that the United States astronauts practised for their moon landings. Sudbury itself is peopled with miners, entrepreneurs and businessmen who are prepared to live in these desolate conditions for the money they can earn.

Our joy and delight was the greater, by contrast, as we drove west, when we espied an inviting creek on Lake Huron, lying between the fir trees and birches, with the ever-moving mauve-blue waters reaching out to a mauve-green island. We read a notice informing travellers that this was an Indian Reserve, not to be violated. Against instructions, we drove down a short unmade-up roadway, and sought the local Indian head of this haven of beauty: we found a distinguished Ojibwe Indian chief, who with his smiling and silent wife and his uncle welcomed us, and invited us to stay on their land. We felt greatly honoured, to be accepted by members of one of the greatest Indian tribes of the continent, for the Ojibwes had once controlled the territory from Sault Sainte Marie along the northern shores of the great Lakes Superior and Huron, and along Huron's eastern shores. The Ojibwes also controlled the shores of Georgian Bay and the greater part of what is now the extensive state of Ontario. We were welcomed into a family and into a tribe; we were guests of people whose roots go back through history. We were straddling two ways of life, with a small village school, several modern bungalow type houses and a number of ruins, including a church and several houses and gardens inhabited by Ojibwe Indians. Our host was deftly preparing blueberries for market. He was a short, yet large man with jet black hair and an alert, bronzed face. He was dressed in European clothes, but I felt that the Indian tunic would have suited him better. His individuality was shown in his choice of hat – a splendid straw hat of 'monsoon hat' shape, that went up to a point in the middle of the crown and swept down to the brim in two graceful curves, protecting his eyes, his face and his shoulders from sun and rain. His wife sat with him on their lawn, cross-legged as he was. Every line of her body expressed a calm confidence that comes from the fulfilment of life. An epitaph to be found in the Alameda Gardens of Gibraltar might well be applied to her: "She has borne twelve children and is a pattern to her sex," for this placid mother was habitually surrounded by ten of her twelve children and her first-born was also with her for that week. He was 25 years of age and living happily among the immigrant population on the outskirts of Toronto, but had come back to the Reserve with his wife and two children for a week's holiday.

"I must come back," he said, "for I belong here. I was brought up here when government policy was to keep us on our own and to provide work for us Indians on the reserves. We used to have a factory here and our own Church. There were more of us in this community then, but many have died and some have moved away. We were isolated and so were obliged to inter-marry or move, but there are currently plans to repopulate this area again. It was found that the factory was a cause of our isolation and also a distinct factor in the cause of the pollution of this lake. The factory fell into disrepair and was removed. Then it became policy to try to integrate us Indians with the modern population of the country. Now our children of 11 years and over are being bussed to schools outside the reserves to learn with the children of the settlers. At this age integration can be natural, but for us things were different. We had seldom been off the reserve before we were 16, and then being shy and impressionable and at a loss to know the ways of modern man, we were pitchforked into 'gainful employment' away from the reserve and all that we knew. Our upbringing had been so different from that of those amongst whom we were working. We, proud Ojibwes, found ourselves feeling inferior and unsure; we, who for generations had ruled these lands.

"A Minister of Indian affairs caused research to be carried out and we endorsed the plan for earlier contact with those outside the Reserve. Children of 11 take things as they find them and our boys have much that they can teach any boy of that age. They have a certain strength in knowing how to face a bear, track a wild animal, find their way in unmarked forests and the like. They hold their own. In this way they are prepared for work in the community when the time comes. I am now in charge of the distribution of parts in a factory in Toronto," he said. "I am readily accepted by the recent immigrants to Canada but there is still distance between us and the families of the early settlers. This is unfortunate but understandable, for they may not penetrate our reserves and we seldom leave them. TV and the radio are great levellers from which we can learn much of their life, but they only see ours through documentaries which are a specialised form of art and fail fully to communicate our way of life to them. They never tell the whole story.

This man's younger brother, aged about 12, came along with an exquisitely executed birch boomerang that his father had made for him. "Do you know what to do if you meet a bear?" the boy asked me. "No," I replied. "What should I do? "I know. All Ojibwe men know. But I cannot tell you. This is a secret of we Ojibwe men!"

Observing this stocky, sturdy boy with his quiet confidence, steady bearing, and his far-seeing gaze that hid his many secrets that belong to the Ojibwe men, I thought how genuine he was, and wondered how long it would be before he was touched by competition, greed and love of money.

I hoped that he would stay true to the standards of life which he had learned from his father and others on the reserve.

I learned that there are ten linguistic groups of Indians, four of which inhabit the vast tracts of land that lie between the Atlantic and the Rockies, while the other six are to be found in British Columbia. East of the Rockies live the Algonquin, Athaspakan, Oroquoian and Siouan speaking Indians. There are many sub-divisions of the Algonquin stock: the Mic Macs of Prince Edward Island, Novia Scotia, including Kejimakujik Park and New Brunswick; the Montagnels of Quebec and the Ojibwes of Ontario with the Cree, Stony, Black Foot Indians of part of Ontario and the Prairie Provinces reaching as far as Banff in the Eastern Rockies. Oroquoians, including the Hurons, are found around Lake Huron, in Ontario and Quebec provinces. The Athaspakan stock inhabits chiefly the Yukon and North West Territories. Tribes of the Sioux inhabit parts of Manitoba, Saskatchewan and Alberta.

The organisation of Indian Affairs has varied over the decades. In 1880 it had its own department, since when it has been a branch of the Department of Mines and Resources, then a branch of Citizenship and Immigration. Since 1956 Indians have been the responsibility of the Department of Indian Affairs and Northern Development. The Northern area is an area of very rapid development. The Pre-Cambrian Shield covers the central part of this northern area. Through the development of the Trans-Canadian Highway it is now partly accessible. This has encouraged the pulp wood industry which provides work for Indians, while mining and other projects are being explored. There is plenty of untapped wealth in that area. This Department, as well as supervising the development of the land has an enormous project ahead of it in bringing Indians into the full citizenship of Canada.

There are at least eleven Post Confederate Treaties made with the Indians including two made between King George V and particular groups of Indians in 1925, who ceded their hunting, fishing and trapping rights in Central Ontario and Southern Ontario in return for a payment of $500,000 which the Provincial Governor of Ontario paid them. The Indians ceded vast tracts of land of the order of 42,000 square miles (the smallest tract!) to 372,000 square miles (the largest tract), and in return the government undertook to provide reserves for the Indians of one square mile for each family of five, and some small annual payments in dollars and equipment to further their hunting, farming, trapping and fishing. The Indian population of 200,000 was declining from 1848 until about 1908. Since that date the population has again been increasing until, in the 1960s, it had exceeded the 200,000 mark. Indians are being encouraged to integrate with the population of non-Indians in Canada and to this end the Placements Programme was formally established in 1957, whereby Indians are being encouraged to give up Indian status. This status entitles them to a per capita share of the Indian Tribal or Band Trust, but it also removes them from the rights and privileges reserved under the Indian Act for Indians only. This step is taken by professional Indians such as doctors and lawyers. Even successful artisans are reluctant to take this step when parents and brothers and sisters are still living on the reserve, for on the Reserve they feel protected by the Department of Indian Affairs and Northern Developments and do not easily feel sufficiently assured to emerge from this protection. Their children may feel differently. For instance, the children of our host's eldest son were typical products of the suburbs of a large and flourishing city, whereas his own children of the same age still had a pride in their Indian ways. This is certainly a transitional stage for Canadian Indians.

When our informant had finished telling me something of this history of the government schemes in practice, and of the present state of affairs as he saw it, he took his leave and went down to the jetty to prepare his boat to take his parents and several members of the family on a blueberrying expedition to one of the islands or promontories which could only be reached by water. The girls came and joined us. Owl and her friend, also 12 or 13 years of age, were attractive and also important members of the family for they were temporarily in charge of the youngest of the family, a girl of just 4 years, and also of Dorothea, a bright little girl of about 8. She had a twinkle in her eye, a sense of fun and a great capacity for arranging interesting things to do. I could see that she was never bored nor at a loss as a 'town child' might be if divorced from TV. She led the way in single Indian file along narrow tracks between the high grasses and wild flowers to a small area surrounded by a stockade in which were tombstones set up to commemorate past inhabitants of the area. It was a proper pilgrimage and we, with the solemn children, paid our respects to those who had gone before and who had left their mark in the community. There were not many graves but they evidently stood for something and, although a Christian burial ground, I wondered if some form of ancestor worship was understood and practised. Somehow, it had seemed necessary for the children to bring us to their buried ancestors: now I felt that we might remain among them with their blessing.

Dorothea next led us to her school playground where several children were enjoying slides, swings or see-saws. A small boy disentangled himself from the group and shinned up an old-fashioned iron pump, took a china cup that was balanced upon its top, gave himself some water, swilled it out and again shinned up the pump to replace the china cup. How orderly, how quietly responsible, how remarkable that this china cup survived. The two children who lived in greater Toronto could be singled out in a moment. They were less confident, almost outsiders, self conscious and somewhat selfish. The affinity with the land was missing, the assured deliberate movements were not there. Dorothea suddenly bubbling with excitement pointed out a good sized tanker that was making its way towards us leaving a white trail on the waters of the lake. "Look," she said, "that is our ship. It comes twice a year to bring us oil for cooking and heating." With a dance-like movement she led the way to a great grey-green rock, stark and bare but for a few blueberries and dwarf wild cherries and raspberries. The great curve of the rock was like the back of a giant tortoise split with fissures here and there in which crevices the succulent fruits grew. We sat and watched the busy little boats bringing the lines ashore. The oil pipes were coupled up and while the oil was being transferred the sailors of the ship enjoyed a prolonged bathe. As we watched we caught something of the excitement expressed by the children. The peace, the remoteness, and the isolation, the quiet tenor of life on this Indian Reserve was creeping into our veins. Birds flew overhead, snakes were said to be in the grasses, we felt that porcupines were likely to emerge, and that bears were not far off, yet peace and a redolent sense of orderliness and fitness of purpose permeated the atmosphere.

We returned to the jetty just in time to see the family return laden with blueberries, later to be sorted, weighed and presented in baskets to a pedlar who came the next morning to collect them and take them to market. This had been a good day for blueberrying and their crop was worth about £35. How surprising to learn later that our hostess had gone off in the evening to Bingo! We were indeed straddling two ways of life. In the morning we bade farewell to our splendid host and his charming family who invited us to stay with them again. We returned to the hustle and bustle of the Trans-Canadian Highway with its streams of fast moving cars and the extraordinary sight of mobile homes and pick-up caravans perched on trucks. On reaching the important port of Sault Sainte Marie, with its factories and warehouses along the waterfront and the fine bridge spanning the water which marks the boundary between Canada and the USA, our retreat was over. We reflected on the eternal problem of, "What is living?" How do we achieve this, and which is real life; that on the reserve or that in the great towns of the sophisticated world? What is happiness, how can it be measured and where is it to be found? Lewis Carroll wrote that enigmatic poem The Hunting of the Snark... Is the 'snark' a symbol of perfect truth or perfect happiness? Are the two interchangeable? The snark comes so nearly within the grasp of his seekers, but can never be wholly embraced. Surely, we were near to grasping the snark during our stay on the Indian Reserve.....

Our encounter with the distinguished Ojibwe Indians, which we had so much enjoyed, brought this whole issue to our notice. This problem is most difficult and pressing just now. It is difficult because the Canadian Indians, as we learnt are of a number of different tribes. This number is of the order of five hundred and they were never unified. They have differing backgrounds and are at differing stages of development. Within any one tribe there are strong differences of opinion, yet their administration is in the hands of the minister for Indian Affairs and Northern Development. What an enormous and delicate task this department has as legislation must apply to all. So long as Indians were kept isolated on the various reserves, the dual problem of providing for them and trying to integrate them did not occur. With the advent of education for the Indian, followed by the radio and TV, many of the younger Canadian Indians are ready for higher education, followed by responsible jobs away from the reserve, whilst the older generations feel exposed away from the reserve and the life that they know. The minister for Indian Affairs gives protection for Indians and subsidises them, however, the standard of living of Indians away from the reserve and the control of their Chief, especially in the Kenora area, leaves something to be desired. All too often Indians have been lured into towns to take unskilled jobs, have been unwise with their money, become unemployed and then unemployable. This reputation of a few has been taken by Canadians in the vicinity as the norm, and suspicion has grown between the earlier settlers in Canada and the emerging Indians.

Neither the British nor the French Canadians has been scrupulous over treaties made with the Indians, and in the States this attitude persists. The incidents of Wounded Knee made this quite apparent. There, land ceded to the USA Government for a specific purpose was to be returned to the Indians when that purpose was fulfilled. These provisions were realised but the land was not returned to the Indians. A mini civil war ensued until the Indians got their rights. Indian lands are sacred to the Indians and no-one may enter them without permission from the Indians. There are large tracts of land sometimes rich in mineral deposits, reserved to the Indians. A crossroads has been reached: should there be a speed up of integration? Should further compensation in the form of money be paid to the Indians for their land – if so, at what rate and how should it be distributed?

Canada is also accepting groups of asylum seekers.. These people remain in their cultural groups on the outskirts of the cities and Folklarama weeks are arranged when the immigrants 'do their thing' and keep alive the cultural customs they have brought with them. Chinese, Jamaican and Ugandan nationals, for example, have kept themselves in social groups with their native customs just as have French, Armenian, Russian and Croatian nationals. This policy is quite different from that pursued in the USA where an immigrant becomes an American on arrival and is expected to speak American and become a full citizen of his adoptive country. Each scheme has its strengths and its weaknesses.

Continuing westwards we headed for Thunder Bay on Lake Superior, a busy port handling grain and timber for the paper mills and also the heart of Indian culture of the area. We were planning to stay with our cousins, Rod and Gerry, at their summer house in Silver Islet on the tip of the great spur of land known as the Sleeping Giant which has long been venerated by the Indians. Nearby are the Kakabake Falls, redolent with the legend of the Indian princess who, when captured by an attacking band of Sioux, led them over the 125ft drop to her and their deaths, rather than give away her father's people to them.

One part of the peninsular, known as the 'eagle' of Thunder Bay because of its shape, is covered in primaeval forests. The harbour and Lion Rock are located here, natural formations of hard rock which remained while softer rock was eroded, rather like the Cornish rocks at Polperro. Lion Rock is nearly golden in colour and some years ago must have looked like a sculpture, but alas the frost and the weather have eroded much of the Lion's head away.

In the entrance to the bay is a small island called Silver Isle, so named because for about five years from 1868 to 1873 some of the best silver the earth has yielded was mined there. The village of Silver Islet sprang up on the mainland and a self-contained colony was established, being reached by water from Port Arthur, as Thunder Bay was then called. The richness of this silver deposit was legendary and after a difficult beginning wealth seemed assured. However, the mine had to be kept free from the waters of the lake by continuous pumping. One year around Christmas time it is rumoured that the Captain of the supply ship with the essential delivery of coal needed to drive the pumps became drunk, and lost control of his ship, which then failed to reach the island and became ice bound. . Without coal, the pumps stopped working, the mine flooded, and silver from the isle has not been worked since that fateful day. The silverworkers' log cabins were deserted and nature took charge again: animal wild life and birds returned and were undisturbed for about 30 years, until Silver Isle was rediscovered. The miners' log cabins in their original state were bought by Canadian families to be used as Summer weekend cottages. Most of these houses have been modernised and refurnished, and a road from the Trans-Canadian Highway has been built down to this haven from the Thunder Bay road past Selby National Park, a reserve for indigenous birds, animals and vegetation. Silver Islet now has a thriving summer community and many new 'A-line' houses are being built to accommodate more visitors. These are situated around the long slow curve of the bay, with just enough space for a barbecue between the house and the water's edge.

Rod and Gerry's house is on the crescent of the 'eagle's' under tail feather, as it were, with a view of Powder House Island amongst others. Together with their neighbours they have built a makeshift sauna. The birchwood fire heats the stones on which water is splashed, to give off clouds of steam. Each naked body, having sweated from the heat, then boldly plunges into the bitterly cold Lake Superior just outside the door! Once was enough for me as the waters of Lake Superior are really cold, although the sun is wonderfully warm.

We visited one of the miner's cottages that was left as it had been found, with a long wooden table and bench on the bare floorboards with some plaited wool rugs, and, of course, no electricity nor even paint, just the bare pine which has now mellowed to a lovely grey-brown colour. Inside, the walls were plastered between the pine uprights, and the sitting room furniture was 'Victorian': in style; a hat stand with mirror, rocking chairs, a three-legged coal bucket were on display, with pictures of the period and photographs of the works, now searing with age, along with a copy of the rules for miners. In the kitchen-cum-dining room there was a board set out with bits and pieces from the mine including mysteriously shaped pieces of metal which we learnt had held the lamps underground; also old flat irons with detachable wooden handles, a butter pestle, candlesticks and so on.

Behind the houses is the jungle where pitcher plants grow. These are one of the insect-eating plants: the lime green leaves with mauve or crimson veins have their sides joined so that rain collects in them and as soon as an insect begins to explore the neck of the pitcher it is caught in a

Eastern Canada

Lake Huron with Ojibwe Indians

Ojibwe Children

St. John's River, New Brunswick

Niagra Rapids

Western Canada

The Rockie Mountains by Yoyo National Park B.C.

Lake Superior

Hoodoos, Banff

Tepees at Banff

Western Canada

Takakkawa Falls

The Mighty Redwood Trees

Maples from Barnaby Park, North Vancouver

A Painting by the Author

Vancouver Island—seen from Lighthouse Park, across English Bay

sticky liquid, drowned in the water and ingested into the plant. The sepals are above the flowers which stand up straight, and if the head is tipped back five soft lime moss green velvety 'pads' may be seen.

There is many a tale to tell of nature's ways here. The jungly woods open onto reed-fringed lakes where pine, birch, fir and aspen trees jostle for position. Fallen branches crackle underfoot and marshy areas make walking difficult. Moss hangs from the trees and carpets the ground, with lumps of pinky-grey granite obtruding. There is a dampness and a stillness creating an atmosphere of calm. Here one is enveloped by nature, and Nature is in command. There are some ancient trails left by the Indians who depended on these wooded hills for their birch trees. Birch trees were cut in the spring to provide the peeled-off bark for canoes. This bark, when it first leaves the tree, is pliable, almost like leather and can be shaped before it becomes 'set'. The canoes on Lake Superior had the bark on the outside of the canoe but the canoes for Lake Huron had the bark on the inside and the smoother inner part met the water. These canoes were built on a frame of young branches, the bark being thonged into position and held there by wood athwart the beam. They were simple, light-weight, watertight and manageable. I made a miniature one from birch bark and young willow. The Indians additionally used to make boomerangs, catapults and aids for cooking from the wood of the birch trees.

Rod and Gerry took us by boat to Lighthouse Island, called Porphery Island, where we met the lighthouse keeper, the third generation of his family to be in charge of the lighthouse – and the last, for this old, hand-operated lighthouse was soon to be worked automatically. The local inhabitants viewed this development with horror as yachtsmen and others using the waters over generations have been dependent on the help that has been given from the lighthouse. The day we were there was no exception. A Scandinavian-American family sailing up from the USA had holed their boat which was shipping water. Being unable to repair it themselves, the lighthouse family came to their rescue. One look at the keeper was enough to judge that here was an experienced and capable man. Dressed in an old sweater with a woolly cap atop his rugged, sensitive, sun-tanned face, he was mixing some well-tried resinous preparation to mend the leak. Confidence had been restored to the boat's inexperienced crew members. Meanwhile his wife was sorting the contents of the boat which had hastily been put ashore when the boat began to sink. She and the lady of the party were working with a will, whilst a tall rather elegant fair-haired youth, smartly dressed in white jeans and a white top edged with dark blue, looked rather lost and out of place. He obviously did not know about patching boats and felt the sorting of the clothes and kitchen things to be women's work. He had only a slender knowledge of birds and things of nature and was finding the delay and disorder tiresome.

The lighthouse keeper gave a knowing nod to Rod and Gerry and we set off for the lighthouse along a road with signs everywhere of the great storm of 1st October 1971. Tall birches and firs had been uprooted, and some had fallen amongst standing trees and were still being propped up by them, whilst others having fallen across the road had had to be cut, in order to clear a way to the lighthouse. Some had been twisted by the storm that had vertical slits on the trunks, and many of them had grey fungus hanging from their branches. Birch trees are beautiful at every stage. Never before had I seen the subtle, soft colours of the dying birch bark. They displayed a pinkish colour with a splash of yellow ochre and a dash of silver, and where the trunks were bared of bark they had turned a deep chestnut colour. The degrees of change were so delicate and so variable.

We climbed the hill and reached the clearing at the top where, in all its glory, stood the lighthouse. It had been freshly painted a brilliant white as had been the house which was adorned with red shutters. The sky was clear and the whole area seemed so well established and secure that it was hard to believe it was shortly to be deserted. Brightly coloured flowers dressed the area: roses, petunias, forget-me-nots, aquilegias both purple and white, and gold coreopsis. The assistant's house looked equally spruce. The power house also was smart and functional, with a grey-blue floor that reflected the light of the sky, and powerful machinery painted red which gleamed in contrast to its white walls. This lighthouse would close at its peak.. The earlier generation of keepers would have been proud of the spirit of the last inhabitants. We told his wife how lovely we thought her home looked, so clean and bright with flowers. She was much pleased, and spoke ruefully of their impending retirement when her husband would be leaving the only way of life he knew. As we got into the dank wooded area that led to the jetty we were plagued with mosquitoes. The keeper said that they were "worse than he had ever known them". They were hanging on our woollen garments in numbers, to be blown away only when we got free of the land on our return boat trip.

In the mountains almost due north of Silver Islet there is an open cast amethyst mine. The way to it we found tortuous and narrow. After some miles a notice warns visitors of the dangers and difficulties of a very steep and sharply curving single track road, so we left *Peregrine* in a parking area by the river, to complete the journey on the moped. Susie and I started up the steep narrow track, but it was soon evident that the moped could not manage the weight of both of us. Susie leapt off and nobly ran by the side of the moped. On we went along this rocky, pitted, sandy road. The hill became steeper. I tried zig-zagging but this was to no avail so I had to dismount and started to push the moped up the 1 in 3 gradient. The temperature was 100^0F or thereabouts. It was midday. This was a mug's game. I found the moped would drive her own weight up the hill and this gave me some respite. Balsam firs grew on each side of the road with a few alders and birches at the fringes. Reaching the top of the hill at last, we looked through the firs and were surprised at this height to see a large, still, deep blue lake – large by British standards but not by comparison with Gitchiecoomie, (the Indian name for Lake Superior) which is more like an ocean.

We mounted the moped and drove along the top of this great hill. In front of us was a wall with a notice upon it indicating that it was built in 1967 to mark the official opening of Thunder Bay Amethyst Mine. The entire wall, standing 6ft high and 10ft long, was built of amethysts. Some parts of the wall were brown, some a real mauve, part was of a pale lilac colour and part almost crystal clear. This semi-precious stone is characterised by its shape, always crystallising in the shape of a six- sided pyramid however large or small. This was an open cast mine and we found we were crunching crystals under our feet as we walked about. There were crystals everywhere, shining bright in a muddy brown stream or tantalisingly 'growing' from the living rock. Where some of the hill had been blasted away the granite covering was split with fissures filled with these gems. We watched a bespectacled lady in bright green trousers and a pink blouse chipping away with a hammer and stone chisel. She told us that she always finds her own pieces, for her hobby is polishing and setting these precious stones. Two men, casual visitors like ourselves, were looking with untrained eyes for the six- sided crystals, and reckoned they needed dynamite not just a hammer and chisel to expose them! A mother and her two boys were choosing small bits while Pa was down in the river bed, offering pieces to his wife who was keeping her feet dry on the overhanging sandy ridge. From these visitors we learnt that we might choose pieces from the display on the trestle tables, or select our own samples. We picked up pieces, though it was difficult to find undamaged shapes, and dropped them into a bucket provided by the company. Returning to the wall at the entrance we found a wooden hut nearby, where wonderful examples of quartz and amethyst were on display, and there we joined a queue of bargain hunters waiting to have their finds weighed. The man in charge was a wag, telling jokes non-stop as he served us. The crowd listened with respect to one old chestnut which elicited giggles of laughter. It was about an Irish nun making her way through customs armed with a bottle of 'holy water'. The customs official established it was whisky, but unperturbed the nun announced that "...another miracle has been performed." This 'wag' allowed us a generous weight of gems for our money, and then helped us to load them on to the moped and, full of jokes to the last, saw us off on our return journey.

Regretfully we left Thunder Bay and our hospitable cousins and continued our drive westwards, now towards Winnipeg and the Prairies spending one night at Iquace, an idyllic spot on Lake Agimack. The eight mile long lake (too small to be marked on the map!) was calm and in the evening reflected the most perfect sunset, a golden red with deep blue streaks, against a duck egg blue sky. In the early morning the gold lit the tops of the trees and only later revealed the many greens that clothe the further shore, and against this, wisps of mist curled away. We found that we were within fifty miles of Lake Kilvert, quite a big one, that lies between two main roads. We heard that the map-makers were overwhelmed by the numbers of unnamed lakes; and it was decided to give them the names of the Members of Parliament at the time – this included a cousin who was also Mayor of Hamilton.

We made our way towards Lake Louise and turned off just short of a large tourist centre and found an isolated hotel by Lake Moraine in the ten peak valley, and stopped under a 'suitable' notice which read 'No overnight parking' and there we stayed! It was a lovely quiet spot facing great glacial mountains. In the morning we drove into the town of Lake Louise and learnt that there had been much disturbance through the night on account of marauding bears!

At Winnipeg we replenished our supplies at a grocery store and when we came out we saw that *Peregrine* was leaking water badly. Later we learnt that our shower, which was heated by its water encircling the engine, had broken into the engine and we were in serious trouble. Mercifully I found a well qualified engineer who enabled us to continue our journey but without the benefit of hot showers. How lucky that this happened at Winnipeg and not in some remote spot!

We found our friends, Lawrence and Nancy and their family in their Summer quarters, on the shores of a lake, in their log cabin, which can only be reached by boat! Lawrence, a thoracic surgeon and Nancy kindly allowed us to stay in their house in Winnipeg while *Peregrine* was undergoing treatment. While we were there an especial festival occurred with displays of art and handicrafts from the different national groups represented in the city: delicately painted eggs from Armenia, brush paintings and decorated chopsticks from China and so on.

Leaving Winnipeg behind we were soon out in the prairies, which at first were quite different from what I had expected. There was plenty of variety and colour with great fields of yellow sunflowers, green and brown fields, and blue flax fields alongside the white and yellow rape, some grown I learn for the oil that they produce. Then this mixed farming gave way to the great fields of wheat, barley and oats, where the skyline was broken only by the elevators. These are often brightly coloured – the Pioneer elevators were painted bright brown and orange, whilst others were red or white with blue and green roofs – and under a clear cloudless sky with unrelenting sunshine and a shimmering heat haze the effect was quite startling.

It was a very hot day and at noon the temperature must have been about 98^0F. The sun was right overhead in a clear blue sky, and there was no shade anywhere. Susan and I had been travelling since early morning and *Peregrine* was feeling the heat and beginning to splutter as she pulled on her feed of petrol and received some of her diet in vaporised form. The heat had affected her mix of petrol and air. Just off the main Trans-Canadian highway we espied a pond surrounded by bulrushes and decided to stop there for a break. We enjoyed the brightly coloured birds that emerged from the bulrushes and wheeled and swooped around us. There was a pair of yellow-headed blackbirds, and many red-winged black birds, which we identified from our bird book. The effect of the red-winged black birds in flight with the sun catching their colours was just lovely. Eventually they settled in amongst the reeds again and were lost from sight.

We calculated our likely time of arrival at Medicine Hat, where friends were expecting us, and were ready to take to the road again. *Peregrine* started at a touch of the button and we trundled down our dirt road and prepared to cross the double track railway line to reach the main highway.

But suddenly our peace and calm were shattered, for *Peregrine* had cut out as she straddled the double track of railway lines. I pressed the starter... nothing happened. I tried again... no response. The petrol had vaporised and no liquid petrol was reaching her carburettor. Nothing we could do would get her to start. This was a busy line: what could we do? At first we tried to push this 3¾-ton vehicle at least off that part of the track that would be reached from a corner about 25 yards away, but to no avail. We were losing precious time. *Peregrine* remained firmly with her front tyres on the outer rail of the first line and her back tyres on the outer rail of the other line. We were well and truly stuck. I tried to suck up petrol from the tank so that we could fill the carburettor, but whilst my lungs filled with petrol fumes I could not get any petrol to flow.

How much longer might we have before the next train would round that bend? We had to try to get help. Susan rushed down the road and onto the highway where she danced a frantic jig in the path of an oncoming car. The startled driver slowed to a halt, to find out what could possibly be the matter, and what response was expected of him. Susan explained our predicament, and he most kindly drove to the railway lines; and there our 'Sir Galahad' looked helplessly at *Peregrine* and feared that his old car would not be strong enough to shift our great truck but said that he would be willing to try to pull her to safety if we had a tow rope. We produced our tow rope and fixed it through our tow bars while he fixed the other end to his towing hitch. The rope was long, but gradually it untwined itself, and then it began to take the strain. Could this old private car pull heavy *Peregrine* from the tracks? Gently, gradually, *Peregrine* began to move. She was over the first rail, with three more rails to go, the noise of the train seemed to be becoming more distinct. *Peregrine* gathered a little momentum and she was over the second rail and the third, but could she get fully clear before the train reached the corner? She was finally pulled clear just as a great freight train rounded the bend and came into view, the railway lines as usual humming with the rhythmic sound of its wheels. What a relief! The thoughts of impending disaster were broken . We were saved. We stood back as the train thundered past, and waved to the driver from the safety of the little road; he would never know of the feelings that were expressed in that wave! We were for ever indebted to our unknown, kind 'Sir Galahad' who, like all real heroes, just went on his way saying in true Canadian style, "Have a good trip." It had been a very close run thing – a very narrow escape.

Once clear of the lines we tried again to suck up petrol from our tank to pour into the carburettor, but without success. When a car approached we asked the driver if he had any spare petrol and he kindly gave us some in a bottle, with which we primed our carburettor; and the engine started – the whole story intrigued the donor, who, left us, but shortly returned to see how we were faring.

We continued on our way via Moose Jaw to Medicine Hat to visit an 'independent' cousin who had made his home in a 'retired' caboose (or guards van) using many bits of secondhand equipment to furnish his home! He was a real Canadian among a like minded group of friends who lived near to a swimming pool, which for us was just what was wanted after the excitements of the day.

Our route through the Rockies to Vancouver led via Calgary and Banff. When we reached Banff, we heard that there was to be an Indian Powwow just a mile away to mark the final day of their festivities. So we beetled off and found a lively scene in a large field at the foot of the great mountains, flanked with fir and alder trees which formed a wide ring around the area. Within this clearing were three centres of attraction: a circular 'course' for flat horse racing, a space enclosed by wooden fencing with high wooden pens on one side for some spectacular horse show, perhaps a rodeo, and a more intimate area with a backcloth of trees on one side and raised seats on the other. All around were the tepees of the Indians, made of canvas with gaily painted designs on them and borders at the top and bottom with triangles in orange, green and off-white, or a design of cats and gold balls, or of bison, or a collection of birds and animals. Tepees are built with a number of fir tree poles about twelve feet long loosely tied together at the top and arranged to form a wide circle at the bottom; the canvas is held up by these ribs. Some tepees had a little 'hood' at the top which made them look like the beaks of birds. Inside the floors were strewn with spruce fir and other branches which have a nice aromatic smell. The Indians sleep at night with their heads to the outside and their feet to the middle, and there seemed to be plenty of room for 15 to 20 people in any one tepee. The doorway was a framed triangular opening and had a separate flap which, like the join in the tepee, was kept in place with an overlap and a six inch stick driven through two holes, like a brooch.

The horse races were varied and amusing, so informal; one started with the contestants having to drink a bottle of Coke, run to their steeds, fling themselves into the saddle and then make the circle, with hats on too! In the evening a group of men and boys of the Cree Indians from south of Calgary put on their finery and danced, the 'music' being provided by a violin and many drums and bells. Their attire was very colourful; the fully-fledged wore two circles of long black feathers with coloured tips, one tied to the backs of their heads, and the lower one over their backs. Underneath the upper one hung a pelt forming a double ridge on their heads with the tail hanging down. Some wore lovely porcupine quill waistcoats, and all wore beads around their necks, in round medallions, or in cuff form, or as a bracelet above their elbows. All wore bells, usually of a square shape like alpine bells, but some were round, and one or two men had two rows of these bells on their ankles. The women wore leather tunics with fringing at chest and hem lines, bead headbands, pelts to cover their pigtails as also did the men, with a medallion of beads to hide the join. On their feet they wore moccasins and sort of coloured gaiters made from beaver pelts were worn from the knees down. The dances were of the Morris dance variety, and included a chicken dance or Spring dance, a marriage dance, a dance to earn special articles of clothing, a war dance and other traditional dances.

The next day we spent on our moped in and around Banff, visiting strange sandstone rock formations called hoodoos. Six or so agglomerates have been left in their grotesque shapes at the edge of a rock overhanging the river; one looks like an otter begging, and another from one side looks like a Sumerian priest while from the other side it looks like a crocodile!

Sue and I had one unforgettably lovely day. We were in Yoho National Park and found the Takakkaw Falls by the Yoho River with many wild flowers which we identified from a special book. There were lovely montane flowers, such as wide leafed fireweed, Parnassus grass, ragwort, 'heal all', special willows with grubberries on them, and so on. The sun was out, the air was clear, and the noise of the falls from the Daly Glacier echoed round the mountains..

From a map that included contours etc. we spotted what appeared to be a super walk right round Lake Yoho, that was high yet not too far. We prepared ourselves suitably and set off, picking our way over trees and boulders left by last year's avalanche. Fairly soon we were in a pine forest of tall Douglas firs, white larch firs and aspens, while at our feet were the red, mauve and yellow paintbrush flowers, white button flowers, columbines, lilies both the snow white and yellow varieties, and ferns and brackens. The short tough grass was covered with fir cones and fallen trees and branches, and there were greens of every shade, browns and greys too, with many of the trees having some black parasite which looks like clinging black bears' fur! However, it is a soft grey-green at first and gossamer fine, before it becomes black and matted.

We mounted a steep hill zig-zagging all the way until we came to a clearing which was not far short of 100ft from where we had started. We were nearly on a level with the start of the falls and had a good view of the Yoho glacier looking steely grey-green with weird dark markings, flanked by golden sedimentary rock, with stripes of grey, fawn and a burnt sugar colour marking the strata. Some are horizontal to the ground, some at right angles, and others make great swirling curves as the rock has been forced upwards from below. We were sitting on warm bark chippings and it was not until we had walked on a bit that we discovered that underneath was packed snow anything up to 6ft deep! We spotted lots more snow when we were on exposed ground.

On we went on our hard clay trail with the shallow roots of the firs making their twisted patterns across our path, until we found ourselves on another side of the mountain. We saw a 'hidden lake' below us, green and still, with the reflection of the surrounding trees, with a slight sandy beach on one side. Eventually we came to a clearing with grey rocks and a profusion of wild flowers, small alpine lilies, stunted yellow paintbrush flowers, and alpine forget-me-nots. We had reached the alpine and sub-alpine level and were very near to the timber line. We crossed a stream which was flowing in the opposite direction from two others that we had crossed and drunk from. The water was so clear and cold, and after crossing this rather boggy bit, we suddenly came upon Yoho Lake. Like 'hidden lake' it was clear and green and had small silvery fish jumping and playing in it. We found bear trails in the wet mud at the lake edge; the bears we learned were attracted by wild currants which grew there, as well as by the water. At the far end of the lake two boys had put up a red tent which was reflected in the green water contrasting with the sparkling sunshine and clear blue sky. One of the boys was gathering and fixing unlikely pieces of wood together to make a raft, so that he would have a better chance of catching fish. There was quite a man-made clearing at the far end of the lake where once had stood a wooden lodge, with evidence of stone fire areas nearby. There were, strangely enough, some old finger posts which indicated trails to Emerald Lake and Field, the next 'place' on the road. No finger post indicated Yoho, but we found a still ascending trail which enabled us to encircle the lake, before somewhat regretfully, we had to leave it.

All the time we had been following horses' hoof-prints and sometimes we spotted the footprints of moose. After a good deal more climbing, and several more rests on fallen firs, we were fully rewarded by the most magnificent view I have ever seen. We must have been nearly 10,000 feet up, way above the falls and the Yoho Glacier, and could see nearly the whole of the Daly Glacier. The sun was brilliant and the firs were black, green and gold, the mountains looking like three gold sisters leading to a high pinnacle surmounting a 'giant's auditorium'. This peak led away past needle-sharp ridges to a further bulk of mountain, more glaciers and three further falls above the Takakkaw Falls, quite another 600ft up. This great range then gave on to a gorge and met another range, which was further away with a high mountain at each end supporting a 'curtain' of beauty in the middle. The patches of snow made various shapes, like lions rampant, bent men, dancing folk and the like. The brilliance, the age, the antiquity, the grandeur, the permanence, the fickleness of the light, all made the world stand still and seemingly get into perspective. How can people quarrel, how can problems ever be insuperable? These mountains give one an inkling of reality – how pigmy is man, and how good it would be if he realised this!

When we emerged from the forest we were above the timber line and in the full sun, above the avalanche and near to heaven. We came down on more snow – snow in full sun in August then on packed ice – and we saw our faithful *Peregrine* below, seemingly no larger than a match box. This was one of our most exciting days. The evening before we had seen a real moose in a wood by the highway. I had no idea how like a horse its head would be, and how like a deer its legs would be. The antlers were covered in soft almost green 'velvet' while its dark brown velvety nose and markings gave it very good camouflage in the forest.

After this idyllic interlude we were heading for Vancouver where I had to try for a real job to cover the cost of the next six months. It was also time for Sue to leave me and to return to England to start her college course.

For most of September and October I stayed in Vancouver with cousins, while earning money in various ways, such as doing interior decorating, broadcasting, and talks on my Uncle Frank's diaries. During this time I went out to Burnaby Park, and on one October morning at about 0945; it was so still that the gentle noise of falling leaves was all about me, reminding me of the sequence of life and death... followed by Spring again with the bursting of the buds now immature and dormant by the new leaf scar. The nearly horizontal light struck the bright maple leaves, resplendent in their gold and flame colours, which responded to the sunlight with a glow of intensity that must be seen to be appreciated. These entrancing maples were reflected in the lake and contrasted strongly with the tall gaunt fir trees, grey-stemmed with dark green tops like a pile of monsoon hats, for the maple bushes seemed to dance holding their heads on one side with their 'skirts' puffed out 'bouffant' fashion and held in place by dark fine stems. The colour of the leaves, I was told, was more beautiful than usual this year. I picked up one or two individual ones in order to enjoy their colour in my *Peregrine*; and found that the very stalks were coloured from a lime yellow near the stem shading through ochre to flame colour near the leaf. The leaf was fringed with gold with some gold marking the veins, while the rest of the leaf was flame coloured with greater or less intensity. Other leaves were almost crimson and the blending of these with the gold, grey, and greens of other trees and the grass of the Park defied paint or photography. This was beauty. Furthermore the dew hung heavily on the grass and the greens of the little golf course had dark patterns on them made by the feet of the early golfers on the grey dew covered, close cropped grass.

I met several people exercising their dogs. There seemed to be a preference for alsatians, perhaps because one of the main reasons for having a dog was for protection. I met the wife of the warden, a 50-year-old or thereabouts, an English woman from Sussex. She was exercising her dog, an alsatian, and had rather fearful stories to tell of goings-on in the park in the summertime. She said that a naked man inhabited the undergrowth and sometimes appeared on the pathways confronting women with this spectacle, she thought that he meant no harm and was just strangely adjusted! But there was also a more sinister man who invited little girls into the shrubbery. She said she was worried by the pushers and drug takers who inhabited the park during the height of the summer, and she found many of the teenagers that came that way on summer evenings drunk and disorderly and up to all sorts of horrid tricks especially in the washrooms. This was a shame, for the setting of the park was superb, the wildness of some areas attractive, and the golf course much used, as was the swimming bath, through the Summer months. The smoking, drinking, smashing and destruction for 'kicks' is a most unfortunate development of the affluent society. I find the careless and thoughtless throwing down of cigarette packets, plastic bottles, newspapers, odd socks, rags, plastic bags, bottles and so on, difficult to accept, for it obviously detracts from the beauties of nature and it indicates an attitude of "Why should I care?"

I passed several pairs of small boys exercising dogs whilst engaging in earnest conversation; obviously there was a large group of responsible young people around – may they predominate. I was much interested in the views of a selection of young people in their early twenties who had gone over to England for visits and to widen their experience. They were finding the costs comparable with Canada but the salaries and wages much lower, yet they wished to return to London as they were aware that life there has more to offer than just material gains; and they appreciated the sets of values pertaining in England.

The sky was cloudless and the sun was really hot as it had been for a whole week. One day I met a pleasant golfer from Kingston, Ontario who was visiting his son in the Royal Canadian Military Police. They had been over to Vancouver Island and he was trying his hand at golf for the first time and had 'put' a ball in the shrubbery. He said that he had no idea that the West could be so beautiful and he found the air clearer than in Ontario and the weather gentler. He was proud that his son had visited England for he had never had that opportunity. He had such a pleasant healthy open face and greying hair, and he obviously got much enjoyment from life, making the most of each experience. The son was rather shy, pale faced and with a self-conscious moustache, nothing like so free nor assured as was his father, but 'in' with the pattern of life he thinks appropriate to his responsibilities! I greatly enjoyed painting in the Park and sat by the 9th hole, well protected in case of a wild shot, as many golfers are amateurs. To my great joy no-one came over to my tree, apart from a black headed and black tailed bird with a crest and blue wings and a pale yellow beak and black legs – a chickadee, I think, colourful anyway – which landed on the fence close by me and made its way to a nearby tree.

How different two days can be from each other. The next day a watery sun shyly emerged from a mackerel sky. The great pine trees swayed and rustled as if taking part in a somewhat sad ballet, rather of the Indian dancing style, with feet fixed firmly to the ground and the upper limbs swaying together in their effort to express some hidden emotion. Many leaves had fallen so that the ground was bespattered with gold, yellow and crimson leaves. The backs of the crimson leaves were a dull purple and they were crisp and wrinkled, unlike the large gold ones which were still pliable and seemed yet to have life in them. The lake was reflecting the trees and the distortion of the water made one maple tree look like a gold and flame coloured pampas with an abundant green base. The gentler light gave yet greater depth to the water and it seemed easily able to accommodate the full 160 feet of fir trees and at the same time do justice to the maples which were like Chinese paintings, fuzzy yet bright and definite in the green lake among the floating logs.

Early the following morning I went for a stroll in the park and found the sun hanging so low that the light shone through the trees almost horizontally, throwing long shadows onto the lake where they were reflected at an angle, thus making a sweeping herringbone effect and giving yet another new dimension to the lake in the park. It was very still again and no leaves moved, but the fallen yellow leaves were drying out, and crunched underfoot and swished as I walked through them. These brilliant still Autumn days were most beautiful and the mountains emerged and disappeared in the mist, accentuating the transience of life.

One day Sallie and I went off in her car to Garibaldi Heights. It was a magnificent drive along the West Coast of North Vancouver. We were always above the Canadian Pacific Railway line that hugs the shore and goes right up to Prince Rupert. The pine-covered islands stooped to the sea and great long fjord-like bays were emptying their blue waters into the main channel. We passed Horseshoe Bay and Britannia Bay, such attractive names for parts of this ugly industrial port. Granite chippings cut from the rocks are brought to the water's edge in trains and elevated 'vias' load them into the ships to be taken by sea to various destinations. Until fairly recently approach to this area was only by sea, but now great roadworks were in operation and this beautiful natural retreat, presently surrounded with great areas of forest, was being offered to the speculator and commuter. This is a volcanic area too, as is evidenced by the shape of the mountains and by the lava which has clothed one great rocky area and relieved it of its trees. The rocks varied in colour from deep grey through silver to a real honey-gold colour and the fir and pine trees were contrasted with maples, alders and birch. The maples here were mostly the gold-leafed variety, though a few cheeky little red saplings were growing among them. Diamond Mountain was very noticeable, with its glacier on the North side, and its angular pyramid-shaped summit. It looked unapproachable, defiant and superior in relation to the other mountains, and reminded me of the Matterhorn.

13th June 1972—6th November 1972
Mileage: Halifax—Vancouver. Total 6,828

West Coast of the USA —Route Map

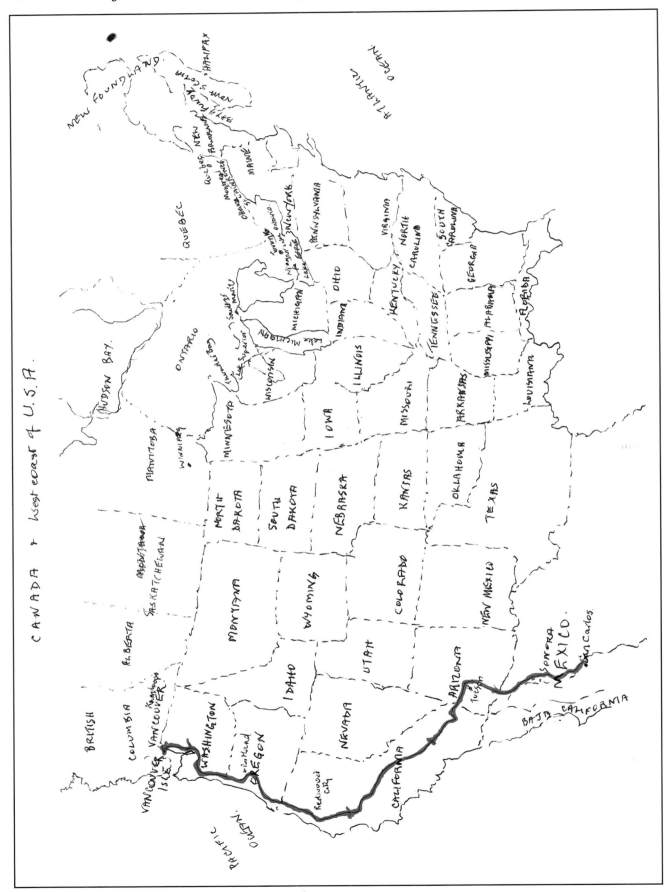

Chapter 3

WEST COAST OF THE USA

In early November, I bade farewell to Canada and set off alone in *Peregrine* for San Francisco. Travelling South from Vancouver with the great Pacific to my right, across the waterlogged farming peninsular, I met great posses of seagulls avoiding the gale forecast for the Georgian Straits, the scrubland gave way to clumps of beautiful golden silver birches, looking delicate against the steely blue sky which eventually took over, leading to the water's edge where piles of well-washed driftwood lay on the shore.

I left Seattle at about 9.00 a.m. on 8th November, under great grey clouds, with sporadic sparks of sunshine, that were weak at first then accompanied by patches of blue sky with white puff-ball clouds, followed by a general clearing of the air, when the mountains appeared from nowhere; a mauve-blue silhouette against the backcloth of swirling clouds. The sun broke through in all its glory lighting up the great towering Mount Rainier, resplendent and snow-capped, strong, silent, grand and imperious, quite dwarfing any other mountain for miles around. The noble mountain, rugged and so white made all others seem puny by comparison. I chose the route by the waterfront with its rows of house-boats, a veritable floating city ... the road became part of a jungle of concrete flyovers, underpasses and throughways, that gave the appearance of giants knitting a new and complicated pattern in rigid concrete, with verticals and horizontals, intertwining each other, All were larded with green placards of instructions; offers of fast roads North, South or East.

Eventually this nightmare of roadways was behind me. The sun came out with that bright light which follows rain and lit the golden maples, alders and poplars, which in turn shone, and were the more striking by the contrast they made with the deep dark green firs amongst which they grew. The whole country danced with beauty. At Kelso three piles were driven together into the river bed and bundles of lumber were kept in place with chains. Lovely red cedarwood, great huge tree trunks, and then a little apart the smaller trees, the more ordinary grey firs, keeping their distance from the superior redwoods which are easily distinguishable at all times – they command one's respect even after being cut down.

I stopped off for three days to visit friends in Portland City, and left in brilliant sunshine, which lit up a lovely scene of golden leafed branches meeting across a river and there reflecting the deep blue of the sky. I drove through good mixed farming land with cattle and occasionally sheep concentrated together, as well as fruit farms. Blueberries are cultivated here and grow on trees like gooseberries, so different from the delicious wild ones that Susie and I had found in Ontario and on the Indian Reserve. Several grain elevators painted a light grey were to be seen and always the wooded hills. Eventually the road wound up and into the forest and followed the Henry Van Duzer Corridor across the mountain range. Sometimes there was a river valley, and I saw a ringed kingfisher, but much of the pass was clothed in really thick, dense forest. I met such a nice fireman on leave from Seattle, when I stopped for luncheon in a National Park. He recognised my fire tender! He and his wife joined me in *Peregrine*, and were keen to know how the onward part of my trip will develop. So am I ... !

The sight of the seemingly limitless Pacific Ocean forever pounding the coast with its powerful dark and heaving rollers, capped with brilliant white foam, appeared to adopt the tactics of a boxer preparing to position himself before striking his opponent. I drove South along this coastline and passed a stone set up at Perpetua Point, to commemorate a landing there of Captain James Cook on 7th March 1778, who is one of our forebears.

One rather misty evening I drove up a narrow road along the Yachat River valley and, seeing a light in a farmhouse window, stopped to ask a somewhat surprised lady if I might park *Peregrine* for the night outside the house, next to a more conventional car. She told me that her elderly mother was very ill and that it was feared they might need an ambulance to take her to hospital in the night, but so long as there was space for it, there was no objection. Relieved, I parked *Peregrine* and turned in and much enjoyed the regular remote sounds of the river as it fell over some stones just up the valley.

In the morning I was invited into their house and I was told that 'Mother' had taken a turn for the better, which was lucky because it was Sunday. The house was full of modern, mass-pproduced furniture, all shining with false veneer. Pictures covered the walls. One of these was a good modern original, of which the owners were justly proud. Flowers were growing in pots, their leaves trailing. It was the scene of well-being for a late middle-aged couple, whose children had grown up and married and established themselves elsewhere.

There was still a gusty wind blowing but the sun was trying to break through the layers of cloud. The gleams of sunshine were accentuating the deep dark tree-serrated hills. The coastline appeared to me to be a cross between the Cornish coastline and the Dalmatian Coast, with isolated rocks stepping out to sea, and with many rios and creeks, though here they are spanned by this excellent road with its wide sturdy bridges, and cars do not rely on ferries as in Yugoslavia! The great sand-dune lands reminded me of various deserts, and of the north Norfolk coast around Holkham. Sometimes the dunes have stunted and dying trees which have not yet fallen; such was a group of three, and until I got out my field glasses I thought that three people were in the dunes, then I saw that three trees, shorn of all branches and bending slightly together as if in serious conversation, were gradually rotting where they stood.

After Eureka the road goes inland into the redwood country. I chose to drive the avenue of the giants and what an experience that was. These ancient, noble, massive trees grow to as much as 300 feet, and any one of them worthy of the name must be over 200 feet. Their stems are deeply indented and in varying colours, cedar, chestnut, varying shades of grey and even black in parts. As dusk fell I was down by a river where my solitude was broken by a logger and his family. It was raining, but little rain penetrated these great trees. Man is dwarfed by the sheer size and by the antiquity of these graceful giants. I was repelled by a sign which invited one to drive one's car through the trunk of one of these noble trees. What will man not stoop to in order to earn some easy money ? What an indignity to so venerable an example of God's creation. A small village in a clearing gave me shelter for the night, but no protection from the torrents of rain, which made sodden the fallen leaves, and deadened all other noise. I retired dreaming of the redwoods, my mind saw again the drooping branches and the straight firm trunks with their long vertical grooves which accentuate the age and strength of each individual tree. Some fallen and decaying tree trunks were harbouring parasites in the form of moss, ferns and even other trees which in turn were growing spindly branches.

I could see the Golden Gate Bridge which to my sorrow was painted a sort of red, as I left the redwoods and drove South to San Francisco. What an amazing place it is, with its narrow waterfront and steep hills to the west, where the famous tram is coaxed up the 1:4 mountain. I was rewarded by the view in all directions when *Peregrine* just made it to the top; the great sweep of the Bay to the East with the Oakland Bridge to the further shore, and the rollers of the Pacific to the West. The skyline of San Francisco as one drives in is fantastic, with the tall high rise buildings, some finishing in a point, some in a dome, while most have flat tops; and these conspire to dwarf the older buildings.

Highway 80 has at least three lanes, and *Peregrine* was in danger of being pushed off the road as her top speed was only 40-45 mph, and therefore she had to occupy the right hand lane, from which traffic was directed off the main highway. I drove South through the city and eventually reached Redwood City, where I was invited to stay with one of my childhood friends. Anne and her husband invited me to park *Peregrine* in their short driveway and introduced me to friends for whom I upholstered furniture and made loose covers, in order to replenish my funds, and lay in a balance for the future. Also, I put a one dollar advertisement in the *Woodside Times* "Available, pre-war Cordon Bleu Cook," which was answered by an English lady, the wife of a millionaire, who invited me to stay in their fully heated flat to cook for their Christmas houseparty and other dinner parties. They also kindly arranged for me to cook dinner parties for their friends on the evenings when they were away from their house. On those evenings I went off on my moped and was usually met by a temporary butler who welcomed me doubtfully, and then helped me to serve a high class meal to the invited company, who often came to the kitchen after the meal to sign my visitors' book! I then rode my moped back to Woodside under the glistening stars. This was a splendid way of earning money and there were also the 'perks'! My employers lent me their cars, including a Mercedes sports model; and although I had never before even ridden in a Mercedes, I much enjoyed driving such a precision vehicle – a contrast to my moped or lumbering *Peregrine*!

Anne, her daughter and seven of her friends joined me in *Peregrine* for a tour to Mexico, but our plans were thrown out when in Arizona the gear box housing cracked, and oil poured out. Unfortunately, the USA has no Bedfords, only Chevs, whose spare parts are not interchangeable with the Bedford's, and the best they could do was to remove the aluminium gear box and patch it together, leaving *Peregrine* with unaligned gears which were to be a problem for the next 8,000 or so miles They calculated that several days would be needed for the repairs.

The young friends meanwhile, found their own way to Mexico, while Anne and I stayed in Old Tucson's caravan park for nearly a week, which enabled us to explore the area., including the museum of the desert. This is a fine place which we reached after enjoying lovely mountain views. The Arizona and Sonora Desert is extensive and unique in many ways even among deserts. In the museum a collection has been made of the mineral rocks to be found, of the snakes ranging from the coloured coral to the rattlesnake, some so beautiful while so venomous: there were iguanas lazing about, or blindly hopelessly searching for insects. Two great jaguars, so sleek and so lithe, were restricted in their cages: a puma was more resigned to the life, as were several smaller feline animals, as well as boars from the desert, desert wolves, coyotes, coon-like animals, a bighorn sheep which had the shape of a zebra with a quite white stern and a goat-like head. From this selection one could imagine the link through time of the animals of the desert.

We found cages, some too small I thought for the birds they housed, such as the great eagles and the golden eagles with their 'plus fours' and yellow claws, Swainson hawks and a bald-headed eagle with white head and tail, and black body and wings. A girl entered his cage to encourage him out for the night. This upset him somewhat, and I felt that he found that the little independence left him in his cage was shattered by her presence. She sat so relaxed and still, but never taking her eyes from him, and I think he knew that she would win – as she veritably did. There were two superb barn owls, aristocratic and academic, superior and remote, white-faced and delicate: and the tiny elf owl, asleep in a bundle.

We watched the underwater antics of the beavers who played to the gallery, and the otters who were enjoying their 'turns' and their rolls, and fish who contentedly swam; ants busy as usual making the 'best' use of time, while desert cats and squirrels slept. We could not pick out the vampire bats that feed only on warm blood, but we could smell them!

On another day, Anne and I visited a 'mock up' of Old Tucson, with a 'stage set' of an 'old' main street. This included a prison, a Doctor's surgery, some shops, suitably equipped, and a beer parlour; and a two storey hotel complete with a balustrade around its verandah.

Then we went off to examine a Papago Indian house built in a perfect half orb. It was supported firmly at the base with desert woods, then with ribs tied together inside to support the thick thatch of grasses. It was cool, airy and spacious, and inside there was an exhibition of Indian articles including a short bow, a spear, a thatching needle, and a broad spoon all made of wood, with lovely pots and baskets of various shape – for grain, for straining and for storage; a picture was painted on packed sand in bright colours; and outside were more cooking pots and a grain crusher so like those found in Egypt. A grey bird perched himself on a crossbar of a light shelter, open at the sides but grassed over against the hot sun. A gourd held liquid, and two 'local hockey sticks' and a fierce looking wooden ball were displayed at the side of the house.

All the various cacti were well marked and given a key to pronunciation too! Sequora are the tall ones that group themselves in such a way that the desert appears to be peopled by giants who go about their business, stopping to caress, cajole, warn, advise, dance and observe all that is going on. We found pincushion cactus, with bright yellow flowers, and diminutives with clusters on their top knots, and others protected by hooked and purple porcupine quills; there were organ pipes, displaying varieties of several tall cylindrical pipes that rise together; chollas various, including the teddy bear which may look cuddly but by gum they are spiky and spiny. The ocotillo has red flowers at the tips like the finger nails of witches – they have yellow and bark coloured stems. Prickly pears *(illus.)* vary in colour from purple to yellow green, willow green, peachy colour and bright yellow, and always with their spines a golden basket colour set in reddish valves.

Living in a desert is a really interesting and different experience. All is still apart from the tumbleweed which blows in the wind. There are miles and miles of sage, scrub broken by ocotillos, desert acacia, sequoras and small grasses and plants. Each plant is fighting for survival, and often a new seed will start life in the care of an established plant or tree; the sequoras kill their host plant as they become stronger and better established. It is plain to see that life is so precarious that if a helping hand is given by one plant to another the 'helper' is likely to suffer. Only the fittest survive, and among them only those which are able to make adaptations.

Dangers include strong winds, abrasion, lack of water, and predators: and elaborate precautions are taken by surviving plants. A sort of natural terracing is evident on the hills, interspersed with great areas of space, some plants have long penetrating roots, or alternatively many plants survive in a roseate shape with roots just below the surface. Great wadis cut the area and presumably water flows down them from time to time. The fleshy leaves or small surface areas, the nestling beside protective rocks, and the using of each other's shade are a few of the means of survival. The air is so clear in a desert, and the early morning and evening light beautiful beyond description: the horizontal gold red lights of sunrise and sunset fill the great expanses, and light up the sudden hills and rocks, throwing lights and shadows, with a soft peach pink and crimson scarlet rust lustre such as I have never seen before. The performance lasts from dawn until beyond sunrise, quite one hour and possibly one and a half hours. Impossible to trap, but wonderful to experience. The calm of the desert seeps into one's veins.

6th September 1972—31st January 1973
Mileage: Vancouver—Tucson. Total 2,100

Josemite Park, California

Douglas Firs

The Magnificent 317 foot Vernal Falls

Paintings by the Author

The Oakland Bridge at San Francisco, USA

Prickly Pears in the Mexican Desert

Mexican Architecture

Raingod from the Toltec area of Chichen Itza

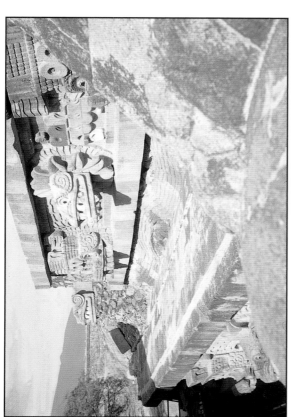

Toltec Quetzalcoatl Temple at Teotihuacan

Mayan Building at Chichen Itza

Jaguar Temple at Chichen Itza

Mexico —Route Map

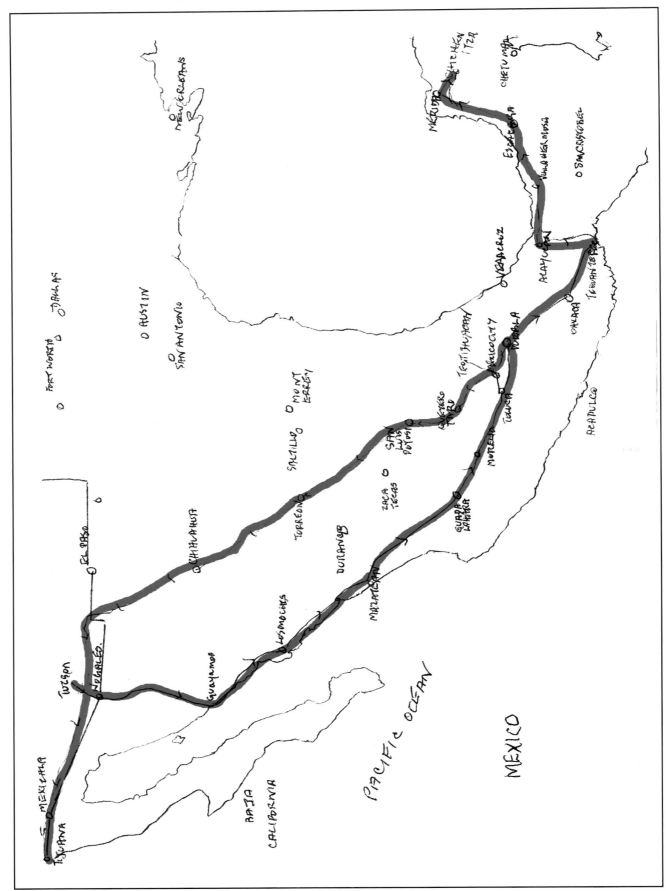

Chapter 4

MEXICO

Anne and I crossed the border at Nogales in the dark, at about 6.30 pm. We were in a stream of traffic three cars abreast … no-one seemed to be stopping from our line. On we went in the rain, slowly through the narrow wet streets of this the first Mexican town we had ever seen. Eventually, after negotiating potholes and traffic lights, and narrowly avoiding cars, unlit bicycles and pedestrians as they emerged from dark corners, we were through Nogales and on our way. We reached a Customs' Post where a Spanish-looking man peremptorily told us that we must return to Nogales, for we had missed the Customs Post there, and were not in possession of necessary documents. Disconsolately, back we trundled. The traffic had eased a little and we were getting more used to the narrow streets. We presented ourselves at the counter in the Customs Office and were given three copies of a piece of printed paper which were to prove invaluable. Armed with these priceless documents we returned to the 'next' post feeling like counters in a game of snakes and ladders. This time we were welcomed as old friends; two copies of the printed paper were exchanged for a sticker which was pasted on to our window; we kept the third copy and this we often had to produce as we went from state to state in Mexico. "Adondo quiere ir Usted?" they asked. "Vamos a Guyamas," we replied. "Buenos noches," we called to each other. This was Mexico and we could find no turning off the road on this dark night, but we were exhausted, so pulled on to a wide grass verge and slept, as best we could for the noise of the long distance trucks that used this main but narrow road from Nogales to Mazatlan and beyond.

"Goodness, how desolate that farm looks," Anne said in the morning, as we looked at several old and dilapidated buildings in the remnants of an orchard. As we spoke, from one of them two children emerged, then a dog and a man. After giving us a keen scrutiny from a safe distance the children took up their position across the road from us. Later a school bus collected them. The dog, a terrier, snuffed around to see what it could scrounge, and the man let a cow out of another of the buildings. As we had our breakfast, washing was hung on the line that stretched from a tree to the house, that was barely distinguishable from the sheds. It was 7.00 am and the day had started for that Mexican family which was striving to coax a living from the land.

We left them and drove out into the desert, miles and miles of open country broken by the strange sequora cactus trees, until we found the branch road that would take us to San Carlos and the coast and drove on past San Carlos, which has become a spot for retired Americans who live in caravans and fish from small launches, and on past a creek full of birds—brown backed pelicans, guillemots, gulls and many waders. We drove on to Catch 22 and there it was! The runway and the half burnt 'Italian' houses, just as we remembered them from the film. Feeling that we must take off and rise over the waves, as we had seen happen in the film, we drove *Peregrine* down the runway to the water's edge and found that several other people had done the same thing. And no wonder, for it is an idyllic spot, the sea so blue in a lovely natural bay, and the beach sandy with a nice sprinkling of pretty shells, from which we made a necklace. We explored a rocky promontory and found more sequoras, organ pipe cactus, prickly pear and lovely little purple and orange flowers, of a kind that we had not seen before. The sun shone, the grey sand was warm to our feet, and the sea was a comfortable 75^0F or so. A colourful young man, who had recently driven down the Baja California peninsular, had pitched a tent and invited us to join him and his friends for supper. He looked splendid in a wide-brimmed Mexican hat and an embroidered

Mexican tunic/shirt on top of an old pair of jeans, in company with about sixteen other guests, who were similarly but less gorgeously attired. We brought wine and a cooked dish and settled ourselves with them out of the wind behind the sand dunes. Fish were expertly cooked over an open fire and we exchanged stories of our travels, and revelled in the crisp air, the peace of the surroundings, the food and the wine. Later we walked back along the shore under a sky bright with stars and a full moon, to the tune of the waves lapping on the shore.

Reluctantly we pulled ourselves away from this haven and drove to Los Alamos. This had been an important city in Spanish times, and the grace of the Spanish Colonial architecture at its best is still to be seen here. One felt that at any minute Spaniards in black cloaks and white lace collars and cuffs would appear to ride round the square to the old hacienda, or, with their wives, enter the large old church; or we imagined we saw rich merchants doing business under the portals by the shops on the fourth side of the square, across the luxuriant growth of flowering shrubs and tall bright red, white and purple flowers. At Los Alamos little has changed since the seventeenth century.

We stayed as guests at a nearby ranch; our hostess was a remarkable little lady, a mere five feet tall but wiry, full of courage and memories of the days when she had worked with her husband as a nurse in the wilds of Africa before the time of refrigerators, fans or aeroplanes. It was easy to see her in her topee with her husband, tending the sick. As we left a red cardinal bird came looking for grubs on a tree, and as we drove along a country lane to rejoin our road we disturbed some blue birds with long unwieldy tails, like birds of paradise. The iron-wood trees were lighting the hills with their waxy gold/yellow flowers burgeoning from their nearly black branches. A flock or covey of parrots flew like a green cloud across our way. We were en route to meet up with the young of our party who had left us in Arizona, although we had no idea where in San Blas we should find them; but as we drove into this Spanish village by the sea, we were hailed by them. They were sitting in the shade of a sweet smelling tree with generous branches and sipping some cooling drink. "We thought that we should spot you if we stayed here" they said, and continued, "we have found a wonderful spot at Los Cocos. We are living in a fisherman's old house". Everyone piled into *Peregrine* and we made our way along a dirt road for about twelve miles until we reached a palm fringed beach and a café, then a hill with pine trees, and in their shade a collection of wooden houses, made from the ribs of palm fronds, with palm fronds tied horizontally above them to make a generous thatch.

We were welcomed into one of these and found the floor was trodden earth., and the rectangle was divided with a partition wall also made of the frond spines. The front of the house was extended and open on three sides; and there on a verandah hung a saddle and harness, rugs, a pick and some tools, fruit, laundry and other things which jostled each other for position. We were joined by a number of other young folk who had found this retreat from the world. These houses cost only $1¾ per week to rent, and a meal in the café could be had for 75c with wine. This was indeed a haven. Horses were the normal means of transport, though a bus plied up and down the road occasionally between the banana plantations inland and the palm fringed pebbly beach by the sea, which gave an intensity of colour. It is easy to see how the artist Gauguin became obsessed with the brilliant greens of this country: in these surroundings a green horse becomes a reality.

After a day or two we left the remoteness of the West coast shore and made our way over the mountains to Guadalahara. This is large and bustling city, thrusting and noisy with its colourful market, and yet representing in its full glory the Spanish colonial culture, with dignified residential buildings. The zocalo with its central fountains, has at one end the Cathedral, rococo and splendid in its unmistakably Spanish tradition. On other sides are a ducal palace, now the city hall, a monastery, now the museum, which we visited, and at the far end an opera house in

Palladian style, a lovely five-tier auditorium in rose-pink and gold with many boxes, that is used as the city's concert hall and theatre; and it also houses a small gallery for exhibitions of art. We heard the Philharmonic at two of their rehearsals, which was rewarding. The city is filled with architectural treasures that reflect the spacious life of the great Spanish colonial period.

In one residential area was a group of young children who sat on the edge of the kerb. Two little girls danced and sang so sweetly, while two impish boys cavorted about, the rest of the group clapping to the rhythm. This innocent, spontaneous entertainment went on until sun-down. Small cafés that opened onto the streets crowded in their clientele, and served them with excellent soup and varieties of tacos. Groups of young men in impeccably clean, gaily-coloured shirts with sleeves rolled up and expensive looking watches on nearly every wrist, were strolling about or chatting at the street corners. Sometimes a Mariachis could be heard playing his pipe and drum, The smart hotels were busy with their American visitors in their well-cut clothes and neatly barbered heads.

In another area, ancient horse-drawn carioles ply for trade, and the aforesaid market makes its very special appeal. It combines Covent Garden, Smithfield and Billingsgate into one and throws in the market off the Portobello Road as well for good measure. Bargaining is keen and no buyer worthy of her salt makes a purchase until prices and quality at other stalls have been compared; and only then an offer is made, followed by a parry from the stallholder and eventually a deal that is acceptable to both parties is established. Time is more expendable than money, and then there is the principle of purchasing according to tradition. We visited this market, where many flowers were beautifully arranged: carnations, roses, statice, gladioli, all rampaging colour, perhaps red predominating; and they had those paper Mardi Gras models of chicken and people, ducks and dogs. There were all kinds of fruit including oranges, grapefruit, mangoes, avocados, bananas, pawpaws, melons, cantaloupe, and all sorts of vegetables, such as egg plants, zucchini, tomatoes, radishes, etc. Then there were baskets of all kinds of fish, pink and white meat, as well as good cooked chickens and freshly squeezed fruit, the whole a riot of colour and fun and pots and people. There was a man selling cured goat skins, and boys trying to shine our shoes, and others trying to sell belts or beads, and women selling wooden spoons or herbs … all go!

We went on to Morelia through the mountains and took advantage of an introduction to the owner of one of the best hotels, and were given a room where there were facilities for laundry, which was marvellous. We found Morelia distinctive, even academic, and most attractive with its great square by the Cathedral as usual, and paseos and many small shops and many craftsmen. *Peregrine* had lost a mirror on a narrow road when a lorry with palm leaves piled high and spreading out in every direction got one of these entwined in the mirror. This was replaced and fixed into position.

The road from Morelia to Mexico City was a great challenge, for Mexico City itself at an altitude of over 7,000ft, lies in a plain surrounded by high mountains that first must be it crossed. Mexico City embraces the island capital city of the Aztecs, Tenochtitlan. The road went up and up, and round and round, on a wonderful pass with a good gradient, but even so much had to be done in second gear. We were up in the pine forest area there, where the pine trees were tapped for their sap, and displayed their channels and their cups, and sometimes their daubs of red paint to stop the flow of sap. I believe that they use the sap for medicaments of various sorts especially for chest complaints and also perhaps for turpentine.

We saw wonderful birds, red and yellow and blue swooping in front of us before being lost from sight in the pine trees that, besides being tapped for their resin, are also grown for their timber. It was nothing to see five ranges of mountains stepping further and further hack into a mauvish haze. The gorges were steep and deep, and little houses hung on the sides of the mountains like flies on a wall. The ground was wonderfully ploughed and terraced, and where there was water it was irrigated and intensively farmed. Eventually we came almost to the top of the pass and found a village in full Sunday swing. Eight men were sitting around a cardboard box full of beer bottles and they invited us to join them. One man was full of his travels in the States to Illinois, Florida etc. while another man walked his three horses up and down a slope, each of which had a saddle inlaid with mother of pearl. In the near distance village folk were making their way across a field track to the white church with its spire pointing to the sky. A brown pig was scavenging around our feet while a sow gave herself up to feeding her young. This might have been a Breughel picture come to life. Groups of men in gaily coloured clothes and, of course, the sombrero were chatting and laughing and the whole place was astir, friendly and waiting for buses and travellers with whom to pass the time of day.

We went on and on along this mountain road and finally reached Mexico City at dusk, taking our place amidst the returning Sunday evening traffic that went at the rate of knots, cars threading their ways past other cars, hooting and taking many a chance. We proceeded in our usual stately manner and found ourselves in quite a pleasant residential area, where we slept the night. The contrast of moving from the rural scene, where little has changed for centuries, to the cosmopolitan modern city of Mexico was most marked. Mexico City has two important streets, Reforma and Insurgente, which go off at right angles to each other, and from which one can always get one's bearing. Since most places are shut on Mondays we set off to the Embassy to look for mail - none - and to see if they would know of anyone wanting a ride to the Yucatan, but no luck. Then we went off to discover the university and found a huge complex with an especially remarkable library building, all four sides being covered in mosaics. As usual the designs were powerful and colourful, and strangely showed, among other things, Copernicus and the Solar System.

We also visited the excellent anthropological and archaeological museum that stands securely in its spacious new buildings in lovely Chapultepec Park. We found the museum a fascinating place. The building itself is remarkable - a great entry from the park giving way to a glass facade, a huge foyer, and beyond to an open courtyard with a great central pillar down which water cascades. Behind this was a rectangular pool with goldfish and papyrus, and around it on three sides were the seven rooms each of which is devoted to one of the diverse regions of the country. Here we soaked up something of the history and culture of this large country that stretches for over 4,000 miles from its northern boundary to the tip of Yucatan, and embraces desert, mountain plains and jungle, fruit farms, arable land, dairy herds, henequen fields, and cotton, salt pans and cement works, oil excavation, ship-building and road making, and over wide areas the remains of the great temples and palaces, pelota courts and astronomical buildings that mark the ancient centres of those sophisticated peoples who had inhabited this land before the Spanish Conquistadors came in the 16th century and destroyed their way of life.

The Spaniards removed gold, treasures and other riches and took them to Europe. Albrecht Durer, who saw some of these treasures in 1520, is known to have been much moved by their beauty, which he thought surpassed anything that he had ever seen in Europe. Most of these treasures were melted down for their gold, to pay for the Spanish wars of conquest... The superbly selected exhibits in the museum included jade, jewellery, the Aztec calendar, sculptures and ornaments. It is possible to see influence of Chinese, 3000-1000 BC, especially in the Yucatan, from carvings of a god, or in the dogs or a grand jaguar, for they have the stance and attitude of the Chinese formal lions, and Yucatan has, for me, a really Chinese 'feel'. I should also like to know the significance of the early place names throughout the country, for it would seem that 'Tepec', or 'Xla', or 'Xian' were very common endings for the towns and villages and vie with new names such Santa Barbara, San José, or San Carlos brought by the Conquistadors.

One of the great centres of the Toltecs and Iater the Aztecs was Teotihuacan - the City of the Gods. It lies to the North of Mexico, in the central highlands, and covers an area of nearly 40 square miles. Here it was believed the gods met and made provision for man. There is the great pyramid of the sun, and a lesser pyramid of the moon before which human sacrifices were made. Around the sacred square by the pyramid of the moon, are numbers of smaller temples dedicated to agriculture, poets, philosophers and other facets of life.

We went to a 'Light and Sound' performance there and received our first impression of this great treasure of a place, which developed in six stages from c. 150BC to 750AD and had much religious, commercial, economic and artistic power, with great influence throughout Meso-America and as far South as Guatemala. We learned that every building was precisely built, and all according to the Aztec astronomical calendar; every step was part of a calculation, each stone of a building having been put in place within a particular time, culminating in the amazingly beautiful rows of temples and palaces, open spaces for markets and ceremonial dances, and a sacrificial mound in the middle of five great squares. There is much symbolism in each building, and in the relationship of one building to another. The precision is remarkable, the wall paintings are colourful and expressive, with processions of plumed persons, or scenes of creation or of achievement.

At the end of the Road of the Dead (so named for many skeletons were found there) is the great citadel Toltec area, with the temple of Quetzalcoatl, the plumed serpent god. On one wall are the great carved, and once painted, snakes heads, naturalistic alternating with formal, above an undulating sea making a wonderful frieze. We found a building in which the original soft, strong, beetle red, green, black and yellow speak out from their rooms and corridors where they have had protection from the hot sun, while on the outside wall of the temple any paintings are less distinct. We spent a whole day walking around experiencing and enjoying this marvellous area. We climbed to the tops of the moon and sun pyramids, from where we had marvellous views of the whole.

On our way South to Oaxaca we visited Cuicuilco pyramid. This site was occupied for 2,000 years until in about 500 AD it was submerged by lava from a nearby volcano. Unusually this was a circular pyramid, and it had a sort of moat around it, which made it most unusual; also on its summit was an oval sacrificial altar. A number of primitive sculptures have been found in the vicinity, which show that it was the centre of an agrarian people.

We then drove on our way down one of Mexico's four-lane toll highways and most fortunately turned off the road as it got dark at Tepotzlan and tucked ourselves in behind the east end of the Cathedral. We were visited by a Swede, who had settled in the area, and then by a nice young couple who told us that the Aztec priests and nobles congregated here and made this their last stronghold against the Spaniards. The villagers who are mostly from noble blood, have a particular independence and rugged pride, noble features and close-knit relationships even to this day.

The village has its own pyramid, way up in the mountains. Bougainvillaea and jacaranda intertwine and rampage together, making a wonderful blue-mauve blaze of colour. The roads through village were or had been cobbled, but to the East we saw houses clinging to the sides of the mountain, served by cobblestone roads going sheer down the mountainside, a slope of perhaps 1:3. It was such a friendly, busy village and this coming weekend it has its own festival, which is pre-conquest in origin, and I would dearly have liked to remain in the village until after that date. So much was going on, cows were driven down the street, boys and men on horses went by, women went off to buy their bread, milk and provisions and a most aristocratic looking old man was sitting on the curb on a corner of the street, in his straw hat, and with a serapi over his shoulder, and his dog sitting patiently just behind him.

All the villagers to whom I spoke were most friendly, and were proud of their village and their stake in it. After we had left this lovely spot we read it had a poet among its citizens who collected Nayarite and Campeche treasures and these are now displayed for four hours a day in the museum. Oh, how worthwhile it would have been to have stayed - certainly several weeks if not months - in this haven for artists and writers, but we had set ourselves to reach Oaxaca, and with the big rains imminent, we felt we must get on before we got caught by the weather.

We had a wonderful drive through the volcanic mountain ranges all day with superb views, sometimes of terraced, quite dry fields, ready and prepared for sowing as soon as the rains came. What faith in the order of things! Sometimes the fields were bare earth - red, pink, and grey, and alternating so quickly that the very hills seemed to have rainbow colours. Sometimes the trees and cacti of the desert abounded, and we saw a fine show of organ pipes and ocotillas with their little red tufted flowers as well as yellow iron wood and pink grasses that flanked the road.

At sundown great clouds collected, and for the first time in many days we had a few spots of rain. The sun was out and a great rainbow rose from the mountains with the sun setting at one side of it. What a magnificent sight - dark valley and mountains, the perpendicular rainbow arch, and the horizontal sunset aflame and copper coloured, with bright edges radiating out a silver light. In such an expanse this was magnificent.

We turned into Nochixtlan, a noble conquistador town, now in the hands of very poor Indians and quite rundown. Evidence was all around that this spot had seen better days. It had an entry arch still just standing, but no longer astride the main road; there were carved lintels to the doorways, a lovely square with its bandstand, and a most important church into which we went for part of Vespers; we found it full to overflowing with reverent men, women, youths and children, singing and joining fully in the service. It was a lovely example of a community living and worshipping together.

We slept by the portales of the municipal building, under the protection of the local armed police, and as we left early next morning we saw one of the finest sunrises ever. It was a cloudy morning and the grey clouds had pink wisps, the valley was dark, and the far hills were lit by the rays of the rising sun, and were aflame in this soft copper pink that abounds here. Oh the beauty of it.

On another day we went to Tula, the home of the Toltecs, who introduced warrior figures and built their temples on the same basic plan, but with differences, notable among them a roofed area, and four carved-stone warrior figures mounted on a platform that forever look south; and behind them carved square monoliths, apart from the fact that they are in three pieces!

Here at Tula one of the first known ball game pitches was invented, and great courts comprising two large squares with a narrower area joining them, were built adjacent to the ceremonial square. A five-inch diameter rubber ball was used, and the players in two teams arched their backs and propelled the ball mostly by their buttocks and thighs, which were covered in leather for protection. The archaeologists are at variance to decide whether the winning or losing team should be offered to the gods for sacrifice at the end! Apparently great betting on the game went on, husbands even laying a wager on their wives!

From there we went to Oaxaca and found it, then as now, a lovely place and this whole area rich in historical remains. The people have a sense of humour and take great pride in their locality. We went out to Mitla and found the Mixtec-Zapotec temple. Here complicated designs have been contrived, by attaching many precisely cut smallish stones of particular shapes, and leaving them white against a background of red - obtained from the cochineal beetle - or green or black. One of the great differences we noted was that the temples are hollow and have underground passages, and also that the four-sided sacrificial area has rectangular rooms on each side; in each wall there is a niche, and in front, pillars. The Spaniards built their cathedral in the middle of the site, using many of the stones from the temples. Nearby, two families of weavers live, and we went up to see them spinning and weaving in their traditional style.

We reached nearby Monte Alban in bottom gear up a five and a half mile tortuous and steep hill. It is a marvellous site, with wide views over the top of a range of hills. We learned that with only stone tools and no special equipment, the mountain top was removed to establish this extensive 'plateau'. It is thought Monte Alban may prove to be one of the largest centres in Mexico, once the excavations have been completed. At least 104 tombs have already been found, along with a good ball court, and a very special observatory building, with Mycaenean shaped arches. It is Zapotec-Mixtec and well aligned for sun observations. Its observatory stands just in front of the Temple of the Sun. Bas relief carvings are to be found in quantity, and some of them have African facial features, some are dancing and some figures seem deformed. There is also the plumed figure of a dancing man, and also a prostrate man, and a good deal of glyph writing reminiscent of the Egyptian cartouches, I wonder if it has been deciphered? This site has already yielded many riches from its tombs, and from these finds light has been thrown on the latter days of the Zapotec/Mixtec peoples.

Monte Alban was abandoned perhaps because of lack of water, or of exhausted soil, or of internal squabbles, or of the disenchantment of the population with the autocratic governors who had to be provided with food. No-one knows, but areas of slash and burn cultivation for food were becoming further from the centre, and farmers may well have resented the extra difficulties of providing this support for the rulers.

In the evening we listened with the local people of Oaxaca to a brass band concert in the square which we all much enjoyed.

Anne had to return home, and in her place I was accompanied by Andrew and Elizabeth, two young Australians, who met me by arrangement near to the cathedral. Andrew, a professional photographer rushed off to take a picture of the cathedral, in its commanding and dominating position standing in its own courtyard at one end of the zocalo. The Spaniards left something of their culture in those honey-coloured stones, with the heavily carved west front that reaches triumphantly to the figure of the Madonna in the topmost central niche.

We drove off towards Mitla and stopped at el Tule by the C16 Church to examine the venerable tree, 40 ft. in girth, which is said to be oldest living tree in the world. What secrets could this tree tell us I wondered as we walked around her, protected as she is by iron railings and a notice of explanation in Spanish? I was glad that we were there so early, for assuredly the bus-loads of tourists with guides would come later.

Then we went on to Yagul, high and commanding on its hillside, complete with the remains of important houses and a temple. It is a lovely site, with the ancient remains of a great palace and a very well preserved ball court 'I' shaped again, with sloping sides in the middle. Furthermore vaults had been excavated, and produced evidence of early civilisations stretching back perhaps thousands of years.

Often we could see six ranges of mountains as we drove South East, ranging in colour from the dark pine green of the nearest ones, through a grey-green to the blue-mauve of the farthest ones, which were barely distinguishable from the sky. We moved into semi-desert country where the hills were of pinky sand and dusty colours with prickly pear and the sequora and organ-pipe cactus breaking the outline of the hills with their irregular and timeless shapes. Every now and then that lovely yellow flower that springs from the henequen plant soared up to 8ft or so above the parent plant, tall and graceful and pristine among the dark greens of the cactus, its last thrust before it dies. A wonderful pair of golden flame-coloured bunting-sized birds were to be seen among the trees that fringed a chortling river that waters the farming area. I wondered if they were of the golden oriole family.

We stopped in one of the many little primitive villages that bestraddle the road from Oaxaca to Tehuantepec, where pigs were walking about the road and in and out of the houses. One of the bigger houses was built with steps up to a verandah, on which sat perhaps a quarter of the village population. This was one of two shops and it was possible to buy tacos but no bread, some fruit or vegetables from the local fields, possibly one of the chickens that walked about if it could be spared, and, of course, one or two of the many varieties of bottled lemonade or fruit juices, but no ice. We looked in wonderment at this scene, so little touched by the 20th century, and they stared back at us, unable, it seemed, to comprehend why we should be wishing to drive through their land, when they seldom went further than their horses could carry them.

We reached Tehuantepec, where the women run the market and are a delight to the eye. They are strong and rather buxom on the whole with strong faces, jet black hair, drawn back and plaited with coloured threads in it, and each is dressed in most becoming clothes; a short-sleeved blouse in black or dark blue with a square neckline that is decorated with two or three rows of dark braid, and a long and full skirt usually of some plain bright colour, cerise, green or bright blue, or sometimes flowered and patterned. In these gorgeous garbs they cut up meat, handle fish, and entirely run the market. The menfolk drive the lorries filled with oranges and other commodities, but the women arrange the prices and control the sales and the stalls. It was a large market too and so colourful with areas of fruit, flowers, pots, baskets, groceries, materials and dresses, arranged around the square and along a street. We bought supplies in the market and much enjoyed watching a group of young attractive girls who hoped to sell us hammocks at a great price!

As we turned north away from the American Highway, the country changed from the flat intensively farmed land near to the south coast, to jungly type growth with an intensity of green. We stopped by a bridge and below it a group of women were standing in the river and scrubbing their clothes on suitably placed stones. They were also washing themselves, hair and all; they emerged from the river with great piles of clean wet washing, each tied in one huge bundle, and this they lifted to their heads, and as if it weighed nothing, stopped to pass the time of day with us. Then, with that grace that comes of a good carriage, they went on their way looking like a frieze from the temples at Teotihuacan.

We wondered where to spend the night in this country where there were scattered houses and small farms, but no villages as we know them. We espied a brick-built house, a rarity in this area, and went up to ask the owner if we might spend the night on his land. We were greeted by a young thin-faced woman with a baby in her arms, and then by her mother, a powerful-looking person. They were most gracious and welcomed us to their farm, arranging that we should park on firm ground right outside their house, a welcome precaution as *Peregrine* is heavy and the ground soft. Asking if we could buy honey, as we had seen the gaily painted hives nearby, they said they had none for sale, but they gave us strong and delicious mead! As soon as we were established we were visited by all the relations and friends from the nearby houses, who came some on foot, by bicycle and even in one case on a horse. How I wished that I was fluent in Spanish for I would have liked to have had real conversations with these friendly people, instead of the halting speech and miming with which we had to exchange our ideas. We were invited into the house, where the mother and her husband lived in one part, which was clean and neat but rather soulless compared with the homely kitchen belonging to the younger woman where several generations lived together. Here in a corner was the centre of activity, the stove, an open wood fire between two piles of bricks on which was balanced a flat piece of tin on which tacos and tortillas in great numbers were being cooked.

The next morning the family got about early and started the generator, while pigs and chickens, dogs and ducks chattered. We went into the house to say our farewells and to invite them to sign my visitors' book. About half a page was needed to allow for the children. Elizabeth drew designs on several eggshells for the children, who were very shy. The fire was alight and the oil drum lid was heating in readiness for baking the tortillas. The well in the garden was deep and always had water but this was not fit for drinking. Food was put down for the chicken and ducks, puppies arrived and a dear little boy of a year or so, dressed in blue, put out his arms and came to me, gurgling with happiness, so secure in his home. Andrew and Elizabeth were given two eggs and some tortillas, and I was given some oranges freshly-picked from a tree in the garden. In return we gave them some of our stores. What a delightful family, the barefoot teenage girls never stopped working, supervising, cooking or looking after the children, fetching water from the well, cleaning the pig house, and so on. Shoes were worn by the parents and small children only. After much hand-shaking we pulled ourselves away and set out for Acayucan and then Palenque where we had a lucky outcome to a nasty predicament at our next stop for the night. I was reversing as directed into the shade of a grapefruit tree when to my horror the right rear wheels disappeared through a thin concrete top to a disused pit. *Peregrine* was stuck at a difficult angle but fortunately the family had invited friends for a shooting party that evening, and in answer to my pleas took hold of the tow rope, after arranging a plank under the wheels. They pulled and I drove and, hey presto *Peregrine* emerged, and the only damage to her was not the broken back axle that I had feared but just a broken reversing lamp. Photographs were taken, everyone clapped, and we were able to enjoy a restful night before driving on to the Yucatan.

I awoke at Palenque to the noise of the jungle birds and the little stream which was making its way down the hill through the lush jungle growth. The grass was very wet from the overnight dew as I stepped outside to get my first view of the Temple of the Inscriptions. These Mayan buildings are so different from the Aztec buildings or the Miztec ones of Mitla. There hidden in the jungle rose the beautiful, restrained, massive yet delicate grey Temple of the Inscriptions and the great palace. While we got ready to visit these buildings, a Chev truck was driven up the hill, carrying a horse in the back. This animal was not tied in in anyway, and a small boy was his only travelling companion. The car stopped alongside us and the boy helped the horse down from the truck, the horse making so little fuss that I imagine it was used to 'hitching' a lift up the long steep hill to the cluster of houses by the ruins of Palenque. The boy mounted and they forded the stream and disappeared into the jungle behind the houses.

The custodians of the ancient site arrived by bus from the village and went to collect their tools and set about cutting the grass and clearing weeds. We noticed that someone collected a wreath that had been left by the steps of the Temple of the Inscriptions. What ancient custom or practice had we witnessed? This site has only recently been excavated and quite a lot is still in the power of the jungle, where great mahogany trees grow among the palms, and the sacred ceiba trees. Primaeval forest ferns grow in profusion with the lush green grass, the intensity of the colour is marvellous. The birds too were brightly coloured and one sang a beautiful song with a theme and - I think - eight variations. The early light was pure and clear, then in came clouds and mist which hung in the valley, and intensified the mystery of this place. By 10:30 or so the clouds had cleared away, the mist was dispelled by the brilliant sun and we could see for miles and miles. I stood on the top platform of the Temple of the Inscriptions with my back to the dense jungle and gazed across ranches with cattle and mixed farming interspersed with waving palm trees, and saw a scene that could not have changed much since the Mayans were there fourteen hundred years ago.

Palenque is perhaps the greatest of the Mayan sites, it once occupied an area about six miles wide on the North side of the Sierra de Chiapas. Within the excavated area of c. 500 yards East to West and 300 yards North to South, fourteen buildings have been surveyed, among these the Temple of the Inscriptions with the unique burial chamber for the great lord Shield Pacal, who developed much of this site in about c. 620 AD, and handed it to his son who continued the development until c. 697 AD. Unusually, there stands a nearby four storey tower with finely carved staircases, as well as the Temples of the Sun, the Cross, and the Foliated Cross. Three of the four Temples excavated show roof combs somewhat reminiscent of Chinese buildings, and they were once decorated with stucco figures and painted. We learnt that this style is known as Palencano, and that Palenque reveals much of the Mayan beliefs of the cosmos, from the tablets and stelae in bas relief, demonstrating their beliefs of death and of the underworld, and the continuance of life perhaps through their sons. Palenque has the earliest and largest known Mayan ball court — c. 550 AD.

Mexico is a land of contrasts. We went off to Escarcega which was alive with noise and bustle. At least three different tunes were being belched forth simultaneously from three different loudspeakers in the square, while boys and a few girls, with great concentration played three-a-side table football. Men sat at tables drinking cold drinks and eating tacos stuffed with savoury fillings. Such a homely nice woman kept a collection of magazines and charged a few pesos for boys to come and read them in her shop, while she did her ironing. A big hammock was slung across her living room in which she sometimes sat, but generally she baked, washed and ate, did the ironing, looked after her children, and slept with all the family round her. She very kindly ironed my trousers for me with great care but would take nothing for this service, so I gave her some tea bags and instructions for their use. I hope she has enjoyed her cups of tea.

From Escarcega we went on to El Kabah, and got there just in time to see the sun set, oh so vividly, from the top of the great pyramid.

El Kabah has a veritable Mayan building, with a wonderful facade carved with rows of rain gods' heads, one above the other, dignified and mysterious, but having quite a different effect if seen from close to, or from far away.

From El Kabah we went to Uxmaal and found wonderful things: the great oval pyramid from the Mayan period and the Governor's house built on a hill with a two-headed animal in front of it – the one, I believe, that the sacrificial victims leant back over for the high priest to make the incision to cut out their hearts before handing them to a runner to scale the sacrificial steps and put it in the fire which was held by the chacmool, a surprised-looking man lying on his back with the plate on his stomach, that we had seen at Tula and in the Mexico museum. Then there was a wonderful courtyard, grassed in the middle and surrounded on four sides with buildings covered in lovely patterns and carvings. On one of these walls were naturalistic chubby carvings to do with farming, rain gods, crops and offerings, and facing it were upside down eight-step pyramids and a sort of Mitla cross pattern.

I find that this kind of pattern is very Mayan, and used at El Kabah and the Mayan area of Chichen Itza too. Uxmal had a ball court and Tiryns Greek-type arches. They were just excavating another pyramid and rebuilding it so badly as they went. The day before we were there they found a rain god in a temple at the top, and they had only covered it with five boards which could be easily removed. It was very fine and unspoilt, similar to those at El Kabah.

We went on to Merida to be there for the Mardi Gras celebrations and found them very slapdash, noisy and oh the noise of motor bikes, revved up for the occasion. The floats all carried advertising stunts, and went round and round; but the crowd was fascinating, children in fancy dress depicted

Austrian girls, Chinamen, Spanish senors in black capes, short knee breeches and hats, while the women were in charming long frocks and coloured shawls.

We escaped to Chichen Itza, but not before two balloons filled with water had been thrown at *Peregrine* - mercifully doing no damage. The excavated remains at Chichen Itza are most extensive, Toltec on one side of the modern road and Mayan on the other. Chichen Itza, the Mayan name for 'on the edge of the well of Itza', is well known as a name and is becoming one of the places to visit. It is pretty certain that Chichen Itza was inhabited by an agrarian community as far back as 1000 BC and there may have been even earlier settlers there. Records show that the Itzas were occupying the site in 514 AD, and the Mayans were certainly there in 619 AD for they left a lintel stone with this date upon it. It has a ceremonial centre and a crowning temple. This site, like several others, was for a time deserted for reasons that are obscure to us. We wonder if a famine occurred, or a plague, or if there was some internal disruption. Some historians put forth the theory that life was too easy and pleasant that encouraged the population to grow beyond the limits that could be supported by the farming techniques known at the time, or perhaps the young wished for adventure and pastures new. The Mayans were certainly in possession from 950 to 978 AD but then the Toltecs defeated them, and established themselves. These warrior people from the central plains north of Mexico City, Tenochtitlan, as it was known in its Aztec days, introduced human sacrifice and a militaristic attitude before they came to respect the cultured Mayans and to fuse their culture and religion with their own. At this time Chichen Itza became the most important city in the Yucatan which accounts for the glory of the site on the north-east of the highway, and for the fact that there is so much evidence of the Toltecs, while the purely Mayan site, on the south of the highway is no less interesting in its display of the decorated facades of the various buildings, in the classical Mayan style.

The sacred well, Cenote, in which the rain god was thought to live, is Mayan in origin, and lies on the north east of the modern highway, at the end of the sacred way. This limestone well with a diameter of about 65 yards has well washed walls of about 60 feet and is thought to be about 40 feet deep. In its heyday it used to receive gifts and offerings, including maidens, who had been doped with copal incense before being offered as sacrifices to propitiate the rain god, a being most important to the inhabitants of the Yucatan. So important were the moods and manifestations of this god that ceremonial knives, jade beads, gold ornaments and other riches were thrown into the well in addition to the maidens. Many of these, as well as the bones of the girls, have been recovered, during the two careful searches made when the Cenote was drained and dredged.

Chichen Itza, unlike several other Mexican sites, has a splendid irregularity, with few buildings being on the same plane. The dominant Toltec building, the Castillo, rises to 97 feet from a square base to a rectangular temple at the top. It contains a Mayan temple within itself, and for those who are prepared to climb a steep and narrow stairway in the heat of the middle of the day (when it is opened for visitors) they will be rewarded by seeing the throne room that contains the famous pink jaguar. It stands four square on its feet with its head turned to the left, and is now a faded red colour with jade eyes, and jade discs let into its body. Its teeth, 'tis said, are those of a real jaguar. For a companion it has a chacmool, or carved stone reclining figure of a man holding a disc on his stomach with both hands. His knees are bent and his head is turned towards us, showing a surprised smile on his face. Well it might, for his function was to hold a bowl of hot oil, and to receive the palpitating hearts of the young men who had yielded them up to the priests, as part of the ceremony at the foot of the pyramid. These hearts, one by one, were rushed up the steps by bearers in order to be offered to the gods still beating and palpitating. The lintel to this throne room has a Mayan design of jaguars facing twisted serpents, with symbolic moons and suns with serrated edges of 52 points. This frieze appeared to encircle the older building, but has been lost to view in its full glory since the Toltecs covered it with the great Castillo. The Castillo has four wide staircases, at the four cardinal points of the compass, leading to the temple of Kukulkan, the rectangular building at the top, where the entrance jambs are carved with Toltec warriors in full regalia.

The platform of Venus lies between the Castillo and the Sacred Way, and near to it the platform of the Tigers and the Eagles, and it was from these platforms that the dancing maidens used to make their final procession to the sacred well. One thing of particular interest now is that these platforms are acoustically in relation to the Castillo: if one claps one's hands near to the platform of Venus, one is surprised by a birdlike echo, a sort of squawk, from the temple of Kukulkan at the top of the Castillo, unearthly yet compelling. The builders must have had great knowledge of acoustics, for they had stones on which tunes could be played by tapping with another stone: and the magnificent ball court, which is 450 feet long and 220 feet wide, can send and receive messages from people from the Temple of the Bearded Man at one end to the wall at the far end with greater clarity than is received on a modern telephone. This is the largest known extant ball court and it is complete with its carved stone ring, high on the middle of the long side wall. Nearby stands the superb temple of the rattlesnakes and jaguars, sometimes strangely called the Temple of the Tigers. This temple has two immense snakes each carved from one piece of stone at its entrance, and a lovely frieze of jaguars encircling the outside of the temple. It is beautifully proportioned and it commands a fine view of the ball court where this ceremonial game was played in the same way as described at Toltec Tula.

A macabre platform of skulls lies between the ballcourt and the platform of the tigers and eagles. One wonders if perhaps the men about to be sacrificed collected here to inhale incense as they danced their final dances, before rendering up their hearts at the Temple of the Sun. This temple, a great memorial to Toltec architecture, like the Castillo, embraces an earlier Mayan temple in which some of the finest pillars in their original colours are to be found. In bas relief are chiefs in plumed head-dresses, with pierced upper lips where sticks have been thrust through, to signify the importance of words emanating from that mouth. The chiefs have straight noses, unlike the curved ones of the Mayans of Palenque. Their heads are shown in profile, while the heads of the 'small men' at the base of each pillar are generally depicted full-face. The chiefs are adorned with belts and tassels and long garments, and the left arm is protected by a shield, while the feet are in profile below the garments. These pillars are painted in green, red, blue and yellow.

There is a lovely Toltec pyramid to warriors with pillars that are painted in green, red, blue and yellow, much as at Tula, and an altar carved from one huge piece of stone, and supported by all kinds of caryatids, small 'Atlas' men with arms upstretched. On each side of the main staircase at the top kneels a standard-bearer; a chacmool is at the entrance to the temple.

We spent three nights and two whole days there, it was so beautiful. The Mayan observatory is tremendous and has eight windows in which were the instruments from which the accurate astrological measurements were made. Also there are two buildings superbly carved, and a number of others which are reached after a rewarding walk in the scrubby jungle.

We were allowed to park *Peregrine* in part of an old walled garden of the hacienda that Thompson, the USA Consul used. It was he who bought Chichen Itza for $75 and started the excavations: From our spot we had a view of the little gathering of huts of the villagers; they were of palm or banana leaf and thatched, and had vertical narrow ribs and rounded ends. Part of the flat sides near the front door, always in the middle, were plastered with the local earth and painted white. The earth in front of the house was swept daily, the chicken fed, and the children turned out to play with each other. The women were up at 5.30am, dressed in their becoming yet shapeless white frocks with bright borders round the neck and hem, and always the broderie anglaise petticoat intentionally showing. The men went off before first light, always walking in single file.

A bus came in at 8.30am and two men and three women, in single file and carrying empty sacks and their luncheon, wound their way among the houses, and out to the fields. They returned at 4.30pm carrying great sacks filled with maize or wood on their backs supported by a band which went round their foreheads and round the base of the sack. They walked with measured tread, heads forward, backs bent, and arms either pulling at the sacks with hands over their shoulders to help bear the weight, or supporting the bottoms of the sacks; either way, the whole thing looked most uncomfortable and dreadfully heavy, and the heat must have been 90°F.

We visited Vera Cruz and had a fish supper at Manchinga in a really Mexican setting on a lagoon, before spending the night at Cholula. Here we mounted the 'highest pyramid in the Western world' which now has a church on top from which we could see the extent of the area that was inhabited when the Spaniards came and destroyed so much. The scene of operations was vast. A good deal of excavation is going on there now, and it is thought that Cholula was the centre of worship for the middle plains, and once vied with Teotihuacan for importance.

I find that I now have a smattering of an idea of Nyarite, Olmec, Toltec, Aztec, Miztec, Zapotec and Mayan cultures, and know enough to see that I am hardly on the fringe of knowing anything at all. The various cultures are really different in their extremes, but merge together and overlap, borrowing from each other. They differ in their interpretation and over the years, their existence is rather like the waves of the sea, each wave in itself discernible, but moving and merging into the next.

Andrew and Elizabeth had to leave me after we had returned to Mexico City, and from there alone I drove back to the Highway leading towards the USA. As I drove North, after seven weeks and over six thousand miles in Mexico, I considered some of the inconsistencies of this varied and beautiful country, which seemed to be full of unsolved mysteries.

The country has areas of desert and deep canyons and many beautiful beaches, a volcano in the high region around Mexico City, as well as a spur of land North of Palenque, the home of the Mayans. Ball courts, so similar to each other, may be found from Monte Alban to Tikal (Guatemala) at a time when there was no known means of communication nor transport.

Perhaps, since scholars have partially interpreted the lid of the sarcophagus below Lord Pacal's Temple of the Inscriptions, more will be understood. It it known that the Mayans had discovered zero, and calculated the 'Long Count' of 90 million years, that they accurately foretold eclipses of the sun and were within 0.0001 of modern scholars' acceptance of the solar calendar of 52 years.

Furthermore, symbolic and beautifully carved jade was found in Lord Pacal's tomb in Palenque and Albrecht Dürer in the sixteenth century was recorded as saying that the Spanish conquistadors brought to Spain the most beautiful golden objects that he had ever seen ... and they were melted down to pay for the invasion!

Mexico had and has a real fascination for me. It has so much to offer, besides being just a delightful country to visit for a holiday.

Just off the main road I found a delightful village, Santa Rosa, with a large Spanish church, a square with its bandstand and the municipal building which is used as a school for part of the day. The inhabitants exhibited a natural courtesy and the night watchman said I might park just outside the municipal building, and that he would look after me. I gave him a cup of coffee to clinch this deal and strolled around to shop and chat with the folk. They obviously were not used to foreigners which was most refreshing. The birds chattered in the trees and children played in the bandstand. First came the tiny ones who played 'ring of roses' and then went off to bed, followed by some boys who played a very spirited game of tag, leaping over the balustrade and the seats, most nimble and energetic. Old men sat on seats around the perimeter of the square, and as darkness fell all was quiet. In the morning I presented a coconut to my old friend, and we had a ceremony of signing the visitors' book, with an 'amigo' signing for 'Julian'.

Such a strange thing happened: yesterday I had looked at the map and decided to take the old road for the last part of the journey, and to stop off at Wellton if I could find a suitable spot. Seeing a turn to Butterfield Park and the Sheriff's Department, I turned up a little hill and to my surprise found a layout exactly the same as the one I had experienced on the outward journey. It was quite uncanny - hedged play area, picnic tables, place for a fire, washrooms, the lot, until I found that I had stopped over at a Butterfield Park en route from Arizona. So Butterfield, like Wells Fargo, must have been a rich and thoughtful man. Wellton was founded in 1878, an age of wealthy benefactors. I had a lovely peaceful night as before - bless Butterfield!

As dawn pink faded to great golden streaks across the desert, massive trains were hooting their way along the tracks. I heard the odd dog barking, otherwise all was still. The desert landscape was broken at intervals by the small adobe square houses, now generally with a real window and door, instead of just openings. The houses are often surrounded by an adobe wall, and are very much on the pattern of the desert houses in the Sudan, flat roofs with poles worked through the walls, and palm, dura, maize or other material used for roofing and laid across for protection. Men and boys with donkey or without, would be threading their way with wood for the fire for cooking, or with water in kerosene cans, carried on an unshapen yoke. Oh, the peak of the brilliance of dawn is here: dark blue clouds, that wonderful gold pink, the duck egg blue-green edged with deep apricot, and all too many folk are asleep and not seeing this impressive and intense beauty.

I set off in a westerly direction, making a detour north in order to visit the Casas Grandes, and this was a wonderful drive. The mountains stood out massive and craggy silhouetted against a cloudless blue sky. The road went up and over and through a pass just here, and lovely black cattle were on one side of the road and white-faced brown ones on the other. The road wound down into a wide valley, with mountains in the distance in ranges as far as the eye could see.

The Casas Grandes are reached by driving over a worn-out Bailey bridge: cross slats had been added to the original lengthwise supports to give confidence to chicken-hearted drivers, and one had to get one's wheels on these cross pieces! I found a pretty derelict adobe village, but out on the hill were the remains of a great centre; the familiar pelota court, though with rounded ends, great storeyed houses that put the puny single-storeyed houses of today to shame, round houses shaped like parrot cages, waterways and doors of a most unusual pattern. The people could not have been very tall, for the space between floors was only about 5ft, and the doorways were low. But what a find, and the houses built of adobe are still extant after about 3,000 years!

Buenaventura, a small town, was the focus of attention in the valley, miles from anywhere, and with its own dignity, pace, calm and courtesy. I stopped to buy bread, and a number of dignified middle-aged men were sitting on a shop window ledge and quietly passing the time of day. A skilled mechanic went about his work while the local police, in a friendly manner, made themselves familiar with *Peregrine*.

It seemed that something of the City or State form of government control still pertained, and all along the river, orchards pink with blossom, cattle and mixed farming, trees burgeoning into bud and leaf, spoke of the calm bred of capable and controlled hands and minds. It would appear from the arrangement of the houses that each family had a stake in the wealth of the land, and each owned his means of livelihood. Horses stood about in any shade available, looking well fed and cared for and there was a lovely air of unostentatious security and wealth - by some standards - I did not want to leave this haven of sanity!

As I drove north I reflected on my experiences of the past two months in this fascinating, vibrant and virile country. A land of many cultures and most variable scenery which is now accessible to travellers by car, plane and ship. I crossed the vast Arizona/Sonora Desert where drivers salute one another for there are so few cars and one is so often entirely alone with nature, there being no single sign of human habitation as far as the eye can see. Here for companions there are the weird sequora cactus trees, standing like sentinels among the lesser palo verde scrub trees, and the graceful waving ocotillos. I drove alone across this desert country, that was relieved occasionally by a collection of small wooden single-storey dwellings with a generous thatch of dried grasses that gave them the appearance of little tea-cosies in groups. Where there were no palms nor suitable slates the houses were made of adobe, sun-dried clay, and had flat roofs of maize stalks and leaves or some similar material. Where there was a more generous supply of water, at once there was cultivation. Alas, the road was punctuated with the carcasses of donkeys and even horses and cattle, which were being eaten by numerous prairie dogs and vultures . The local farming population of villages walk for miles carrying great loads in sacks on their backs taking much of the strain of the load on ropes which they wear around their foreheads. Their houses are rounded at the ends, and they are built of the tough ribs of the palms that are bound together so that the air passes through the space between the slats; they too have a roof made from a generous thatch of grasses or of palm fronds laid horizontally. There is generally a second building nearby in which the cooking is done. Every house has its hammock and one can see people gently swinging in them on any afternoon.

Mexico seems to take charge of one, and it is extremely difficult to turn one's head for home. The pace is deliciously slow, the people so colourful and friendly, with a grace that comes from living to enjoy the present, and not to worry unduly about the future. There is a spontaneity, a self-reliance, a capacity to overcome problems... one only has to watch a skilled mechanic at work on an ancient farm wagon to appreciate this, and an identification with the land, and above all a gaiety that is reflected in those laughing dark eyes and the tilt of proud heads.

The United States, by contrast with Mexico, is sterile and urban and there are no paths through the desert. Men do not live among the fields but in small towns, and 'bus' out in great parties to attend to the land, accompanied by much machinery. Houses are prefabricated, and gas, not wood, is used for cooking. Life is far removed from nature, and is not the personal individual's concern, as is the case in Mexico. Which is the richer? What is poverty?

To my surprise just west of Yuma great sand dunes appeared. They were golden in the early morning light, with their sweeps and ripples carved by the wind and the rain. I quite thought I was back in Egypt, and that the Sphinx and Cheops Pyramid would appear.

I was soon out of this area and one side of the road was irrigated with water from the Colorado River by the Eastern Central and Western Canals, as well as the earlier all-American Canal. It was grand to see the water swirling down the locks at the field edges, supplying acres of green fields. The hay still green had just been cut by machinery and bundled up, in some cases being piled at the field edge.. Contented cows were eating the left behind short green grass.

There really is a place called Ocotillo and it is surrounded by the desert plant of the same name, green stemmed, with long red flowers at the tips. The road soon rose to over 4,000 feet to cross the Californian Range, the tail end of the Rockies. First came sedimentary rock, then moraine, then boulders and back to sedimentary rock, faulted and upended. From the top I had a marvellous view of the plains below, and range upon range of mountains, some with snow on top. It was very cold at this height. I discovered there is a Butterfield route, rather as there is a Wells Fargo route for stage coaches, and this accounts for the well-spaced Butterfield Parks which I had encountered earlier.

I reached San Diego on 24th March, a distance of 1,937 miles from Mexico City much of it across one form of desert or another. A friend took me around San Diego and showed me the sights including the first Christian mission and trade station. For me, the highlight of the tour was the old Spanish lighthouse from which one gets a superb view of the city, the harbour and the sea. The harbour was dredged to deepen it for shipping, and spurs of land were thus formed on which palm trees and pines of many varieties were growing in great profusion. I learnt that, from December to February, the migrating grey whales can be seen on their way from the Bering Straits to Mexican Baja California. The mountains with their distinctive shapes vie with the many masts of yachts in the harbour, or with the aircraft carrier that brought the POWs home from Vietnam.

The sun was shining brilliantly and a light wind was blowing on Lighthouse Point, showing its rich variety of flowers, such as desert lilac intense in its blueness, five-petalled white waxy desert plum, white thistle poppy, orange Mexican poppy, mesembryanthemum, purple and white, blue desert lupin and bush acacia. In contrast rectangular yellow clapboard Naval buildings demonstrated their claim to this corner of San Diego.

From San Diego I drove north back to Redwood City and spent many days trying to arrange a crossing of the Pacific for *Peregrine* and me. The holds of most ships allow for the recent 8ft 6in high sealed containers, but *Peregrine*'s height was 10ft 6in. Eventually I was able to make arrangements with the Scindia Line for passage in the Jalamohan, a cargo ship without passengers, and was given a sailing appointment for 10.30am at quay C22 Los Angeles on 8th May 1973. *Peregrine* and I passed the noble old Queen Mary, whose photograph I had taken with a small Brownie camera in 1936 as she set out from Southampton on her maiden voyage to New York. Two years later she won the Blue Riband for Britain by achieving the fastest crossing of the Atlantic. As I glanced at her now in dry dock, all dolled up for the tourist trade, I just remembered her glorious past.

I found berths C2O, C21 and C23, but nowhere could I espy C22. It was like a nightmare. The Press had been invited to photograph us, too. Oh, where was berth C22? After further enquiries I was directed to an open berth where there was no bonded shed and therefore no number shining out, and at 11 .00am, half an hour late, I drove alongside. Two of the shipping line's agents were there to meet me. The Press reporter was found, and so were three girls from the Trade Fair, being held that week in Los Angeles who were to be my companions in the photograph on this chilly bright day. Miss World Trade, Miss Export and Miss Import were dressed in long thin frocks, with the explanatory sashes across their chests. Clearly they did not relish standing about so lightly clad in this wind . The Captain of our ship arrived and together we five were photographed, with the stern of *Peregrine* and the stern of the large Indian freighter behind us - perhaps this was symbolic. So started my acquaintance with the Captain who would sail us across the great Pacific Ocean with a cargo of Californian oranges, building materials and several cars.

Mexico	***West Coast of the USA***
31st January 1973—23rd March 1973	***23rd March 1973—8th May 1973***
Mileage: Tucson—Yucatan—San Diego. Total 6,362	***San Diego—San Francisco. Total 1,282***

The Pacific Crossing: Going Aboard—and a Painting by the Author

Giant Saguaro Cactus in the South West Desert

'Peregrine' Going Aboard in Los Angeles

A Safe Voyage —The 'Jalamohan'

Mexico—Historical Map of Civilization Development, 1600 BC to 1600 AD

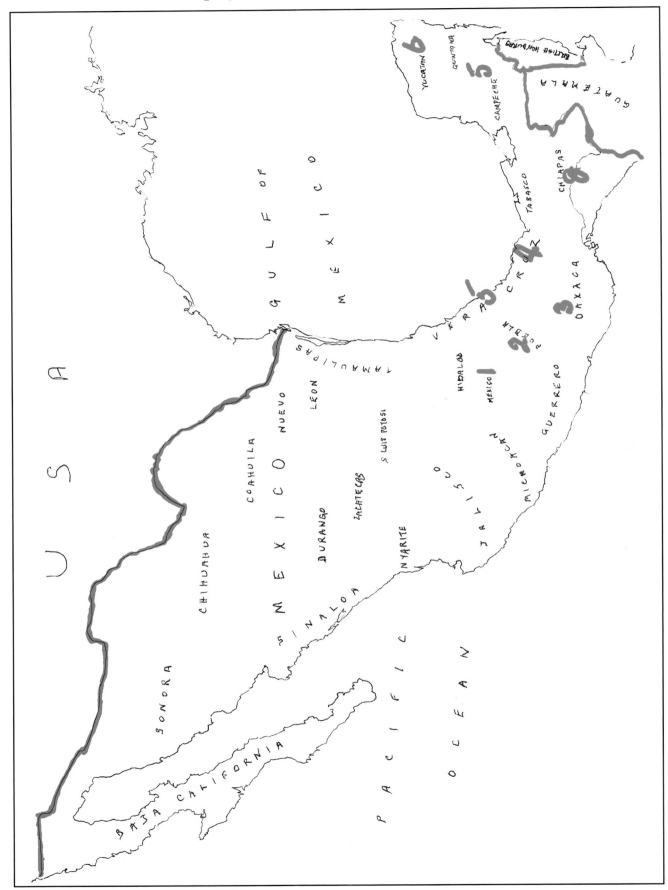

Mexico—Key to Historical Map

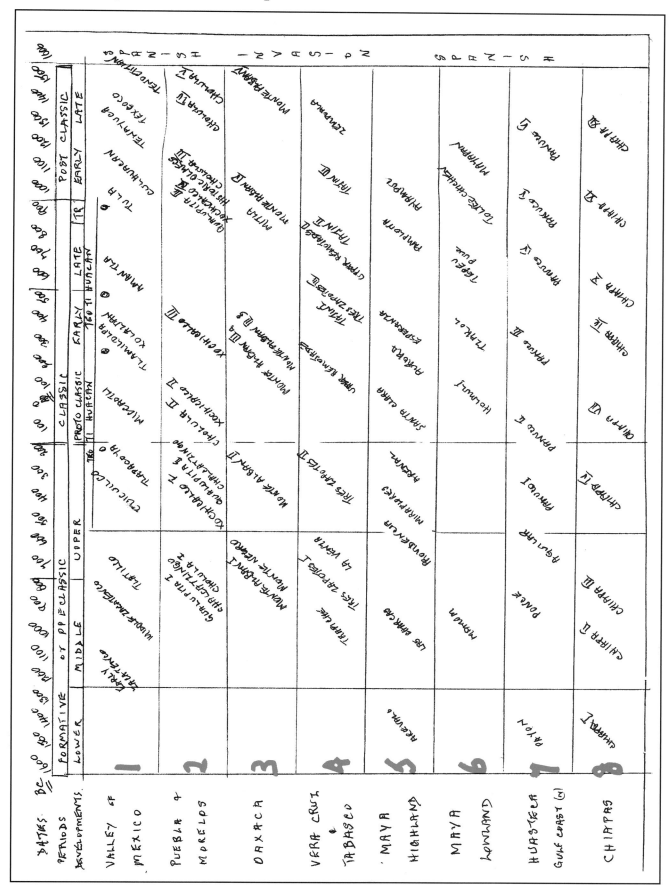

Two Paintings by the Author

Hong Kong Harbour

Singapore - Houses on Stilts

Chapter 5

ACROSS THE PACIFIC TO BOMBAY

I was allotted the accommodation provided for the owner which included a large day cabin measuring perhaps 20ft by 10ft and a night cabin and a bathroom - luxury indeed! I unpacked my deck-lounger, my books, my flute and painting apparatus and some clothes. I was lent a typewriter and so was equipped for the sea journey of two months across the Pacific to Bombay.

The day cabin had two forward portholes and three on the port side and was supplied with a large executive-style desk, a smart leather chair but too low to be of any use for writing at the desk, a table and wall bench for three to five folk and three arm chairs set around the table. In spite of all this provision for seating I preferred to use my own deck-lounger. There was little space for exercise and food was served with intense regularity.

Everything seemed quite normal as the ship weighed anchor at 0530 in the morning and we sailed up the Californian coast to San Francisco, catching sight of the purple edged jelly fish en route. These jelly fish, the sunrise and the sunset are sights only to be experienced with others at sea, and they are thrilling. As we approached San Francisco we saw the spouts of whales, quite close in-shore: fountains of water were puffed up by these great mammals. Alas, we were too late to see the Southern migration that takes place in January - a wonderful sight it seems. Whales which are 30 or 40ft long and weigh, perhaps, 30 tons, leap 30ft into the air and the sun catches their silvery steely grey sides and accentuates their grace and power. We entered the beautiful natural harbour that is protected by the spur of land that rises majestically to a point and supports the gracious and lovely city of San Francisco. We passed under the great golden gate bridge that spans the opening and joins the Northern Californian coastline to the city of San Francisco. We passed the old convict island, now being transformed into a luxury tourist attraction. We passed Fisherman's Wharf and sailed under the lovely long graceful Oakland bridge to our berth. San Francisco is both consciously and unconsciously beautiful; and as one looks at the juxtaposition of the buildings, one is struck by the blend of the old and the new, of the low and intimate on the one hand and the high and functional on the other. There are rectangular and triangular outlines, and there are black and also white buildings; some of the buildings have many large windows, and these catch the light of the sun and add an extra dimension to this city that is linked across the bay with freeways, which carry great volumes of traffic to this city built on one of the sharpest of hills. One cannot help wondering at the faith of man, who can lavish such care on a city that may fall victim to an earthquake at almost any time.

Man is a creature of faith and of superstition as this long sea voyage was to demonstrate. I was the only passenger aboard this freighter, and I was welcomed by the Captain and Officers, with whom I ate, and by the crew whom I saw daily at work about the ship. The ship was bound via Hong Kong and Singapore for Bombay, its home port. There was a well defined routine aboard into which I fitted, although I was the only European and the only 'drone' and I was making my first trip across the Pacific, in this fairly new and large ship that carried Christians, Hindus, Buddhists and Mohammedans. Remembering the story of Jonah and the whale I was reassured that there could be no 'guilty' person aboard, for day after day the seas were calm and the sun shone; sights were taken, our course was plotted and the ship's routine went quietly, relentlessly on.

I found being aboard ship a strange experience. Having foregone a good deal of one's liberty, it is a bit like being a hospital patient at the pre-operative stage -nothing wrong with one but bounds set upon one's activities such as exercise and casual conversations.

The officers and crew were pleasantly friendly. The days aboard were punctuated by meals: breakfast at 8.30 when liver and onions may well be served as well as cereal and toast, luncheon at 12.30 when a choice of three dishes was presented, a meat or fish dish, a curry and a cold meat dish with salad then fruit and cheese, and dinner at 6.30 which was similar to luncheon but with the addition of soup, a terrible 'sweet' and coffee. The food reminded me of my experiences in the WRNS, and 'nuts and bolts' adequately describes the presentation of many of the meat dishes! The curries were neither very hot nor imaginative by Ceylonese standards, but the sauce did provide some flavour, so perhaps my weight might not increase on this voyage.

I tried to re-learn Arabic and as I plodded away at it, something of what I had learnt when in the Sudan came back to me. I just hoped I would not forget it again during the two or three months in India, Nepal and Afghanistan. I had just finished reading Robert Byron's The Road to Oxiana which describes his thrilling adventures on his route across Asia in 1933/34. The modern roads and increased traffic may have stolen some of the thrills, but should have made the journey a more certain affair. The book is beautifully written by a scholarly pen and as well as painting with words Robert Byron also paints with a brush and has a sound knowledge of architecture. If only I could write with something of his clarity, freshness and perception.

I was invited to the bridge and witnessed the sunset and the green flash as the sun dipped into the sea. At other times, I had a good view of whales spouting off San Francisco and way out at sea. I saw seals, sharks, and lovely umbrella-shaped jellyfish with clear mauve markings as if delineating the ribs of a brolly and decorating the edges with this mauve pattern. Small Portuguese men-of-war, a type of jellyfish with a harpoon or fin, were also to be seen.

A group of seven or eight albatross accompanied the ship at first and remained with us until we reached the longitude of the Hawaiian islands; there these noble birds with their great wing span and their effortless graceful flight left us, and in their place we were joined by a gannet. This was no ordinary bird, he was a gannet of character and of inspiration, a singular and spectacular gannet. I felt sure that our Hindu and Buddhist seamen friends could readily see that this bird was a successful reincarnation. He quickly established his regular routine and could be counted upon to rise at about 0530, half an hour before the maintenance sailors came on duty. He left his night perch atop the jumbo derrick, that is about mid-ships, and took up a new position on the upper starboard safety railings, more suitable for his morning toilet. From this position he could keep an eye on the ocean, yet have a sure footing as he gripped the rail with his feet, and undertook his daily tasks and generally got the feel of the day. He was a most thorough gannet and seemed to run every feather through his beak, before positioning it. He systematically attacked first one wing and then the other, then his breast and finally his tail feathers. Then, balancing himself carefully, he dealt with his neck feathers, giving first one side and then the other swift smart treatment with one of his webbed feet, perhaps to rid himself of any infestation of fleas. When he was quite satisfied with this undertaking, he shook himself, held his head high and looked like a veritable king. We were proud to have such a distinguished bird with us, and he proved to be an interesting diversion from shipboard routine as we daily observed him going about his independent business in a purposeful, orderly, skilled and confident manner.

He now turned his attention to breakfast. Looking keenly at the sea a little for'ard of our bows he espied some delicate transparent pale blue flying fish which had been disturbed by our division of the waves. Concentrating hard he noted the speed of the ship and the paths of the fish then left the railing and flew around at a comfortable cruising speed, holding his head first on one side and then on the other, the better to focus on the fish. Having espied a suitable victim he suddenly plummeted down almost to the surface, then levelled out and caught one of the flying fish in his strong beak before it was able to dive for safety. He repeated this manoeuvre several times, and though not always successful more often than not he scooped up a fish, swallowed it and returned to his attentive cruising flight. The whole operation was a masterful demonstration of the art of fishing. Once he was well fed he flew off to enjoy himself and did not return until evening, when he again benefited from these beautiful flying unsuspecting fish.

This gannet demonstrated character, skill and appeal, and he made himself quite at home aboard our ship, but was careless with his excretion, and his droppings bespattered the freshly painted derricks and decks. Being en route for her home port the Jalamohan had to arrive looking spick and span, so the Chief Officer gave orders that the derrick upon which our gannet rested should be greased, to dissuade him from settling there. This was done, but our experienced bird coped easily with this little trick; and it made not the slightest difference to him. He continued just as before...

I began to think of the Ancient Mariner aboard his ship, sailing south to the Antarctic through the ice floes, alone, alone; as we were sailing westward on the great wide Pacific Ocean, seemingly alone, alone. The Ancient Mariner and his crew were blessed with an albatross and we were blessed with a gannet. His was no ordinary bird and ours too was a very especial bird.. How far should the Chief Officer go in disturbing our gannet? The painting programme must go on. The derricks had been painted when we were in San Francisco harbour, and now the jumbo derrick was covered in the gannet's excretion. It was time for the deck to be painted and the Chief Officer could not chance this work being spoiled by the fishy greasy droppings. He gave orders to a sailor to dislodge the gannet. This was no shot with a bow and arrow. Confrontation yes, but murder had not been mooted. The sailor, intending to discourage the bird from making so free with the ship's paintwork, started to climb up the jumbo derrick watched by the gannet from above, his fellow sailors from below, and the Captain and Chief Officer from the bridge. As he got nearer to the gannet he realised that he had no clear idea of what he was to do. The Chief Officer had said, "Dislodge the gannet," but in any case, he and all of us knew that shortly the gannet would be away for the day. Why not wait and treat the derrick in his absence? But orders were orders.

The gannet watched the sailor swaying as the ship rose and fell to the rhythm of the waves. The gannet wondered what fool thing would be tried this time and what action he would be called upon to take. The sailor was nearing the top of the derrick, and could see that the gannet was watching him. He prayed fervently that the gannet would fly off and that he would be spared any confrontation with him, but this was not to be. The sailor gripped the pole that he had brought with him and steadying himself reached out to give the gannet a poke. Surely the gannet would understand that he was just suggesting that the derrick was not for use as a perch. The gannet appeared to be outraged by the insulting dig. He had often chosen ships for his passage and pleasure and had never experienced this sort of treatment, rather being welcomed as a guest and a token of God's grace, as it was generally understood that a fair wind would blow if he was aboard. The sailor with the pole was not playing, and although he was only using one hand and steadying himself with the other, he gave a vicious prod. The gannet much disliked this treatment and could not understand why none of the sailors from below nor the officers on the bridge intervened on his behalf. Unlike the Ancient Mariner, who with his bow and arrow shot the albatross and was alone guilty of its death, here the greater number of the ship's company were involved in the disturbing attack that was being launched. Well, if that was so, he must act and act quickly. An assault on the sailor's head should soon settle things.

The gannet rose from the derrick and went into the attack, and taking aim dived at the man's head. This did not move him. In fact the sailor gripped the pole more firmly and moved his position for a further attack. The gannet dived a second time and as he reached the head he made a sharp beak movement that drew blood. The man looked less confident. Would he retreat? It seemed that the sailors on the deck and the officers on the bridge strengthened his resolve for he was 'under orders'. The gannet dived for the third time. The man tried to hit him but failed, then abandoning the pole he tried to catch the gannet with his hands. At the fourth dive the man judged it well and caught the gannet with his hands, gripping those strong wings, leaving the gannet only his head and his beak with which to attack and to defend himself. The sailor was now in a quandary: what should he do with the bird?

A strong wind was blowing and the swell was increasing so he had to hold the rail to prevent himself from being thrown into the water. The gannet's beak was sharp, the sailor's head stung with pain from the wounds that had been inflicted. He should have been warned, but without thinking what he was doing he hit the gannet's head against the rail. The gannet struggled and again drew blood from the sailor. The man became frantic and hit the bird's head on the rail again. The world for the gannet became blurred and he struggled less. The sailor hit the gannet's head for the third time on the rail. There was a sickening noise as the proud neck broke and the body became limp. The sailor realised he had killed this lovely bird, one of God's creatures, which was perhaps an important reincarnation. The crew stood silent on the deck as the sailor tossed the body into the sea. As the sailor climbed down and rejoined his mates on the deck there was no rejoicing, but rather a feeling of apprehension. The sailor went over the incidents of the last fifteen minutes in his mind: he had been hard pressed, he had caught and struck a struggling bird, he had been in danger of losing his balance, he had been under attack and he was 'under orders'; but he had killed this lovely creature, albeit in self-defence, and had thrown the gannet's body overboard.

However, although the gannet, unlike the albatross, was not physically tied around his neck, the sailor was much disturbed by these memories and could not get the gannet from his mind. The crew eyed him strangely. The wind strengthened, the sea became rough, as the ship continued on her way. The daily routine bore the crew along but our sailor was uneasy. At night he paced the deck and was sure he saw a phantom ship. He returned to the cabin he shared with his brother-in-law. He seemed to bring some lone spirit from the deep into the cabin with him as if a ransom for the death of the gannet was required of him. These spirits of the deep may well avenge this untimely death.

Morning came, a bright and sunny morning. The painters returned to their task but a gloom hung over the ship - life seemed to have gone out of the men. Our sailor found this atmosphere oppressive and he and his brother-in-law gave each other some beer at luncheon time and had a convivial, if brittle, time, so that temporarily he forgot the gannet and all seemed to be normal.

Suddenly, without warning, his brother-in-law doubled up with pain and could not breathe. He felt as if strong hands were clasped around his chest and his head throbbed. His world was becoming blurred. Our sailor saw himself with his hands around the gannet's wings, and he looked on helplessly as his brother-in-law collapsed in a dead faint beside him. He helped to carry him to their cabin, doing all he could for him in an effort to expiate his responsibility for killing the gannet. The Captain and the Chief Officer were informed and with grave faces they each tried to find the man's pulse. The crew seemed to accuse our sailor. After two or three hours the sick man felt better, and he moved about a little, then said that he felt tired and that he would like to be left alone to sleep. Our sailor left the cabin, but positioned himself outside the door, anxious to be of help, should this be required. He wished he could be freed from the thoughts of the spirits of the deep, but he felt cheered that his brother-in-law, a strong man, seemed to be recovering. Suddenly, while so musing, a noise was heard from the cabin, a little cry, followed by a mysterious gurgle. The Captain and the Chief Officer were informed, and came at once. Their faces were grave as they emerged from the cabin and they confirmed our worst fears – our sailor's brother-in-law was dead. The spirits had called for the life of a man to expiate for the life of one of God's birds.

The whole tragic story of the Ancient Mariner seemed to be being replayed but this time the whole crew felt some part of the blame. A deep freeze was emptied to give space for the body, wrapped in a rather heavy tarpaulin, thus preserved as it was to be taken to Bombay for burial.. Along with the rest of the crew our sailor made a vow never again to kill one of God's creatures, but to set an example of love and reverence for them.

As we passed the tip of Taiwan we saw several local fishing boats. I was thrilled to see one really near to us which was, for me, such an unusual shape, high in the prow and stern and only just above sea level athwart the beam. It seemed that one man and one woman were aboard, the man with a large round hat going to a peak at the top, and the woman with her straw hat tied on with a mauve-grey scarf. Why should hers and not his be in danger of blowing off, or is the scarf to give protection to the face? It seems they were fishing with great nets which they let down deep into the sea. I hope that they may be successful, for we were only several feet from a marker, a black plastic flag, and I would hate it if we had torn their net and spoiled their catch, for they surely do not have much spare money.

With a member of the crew, I looked at *Peregrine* to see how she had survived the voyage and to find what needed to be done to get her ready for the road again. One of her mirrors had been smashed in handling and when one of the engineers looked at the gearbox, he discovered that brass had worn off into the oil which had been overheated, presumably during one or more of the four separate occasions that she lost her oil during the 8,000 miles. The engineer said that the springs on the oil seal were probably faulty, so I must find a sound and sympathetic garage in Bombay to set things really right before taking off for Nepal. I learnt that driving is on the left in India and Nepal and on the right again in Afghanistan and thereafter -until I get to the shores of England. I hope I shall remember! The speedometer stands now at over 21,000, so we had covered 17,000 miles on the continent of the Americas.We arrived in Hong Kong on 30th May 1973 in the pouring rain with everything shrouded in cottonwool clouds. In the evening the sky lightened and lights twinkled from all around this great natural harbour which was full of Chinese junks, motor launches, strange craft the like of which I have never before seen more like Russian sleighs of the 19th century than any vessel for the sea, sailing among the ferries plying to and fro every three minutes. It was all go! After unloading, reloading and a short stay we sailed off towards Singapore where the process was repeated

We put in at Singapore, then sailed up the Malacca Straits and near to the coast of Sri Lanka so that I was able to distinguish the old Portuguese Fort at Galle, which I had known in 1954 when I was helping to run a school on the island. On 6th July we landed at Bombay.

8th May 1973—6th July 1973
San-Francisco—Bombay aboard the Jalamohan

India—Route Map

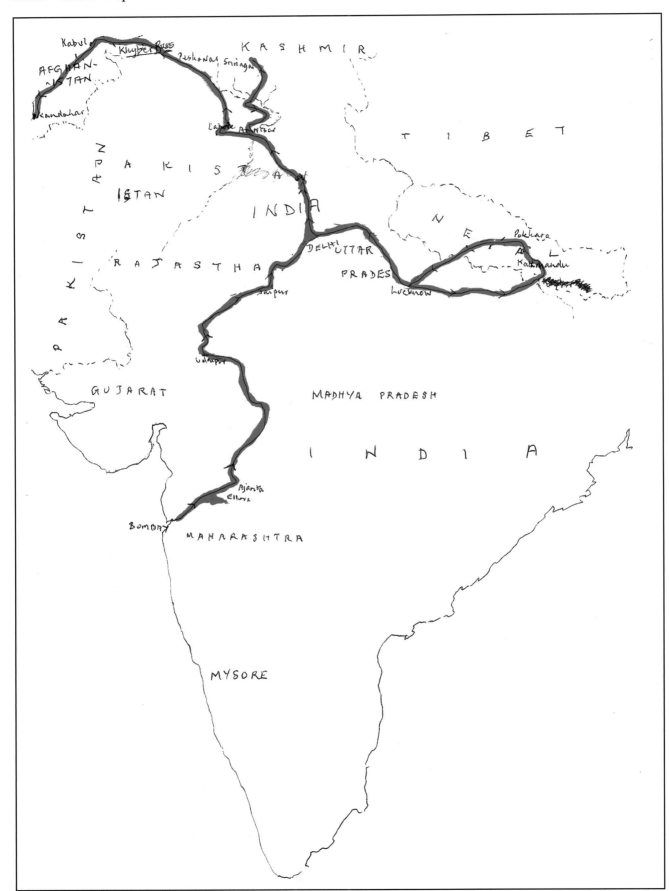

Chapter 6

THE INDIAN SUB-CONTINENT

This sub-continent includes India, Nepal, Pakistan and Kashmir.

INDIA

My arrival in Bombay coincided with the centenary celebrations of the Port Trust Authority. Ships in the stream and at the dock sides were dressed overall. A Naval ship sailed out of the dockyard similarly attired, anchored in the stream and added to the festal air. Two clocks on the jetty, in towers just 50 yards apart, proclaimed the time: they were ten minutes apart! The dock gates displayed the Port Trust centenary in bright blue letters upon a peerless white ground and the Port Trust building in Ballard Street re-iterated it. Old red Leyland Buses, redolent with the past they had spent in England, now with B.E.S.T. upon their sides, rested in the shade, and taxis, gaudy in yellow and black, plied for trade.

I found Bombay seething, teeming, hot, sticky, a noisy place both colourful and drab: stately and beggarly, sturdy and trashy, courteous and arrogant; leisurely and bustling; green and muddy, elegant and shabby; dignified and degraded; luxurious and unpainted; houses and hovels, great riches and abject poverty … all this and more describes Bombay … a city of contrasts.

Life in the smaller streets in Bombay was full of incident: the peregrinations of the sacred cow, being hand fed with indigestible looking coarse grass; the circles of men round the vendors who were demonstrating their wares; the rickety old bicycle threading its way through the crowds; laundry being hung up to dry behind open windows and shutters; shoes were being soled, and metal filed; and all about were the markets where transactions were being made after keen calculations. Railway stations and shady corners provided space for lepers, and popular spots for prolonged sleep; the dead were covered with flowers and wheeled or carried to their last resting place, while the maimed asked alms of their more fortunate brethren. The old life and the new; the 'good life' and the struggle for existence; the educated and the illiterate are side by side in the streets of Bombay. Where should the responsibility lie? Should there be generous social security schemes, the supporting of the poor by the rich? Is the division of wealth tenable as it is? Should a man have to demonstrate that he can support the children he gives his wife? Is there no plan to aid the destitute? The degradation of man affects us all. The pulsating life of Bombay goes on. Bombay that rich city, that has so much to offer, but in such variable amounts.

The High Commissioner's Office was thronged with would-be emigrants from India to the British Isles while the papers spoke disparagingly of British rule in India. A gleaming, air-conditioned Mercedes, with a well groomed passenger was at the traffic lights alongside a two-wheeled vegetable barrow, that was being pushed by a sweating half-starved man in a doubtful dhoti. An impeccably dressed Hindu lady, graceful in her coloured sari, and shaded by her parasol, crossed the road next to a half naked man, with his heavy load of lunch-boxes balancing on his head. Although half-starved himself, he hurried to deliver this food to others in the heat of the day. A young man, hair neatly brushed, in a clean uncrumpled shirt and well tailored trousers, found himself passing an old man with shaven head, in a drab dhoti, balancing a wide round basket of fruit and vegetables on his head … these he must sell this day if he would eat. Neat little boys with white socks and satchels, and girls in outdated blue cotton gym-tunics, contrasted with attractive, dirty, dishevelled little imps, who were being taught to be professional beggars. Solid spacious old Victorian buildings, verandahed and shuttered, rubbed shoulders with brash concrete edifices, with much glass and little shade. Open plan, air-conditioned offices contrasted with small shops in narrow streets, with not a breath of air moving, where artisans and craftsmen plied their trades. Distinguished five-star modern air-conditioned hotels, with bathrooms attached to every suite and the degrading 'kraals' with little protection from sun or rain, no water, and human excrement on the roads, lie within half a mile of each other.

Old world courtesy is to be found cheek by jowl with brash indifference ... the brusque command to the suppliant hands, the 'haves' alongside the 'have-nots'; genuine help, given so generously, contrasting with the studied 'brush off' veiled in polite blandishments. Big firms, important in world markets and the surreptitious man who approaches every European with "change money, very good price, German, Eenglish, Americarn". The peace of the University precincts compared with the pressures of the pavements.

The rich tourist may gain quite another picture, for he may be driven from the Gateway of India to the well architectured Marine Drive, and then to the Jain Temple, and the famous Hanging Gardens on Malabar Hill. He will see the spacious Kamala Nehru Park and may bathe in the Beach Candy bathing pool, before going to the world-famous Bombay Race Course. He will go everywhere by car, stop off at the Zaveri Bazaar and be pleased with the jewels he finds there; before making his way back to his five star air-conditioned hotel. This picture is as true of Bombay as the earlier one. Bombay is a rich and varied city; full of the past; and confused with the present.

I had to wait for about a week for *Peregrine* to be repaired, during which time the monsoon rains somewhat complicated my days. I was parked in a garage forecourt, but I was allowed to read in the nearby University Library which was both spacious and cool. There were necessary documents to be acquired for *Peregrine*, and I went off by train for them. The railway station had many sick and lepers lying about, a scene I had never previously experienced nor imagined.

Also during the week I visited Bombay's Museum and met a French 'girl' and together we tried to decipher the meanings of the Hindu artists. She told me she had been staying in an ashram, and had met Bailey, an American boy, and they were hoping to tour India. I agreed to take them in *Peregrine* when she was roadworthy. This was not to be, for the girl developed galloping hepatitis and had to be flown home to Paris, so I arranged to take the young American with me.

A week later I went round to Dixon's garage at about 9.00am, and more or less woke them up. I waited for the shop next door to open. This eventually happened at 10.30am! but no handle was found for the door. At last Maxie went off to get an oil filter and a handle; he returned at 12.30 with a handle but no filter. In the meantime, I had met his father – a clean, moustached, grey-haired dapper little old man who had had to leave his good garage premises when the Indian Navy sealed off his part of the old road as docks. Three sons carry on the garage, and still do a good job. The firm is of 35 years standing. *Peregrine* was nearly ready to go at 2.10pm when Maxie broke the mirror as he was positioning it. Eventually the costs were worked out and I left shortly after 3.00pm and *Peregrine* was going well.

I left the Sassoon dock gate and by arrangement, picked up Bailey, and drove off past Flora fountain, the Times of India (which had bought one of my articles) before reaching the four-lane Nasik/Agra Road. This road shortly became a two way road, and then deteriorated still further as we passed rice fields, then factories, en route to real country scenes. There were men and women with boat shaped leaves to give protection from the rain on their heads as they worked. The land became more wooded, and we began to climb the strangely shaped volcanic hills.

Dixon's Garage.

As it began to become dusk, we stopped at Khadi, a hill village, and parked by a garage for the night. Khadi is a busy farming community, with s and stalls providing goods that would have a sale at the bus stop, as well as having small shops selling nuts, chillies, spices and dahl, all laid out on the floor of the shops, with brass scale pans to weigh what was required; and other shops had men who were machining and repairing shoes. There was evidence of Christian, Hindu and Muslim religions in the village of c. 5,000 folk, a few of whom spoke English, such as the electrical engineer and the men at the garage. Men flocked round and borrowed my 'India' book and escorted me up the hill to buy bananas; they were most polite and nodded to the local doctor en route. It was pretty quiet after 11.00 pm.

Early next day we left Khadi, and a great family of girls lined up on their balcony and waved. We drove up beside a lovely gorge, flanked with trees displaying such big leaves; then up and over the range of hills, with wooded slopes that gave way to paddy fields, nuts or sugar cane. The land became flatter, the Deccan was sparsely populated but densely cultivated; cattle, strange sheep, often brown, were to be found along with goats either on the farms or on the road. Where the roads were under repair, men and women were shovelling up stones into small round baskets or tins, and emptying them into a lorry or putting them into a pile. The torrea, an agricultural tool, was much in evidence. Women were also breaking stones by hitting them with a hammer, when bits flew all over the place. Road accidents, and the results of accidents were all pervading.

The locals of the Armpalgaon village took a lively interest in *Peregrine*, and helped me to fix the handle from the unused door to the offside locker, and then sharpened my screwdriver! The road to Aurangabad was very narrow, making it really difficult to pass oncoming traffic; it became a test to see who would 'give way' and leave the hard centre of the road.

We reached Ellora, standing as it does in its great sweep of a rocky mountain from which there is a view for miles across the valley. It is an amazing site, having one to three storey caves that are hewn from the living rock, while in front of them are pillars, with decorated capitals, light in colour and evenly arched, displaying a regularity and beauty which through the simplicity of the design, contributes to the utter peace of the place.

The great domed and crenellated temple stands out because all the rock above it has been removed. This eighth century Kailasa has an unsupported projection of about ten feet, which overhangs an open space with the heavily yet delicately carved temple in its centre. The underside of the projection originally had a lotus leaf decoration in painted stucco, but little of this remains. There is a perambulatory with more than life-sized figures – Siva, Vishnu and Brahma – all well flanked by a huge elephant and an obelisk. The obelisk takes ones eyes upwards to the lofty carvings of the outside of the temples, some of which give details of battles of the Maharansas, while others form a frieze of battling elephants, and are followed by formal designs interspersed with several individual women in leaping positions. The whole, though so massive and so closely enclosed, contrives not to be heavy, the artists have used much symbolism, such as Siva the destroyer opposite to Siva the contemplative. Durga killing the buffalo, Siva killing the elephant demons; the power and the restraint, the naturalistic and the symbolic, the lotus flower and the designs of pillars and the occasional caryatid, of a man with upraised arms, rub shoulders with each other.

My amazement when I saw a doorway in one of the three-storey viharas with a square upper part, and a small rectangular lower end, which is so similar to those doorways at Las Casas Grandes and I have never seen them elsewhere; was there any link between the two, I wondered? They were each built at roughly the same time, circa 8th century.

These caves which, unusually, combine provision for Hindu, Buddhist and Jain followers, exude a stillness, and the power of the contemplative is there, even with the swarms of sightseers, some with radios or guides and their shouting and singing. The Buddhist caves are especially magnificent, e.g. 21 and 29; and the Jain 32 that leads into 33 with their ornate Victorian bowl pillars and in contrast, their nude figures; the fat man on the elephant and the girl on the lion. One temple with the ways guarded by lions, each with a paw upraised, so reminiscent of the Chinese lions with paws on a ball or sphere. Although not finished, this cave is most impressive, and the view of the waterfall focuses ones attention on the force of moving, flowing water as it threads its way through and over the powerful solid rock that has been shaped by man. Where does power lie, in the solids, in the water, in the mind? The valley below with the changes of the seasons tells of God's plan for life and of man's dependence on Him.

We drove on to the foot of the great Mogul castle (*illus. next page*) and met an elderly lady, who gave us gave coffee and invited us to park *Peregrine* on her property. In the morning, I awoke to the noise of peafowl, donkeys and birds. Later, we climbed to the top of the great fort Dalautabad, through its surrounding walls, past a great cistern, up by a beautifully chased and decorated canon, with a ram's head, curling horns and over it all a regular pattern of grasses and plants: and on its mouth an Arabic inscription, with two very worn lions. From here, we made out the facade of a palace, once with much stucco and decorative scallops. Originally this was an 11th century Hindu castle, and was only conquered by a siege: it had a decorated dungeon that once had housed the

conquered king. Blue and white tiles, reminiscent of Portuguese tiling, had covered the walls and some of them remain. We reached the very top of this building along a 64 metre enclosed passage, and found a modern flagstaff and a canon. We looked down from this impressive sandstone rock with its sheer walls and rock face, reminiscent of Sigirya, in Sri Lanka. Just below the summit, was a lovely throne room with wooden, carved, supports for the roof or extra floor and iron rings to support a canopy over a raised area in the middle. We found a covered arched 'portales' then an idyllic dwelling room. This was pillared with an hexagonal verandah that commanded a wonderful view for miles. It had a lovely stuccoed ceiling, fluted to a central motif. Three doors led to a verandah and three doors led towards a throne room, giving a feeling of space and beauty in this 17th century Mogul area. One wall of the 'room' off the throne room had a wall decorated with formal designs in cartouches – loosely reminiscent of a temple wall at Palenque.

On our way down we visited a nice square and domed temple dedicated to Ganesh, the elephant god, with his trunk twisted sideways, sitting there to help his worshippers. We found another Hindu temple certainly earlier, with carved pillars and a niche. From the top of the hill the whole design of the castle could be seen, with its outer wall enclosing much land, making it seemingly a walled city with a moat. Further walls following a line of the land, were studded with half-circle gun emplacements, and finally there was a moat around the 'keep' rising from the sheer rock that drew its water from a cistern which was fed by the surrounding mountains.

We found a carved stone with an ornate Venus design, like those at Palenque: could there be some connection between the two, I wondered? The inscriptions, the Venus signs, and the decorated columns seem so similar to those at Uxmal or el Kabah.. How lucky we were to see all this in sunshine, for on our return to our hostess, down came the rain.

We next found our way to Ajanta - Oh the beauty of this deserted Buddhist retreat. It was re-discovered by Billy Smith, a British officer when chasing a panther in 1819. The caves follow the curve of the Waghorn River that enters this gorge by a busy waterfall. In this monsoon weather, the river is cedar brown in colour and the flow is constant, noisy and reverberating. The sandstone rocks are of different colours, some cedar brown like the river, others darker red. The birds, the stillness, the care being spent on the conservation of the caves, the variations in design of the carved pillars, and the balance and power of the still and the moving – the intensity of it all and the utter calm. The earliest caves are 2nd century BC and the later ones 7th century AD. The perspective in the wall paintings is well ahead of European paintings of the same date.

Bird of Paradise

The certainty of the artists, the casual mixing of themes, the formal 'Italianate' acacia swirls similar to those of the 16th or 17th centuries, and all hidden and unknown for 1,000 years because of the eclipsing of Buddhism in favour of the 'new Hindu'.

As I walked up the steep steps to the fairly narrow platform and looked up at the sixty or eighty foot of carving on the face of the rock, and then walked inside and saw in one cave temple an apse and a rectangular building, so reminiscent of San Vitale of Ravenna of the 12th century AD, with its intimacy, its overall symmetry, its careful juxtaposition and movement, vital and stirring, yet calm, controlled and alert and contemplative it was very possible to imagine the young monks at the feet of their gurus learning to control their desires and to direct their energy to eternal truths, to the absolute.

The world is indeed shut out from this valley, which ends with the Ajanta Caves. This in itself is symbolic as one drives down the narrow road flanked on each side by green fields which lead to the steep and wild sides of the gorge, only to be suitable for the rearing of sheep or goats, though it was said that there are plans to plant trees, to be tended by the Forest Commissioners, one leaves behind the living social world in exchange for the timelessness of nature. We had a chat with a professional guide at lunch time, a nice boy who has had six months training and earns about 5,000 rupees p.a. Young though he is, he complains of rising prices and was acutely conscious of the dependence of the countryside on the monsoon rains. He told us that after three years of drought, the area was benefiting this year from a good rainfall.

The following day we walked to a viewpoint and saw a pair of very brightly coloured kingfishers, displaying that heavenly turquoise blue/green colour. From the viewpoint, we saw that the sheer rock made a great horseshoe, with the caves nestling so contentedly under the shoulder of the secure background. We visited more of these superb caves, and just at lunch time had the good fortune to find two tours in Cave 1, with an informative guide, who was enlarging upon the most superb paintings, very much of the 'Sienna' school, with that red and dark green, and the almost Titian treatment of the human skin. The pictures were of lovely scenes with pillars, in good perspective: and since they are 5th or 6th century, they are about a thousand years ahead of their time. *(Illus: Cave Twenty-One).*

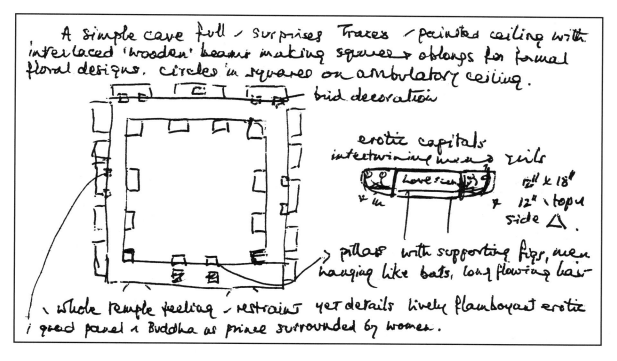

Here too stands the pillar with the capital of one head for the four deer – so skilfully carved in stone that the head could belong to each and any one of the four; it dominates the whole. The ceiling, divided into rectangles, has floral designs, and the whole is a marvel of achievement We visited more lovely caves in the afternoon, including No. 6 with the four 'ringing' pillars, decorated with lovely ducks and birds. We saw the green elephant (one of the Buddha's incarnations) and also a lovely group of Buddha and two disciples on a pillar on the left of the stupa.

India presented me with various difficulties – apart from my lack of knowledge of the language! For instance, money changing was difficult, because the opening times were limited, and the rate of exchange was very variable. Petrol stations were few and distances between one and the next were unknown. Drinking water, too, was often in short supply, and at the same time the floods necessitated my making an 800 mile detour en route to Nepal; but in spite of this, I was only 24 hours late to meet my next companion. Great areas of water had to be forded whenever we came across rivers in flood. One such was so deep and wide that six foot plus tall Bailey, who kindly waded through to establish conditions, found the water well above his knees at one point where the uneven river bottom was very low. *Peregrine* drove through and reached the further side of the river, but by about 6 pm we came upon a line of stationary traffic – a new Tata lorry had been trying to avoid a hole in the causeway, and had slipped off into the river. Help from Navapur had been sent for.

We were fortunately befriended by a jolly fat truck driver from Dhulai, whose friend was the driver of the wrecked new truck. We were going to return to the last village, but the jolly driver said there is a 'bad man' thief there and not safe, and advised us to stay in line with the truck drivers and take our turn at getting across the river. He said first the overturned truck will have to be emptied by 'labour' from Navapur, then an attempt to tow it out will have to be made, and then we should be invited to drive across this raging river. Men have been filling the hole with rocks and boulders and it is to be hoped that they have so strengthened the weak spot that it will support us. Meanwhile it is still raining. Most drivers are retiring to their trucks to sleep. The buses are turning at the ford and returning the way they have come, while the passengers often paddle across the ford.

As it became quite dark, villagers came to see the fun – with plenty of talk and speculation, and then a sort of chanting started, so perhaps the 'labour' has tackled the barrels of bitumen, the load that was on the wrecked truck. Some men rolled a cement main drainpipe into the river and packed it with stones, and two trucks drove over it and went on their way. We ate and slept the night, and were awoken as trucks drove by. A further wait for 40 minutes while the wrecked truck was re-loaded, and it and two others drove by. We went through with two before us and several following, and reached Navapur. Our gallant fat friend who had earlier offered us brandy spoke for us, at the 'hotel' where food seemed to be served all night to truckers, and asked if we required eggs or bread. We made a rush for bread, only to find it had all gone. Another trucker stopped and gave us two rolls. We parked where it was suggested and again slept well. The village was busy and alive by 6.00 am or so, though the sky was very dark and it was wet all about us. What a day, the calm of Ajanta, the surging boys who swarmed over *Peregrine* and hurt her, and the fording of the great rivers, and then the taking of our own place among the truckers, and finding such chivalry .

The village was alive early, and many girls and women in bright saris, were carrying brass or clay water pots. Apart from one girl in blue and white wide trousers, more usually girls are to be seen in bright blue skirts with a blue apron-like front and with dull reddish 'shawls' over their heads and back. The two lengths of cloth are quite usual at Navapur, and over all bright flower patterns and tie-dyed material are also quite common. Men have various head-dresses, from the large magenta turban to a triangular cloth tied round with a knot in front and a way of rolling the material and making three rolls around the head.

We found that Gujarat was prosperous, with intensive farming, and enough water which was not directly dependent on the monsoon rains. Mercifully there were bridges over the rivers, so for the present, no more fording of rivers: but as we went along a very long causeway, we saw the land was flooded on each side, and as far as a railway embankment to the left, and on the right for miles. The 'local roads' were flooded and impassable for all but oxen and their wagons

In torrential rain we reached the main Bombay/Ahmedabad road, passing black faced monkeys en route. Many beautiful girls were repairing the road, and cattle drivers, big and strong and often moustached, were to be seen in smocks or dhotis, and magenta turbans with a red 'tail'.

Ahmedabad was a prosperous place with industry, and many small shopkeepers, and with ornate houses with carved balconies. This contrasted with its neighbour, impoverished Rajasthan, where we watched a boy of about 10 who went up the hill with a herd of goats, paying no attention to them; they lay down all over the road, causing buses and public carrier lorries to stop, hoot, and proceed by courtesy of the goats. The boy sat on a milestone observing the beauty of the green wooded land across the river and did nothing. The goats came back to observe us. Still the boy sat and did nothing. How wonderfully detached – I wonder what he thought of all day each day when out with the goats.

Then we passed some rollicking ragged 'gypsy' children, and also men proudly riding camels. We came upon great road works in Rajasthan started by the Government last year because there were no rains and the folk had no water in the wells, and no food and no money. A great plan was put in hand to make a double track road and to level the road by lowering parts of it. Great rocks were attacked with picks, smaller rocks were hammered and chipped, mud was used to bank up the edges. All done by human labour, much of which was done by beautiful girls and women. This should become a splendid road, but just now it was a shambles. In order to avoid the deep ruts, I chose a path to the left where other cars had been; but slipped off the wet clay shoulder and embedded one side of *Peregrine* in the soft shoulder. We were stuck fast at 5.45pm, near a road gang that had just knocked off. They tried to push *Peregrine* forwards or backwards, but to no avail. A truck driver stopped and I produced a jack, and he had one. *Peregrine* was eventually lifted, after five attempts, when each time hard core was put under the rear wheels, then my tow rope was attached to his lorry, willing hands pushed and I got into reverse and hey presto – we were out in about 30 minutes of this professional treatment! No recompense was expected, it was natural to help someone in need. Girls and men watched and clapped at our success; I gave them sweets. It was a warming experience. I drove on to a lovely valley and put up with the Government of India Mineral Exploration team, and found such courtesy on this lovely starry night.

 Next day, we learnt that it was only 24 miles to Udaipur, but what a road! Two thirds of it was churned up wet clay, with hard core rapidly sinking and becoming useless. We slipped about all over the place, as if on a skid pan. However, we managed to reach Udaipur by 10.30am and went to the Lake Palace of Nomen, still used by the Maharajah of this area, whose family sign is the sun with a face on it. This palace has a wonderfully commanding view, being at the highest point of Udaipur. We drove through two great stucco gateways with fine green iron gates. Large jasmine, oleander and bougainvillia were forming an avenue, and three young well-cared for elephants in stone greeted us on the final turn to the palace, with their trunks in their mouths, and anklets on their legs. The old palace was open to the public.

Only one of the elephant stables is in use now. There used to be several elephants who played in the long courtyard, with paintings of elephants on the stable walls. There is a fine view of the lake, and a palace on an island, which is now a luxury hotel. The straggling city where there are often no roads between the creamy white houses, built so close together, and depending only on walkways and steps, yet the old town seems to have adjusted well to modern times. We lost our way on the way out of Udaipur, and mounted one of these steep narrow roads and had to back down to get around. Eventually we met a social worker on a motor bike who advised against the main road because of road-works, and suggested a route to Delhi via Chittor, which is quite 600 miles away. We have only a slender chance of reaching there before Thursday at the earliest.

We reached Chittor by 6.45pm, but I had put *Peregrine's* front left wheel in a pit. Mercifully, Bailey's strength and reverse gear got us out! . Houses here have processional paintings on them, with tigers, elephants etc. – we found this lovely place, with a suitable spot for the night, in spite of the noise of trains; Chittor is a railway junction, and also has an imposing fort, a most extensive building ranging over two hilltops with a minaret, good sheer walls and other buildings. The wall must be about five miles long, as it encircles several hills.

The road to Jaipur was in good condition, and the sun shone; the women and girls we passed had heads with carrot shaped adornments along their central parting, ending in an ornamented and chased silver cap. They also sported nose ornaments, ear rings and necklaces. They wore full skirts and well decorated tops, often dark with sequins or brilliant designs in the Persian floral style. Then fine head scarves covering hair, jewellery and sometimes another length of material, giving an apron effect. The full skirts were usually dark with many small flowers in red or green and a plain red border at the hem. One girl wore a solid silver collar like an Egyptian's collar, decorated with flowers in square cartouches and weighing perhaps 2 lbs.

Jaipur is a mogul city painted a coral red relieved with white; with fine gateways and great courtyards like the zocalos in Spain. It is exceptional in that it is 17th and 18th century throughout, and it has many palaces. The Rajah is extremely wealthy as Rajahs here have been for generations. We saw the observatory built in the 18th century which is now little more than a curio. The Amber Palace built of light yellow stone graces the top of the mountain The lattice-work gateway and wall, the many windows and oriels supported on pillars all tend to lighten the whole massive structure built in true Mogul style. This lightness was achieved, for example, through the use of pillars, such as those in front of the important arch of the museum. We saw the six elephants that daily carry folk up to the Palace.

We reached Delhi in a downpour after crossing desert country and experiencing a real oasis with palm trees surrounding a lake that was supplying water to many. We encircled the Red Fort and with difficulty I got a visa for Nepal. I tried to find the way out of Delhi for Lucknow, where Bailey planned to leave me, and got hopelessly lost – passing the Red Fort twice! - before finding the road, and later, a village with a nice Government Inspection bungalow for the night.

Next morning, the road led to a little town so thick with peasants that one could certainly have walked on their heads. They were like ants en route to find honey. A policeman there said left turn for Indabad and this seemed strange; Bailey checked the map and found we were south of the main road, on a B road and we had about 50km to go to get back to the main road. It began to rain. Eventually at Garli we joined the main road and had not gone very far when we saw two buses facing in the same direction but off the road, one on each side, each a wreck and fixed into trees. Later, two trucks had run into each other from behind and coal was spilled about. Later, a very big truck had had a head-on collision with a truck and was off the road, and all traffic had come to a standstill.

We were waved on and started to crawl round the line of trucks which had accumulated; they had commandeered the road and we were forced into the wet mud and became stuck. We demanded that the driver of the truck should tow us out, we produced our tow rope and within ten minutes we were towed clear and on our way. The next big excitement was a lorry coming towards us round a corner and quite out of control. I drew right over to my side and stopped and somehow with a fearful lurch he went by. Mercifully, a canal inspection bungalow loomed into sight where we were given permission to stay. Our days and nights were interrupted by our efforts to get rid of the rats that had sought shelter in *Peregrine* from the floods. Eventually we won!

My next concern was the electricity supply to the fuse box: several men claiming to be electricians said all was OK but I was not happy, and later saw the main fuse go! Bailey left me at Lucknow, and on my own I made for Sirwan; but I cannot read the road signs in the local language, and found I was not on the road to Sirwan – the road turned to mud, and I was in a village. The villagers came out to give advice, and I gave a lift to one man who spoke a little English, and we reversed for seemingly miles, until I saw a spot for turning. The Pied Piper could not have attracted more little boys from such a remote spot. At an unmarked junction, the man dismounted and off I went to Sirwan, amid lots of flood water and acres of paddy fields.

Painting by the Author

Bhadgaon—The Golden Door

India

The Taj Mahal

Archway Detail (Near the Taj Mahal)

Ajanta—Buddhist Temples

Ajanta—Buddhist Temple.Pillar Detail

Nepal—Bhadgaon

Malla Palace of 55 Windows

Violin Boys

Golden Door

Kashmir and Kathmandu

Srinagar—Kashmir

Kathmandu Market from the Palace

Exhausted, I reached Mazzafarpur and was allowed to stay at the Bihar Electrical HQ. It was a full moon, and boys carrying flowers and lanterns on their shoulders went chanting along the road to their Puja, surrounded by a lovely sunset, one of the recent few there have been. The local people were so kind and had gone for a loaf of bread for me. I gave a girl and three younger brothers some nuts and four sweets, and one man a US coin. They seemed pleased, and off I went to find the NH28 road to Nepal. Believing that I was in Rakaul I stopped for petrol, only to find I was in Bettiah, and it was 18 miles back to Chapour and a right-hand turn from the south to get me to Birgong. What a crushing disappointment – still, *Peregrine* was in great form, so we retraced our steps and found the sign at the crossroads that I had not correctly interpreted, and took the road to Rakul and the border, between India and Nepal.

6th July 1973—29th July 1973
Mileage: Bombay—Kathmandu 2,192

NEPAL

After a wait, the Customs man asked "Are you alone in that large vehicle? Are you driving?" Astonished, he allowed me through to the Nepalese Immigration Department, where I was given such a welcome, my passport was examined, and everyone was friendly, and many were wearing 'the cap'. The road was both steep and narrow and sometimes muddy, and now and then had water coursing across it. I drove up and up, until I had almost an aerial view of the beautifully terraced land. *Peregrine* was beginning to be noisy and was using much petrol, so I visited a Government agricultural station at Palvag in the hope of finding petrol, but there was none there, as recently their machines had gone over to diesel: but I spent a safe night there.

As I left next morning, passers-by waved to me, with jolly, carefree smiles. *Peregrine* was very noisy but still pulling. A bus had recently gone over the edge; I heard the driver and nine passengers had died. The seats were lined up on the roadside. How ghastly, buses are always so full. I stopped in a larger village for petrol, and found a nice boy in uniform who spoke some English. We went off down the road to the general store, where a boy sitting on the floor unlocked a store and from barrels drained off some petrol for Rs.16 – twice the price, and of doubtful condition. So I thanked him for his pains and declined his offer. Later, I heard the 'boy' was the policeman in charge of the village! I stopped by a tractor and a tiny village shop and there I met a nice old man, toothless and moustached, and a charming girl with dancing eyes and a ready smile, and we had much jolly chat, and two gallons of petrol were found for me, and funnelled into *Peregrine*.

I arrived in Kathmandu at 10.30am with almost no petrol, found the Embassy and there met Rita and Terence, Sarah, Roderick and Harriet and friends. We sat in a huge drawing room, with green carpets, and orange covers, and together drank lemon squash. Eventually I rang Helen at Manash, my companion for the onward journey, and got round there just before luncheon. Together we found the beautifully carved overhanging houses and narrow market streets, like London before the Great Fire, and a temple area with the three-tiered pagoda shaped roofs.

The next two days were given up to cleaning *Peregrine* and getting her ready for our homeward journey. By chance I met an Anglo-Indian who took us to a Sikh friend who traced the electrical fault to the right winker, and repaired it.

The next day we both went off on the moped to Hanuman Dhoka and there saw the hideous monkey god Hanuman draped in red and covered by a garden 'brolly'. The fine brass doors, the great 'coronation' square, the platform and the tall carved buildings were surrounding it: at the far corner on the left were the four seven storey 'towers' of Kathmandu, the last three being in the pagoda shape. Patan having been knocked sideways by the 1951 earthquake offered a rectangle graceful in its simplicity, with a red tiled roof, and bricks between wooden uprights. Badgaon, with its Moghul upturned boat style roof was similar to the Amber Palace, at Jaipur, while the fourth, a complicated octagon, had its roof divided into triangles. Many of the dark wooden supports and beams were decorated with stylised floral designs and white carvings, painted, while the beams on the outside of the Numismatic Museum were carved with a double row of dogs at full stretch, brightish brown in contrast with the usual dark wood. The supports in front of the large temple were carved, often with dancing wooden figures and painted using a lot of yellow, gold and white. Two large drums were housed across the way, and a beautiful great bell hung from its carved niche, near a black, red and yellow painted hideous god figure; and all about folk were selling knives and trinkets, pictures, postcards etc., while other vendors were selling fruit. We sampled a good deal of custard fruits, and found them knobbly on the outside, with little fruits arranged in rows and protected by fleshy bits on the inside.

KATHMANDU

A PAGODA-Type Roof claims to have been earlier than Chinese Pagodas.

We found Kathmandu really lovely, with small 'clearings' at intersections where folk grouped themselves round still fountains or temples, and there they sold fruit and vegetables. Small shops sold material or grain, umbrellas or pharmacy things. When 'shut', spider's web netting was stretched across the doorway. Everywhere were bicycle rickshaws brightly painted, rickety, but skilfully managed by the boys.

We gravitated to the religious centre at Hanuman Dhoka and found women on the left, men on the right, sitting on mats. Music was provided from two drums, a 'piano', a concertina, and an electric microphone. A throne was prepared, men and women brought gifts of flowers or money and put them on a tray. A book was put there too, on a prepared cushion. A 'Guru' arrived, with a flowing beard and long grey unbrushed hair, dressed in grey and red striped 'pyjama' trousers. Men kissed his feet. He took his position on the cushions by the book, and was garlanded; said a little and led a chant. It was very wet indeed, and as the proceedings seemed to be going to be interminable, we returned, cold, to *Peregrine*.

In good time next day we both went off to Patan on my moped, after collecting my repaired umbrella. We went up the Chinese road then down a muddy lane, and across a river, savouring such a pretty view of the riverside temples etc. Here there must have been a Buddhist Monastery, now the remains are just weathered red brick and beams. Rain started and down it came. We shared a tree with a pretty 'cow' girl and got soaked to the skin. I had to wring out the water from my yellow shirt. We transferred for shelter to cowsheds, once temples, I suspected.

When the rain cleared, we went on to the great temple complex, and found an old man in charge. There were three great figures, Hanuman, Vishnu and Ganesh, the elephant god, and behind these three a crude turtle, and from this a great pillar with a lovely gold bird figure on its top, facing the temple. We went down some steps to another temple and thence to the water front, and then on and up to Patan via the great dagoba/stupa to the market square. We found a lovely courtyard, with elephant carvings at the golden temple, before returning to Kathmandu.

We left Kathmandu and headed towards the foothills of the Great Sagarmatha, or as we call her, Mount Everest. We immediately started to climb through woodland, along narrow roads, until we came to the outskirts of one of the cities of the Kathmandu valley, Bharatpur, which we learnt means 'City of Devotees'. Bharatpur was established on a hilltop shaped like a conch shell, which is the symbol of the God Vishnu, the god of creation. Bharatpur, now known on

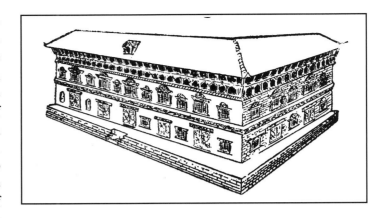

modern maps as Bhadgaon, is about nine miles from Khatmandu. It boasts no hotels. Its area of four square miles is riddled with steep cobbled, and often stepped, roads. This obviates the use of motor cars on most of its roads, and has been a big factor in enabling Bhadgaon to continue its full and self-sufficient life. Bhaktapur was founded in 889 AD, and then in the 15th century, with its King Yakshya Malla it had a number of lovely buildings added to it, notably in 1427 the palace of the 55 windows, with its gem, the golden door. *(Illus. above)*. *"The most lovely piece of art in the whole kingdom and placed like a jewel flashing innumerable facets in a handsome setting in its surroundings."* So wrote Percy Brown, an English art critic and historian.

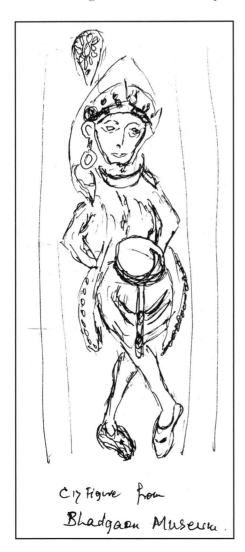

C17 Figure from Bhadgaon Museum.

Towards the end of the 17th century and the beginning of the 18th century further temples were built, including in 1708 the tallest temple in the Khatmandu valley; this Nyatapola temple is pagoda shaped and has a roof of gold and brass. Its five stage plinth staircase has a pair of men, elephants, lions, griffins and deities, in the form of tiger and lion faced animals – baghinis and singinis. The belief in this arrangement is that each pair of figures is ten times stronger than the pair below, and man comes at the lowest stage! The Batsala temple consecrated to the goddess in this square has a very special bronze cast bell, nicknamed the barking bell, because when it is rung, dogs bark and howl in agony. The bell in the upper square is rung each morning and night. It has a most melodious note, which marks the official beginning and ending of each day.

Against this background we were confronted by two young boys. The older one, of about 12 years, was dressed in a homespun tunic with a jaunty Nepalese cap. He was clutching a slipper violin, upon which he could play just one tune. He knew one useful sentence in English, too: "This is my brother, we are orphans, we need money." This seemed a most unlikely situation for the child was full of confidence and although a bit grubby was obviously well fed and set up. He was an attractive young imp. His younger brother was silent behind a cheerful smile and trusting eyes. With them, we agreed to be shown round this wonderful city, dignified, busy, and purposeful in its mediaeval splendour. With pride they took us down a cobbled narrow road that had steps as it neared the Nyatapola temple. We paused in this unspoilt square. Into it in single file came a number of women each wearing a broad cummerbund in which was tucked a sickle. They held their heads high, and their dark hair in pigtails added an air of simple efficiency. They walked easily and erect on their bare feet across the cobbled square. Our guides took us to the main street. The city was quiet but the sound of looms was noticeable everywhere, in this ancient city surrounded by flax and cotton fields which later is carded and spun by hand. Children and women then wind it round iron pegs stuck in the road as they quietly sing to themselves. Having prepared the warp to the required length they thread up their looms, to be found in the upper rooms of the two storey houses. A bench and rice mats are the only furnishings in these rooms. Garments are still made by hand and fastened on the shoulder with hand-made worked buttons and loops.

Pigs, chickens, goats, water buffaloes and cows were in evidence. Rice, cotton, peas, beans, fruit trees and figs indicated the farming pattern. A man was cutting up goat on a slab in the main street,

At Bhadgaon.
*On the left, a typical brass pot.
The dolly stick 'washing apparatus'
is depicted on the right.*

sheltered by a miniature lych-gate structure. Two girls were working dolly sticks in long wooden tubs while others were scrubbing the clothes on well-worn flagstones, or rinsing them in burnished bowls. A potter put a tray with small pots on it into the sun to dry. We were led on towards the outskirts of the city and were met by a jolly looking thin man in his homespun tunic and typical cap. He greeted the boys and we were aware that he was their father! We were invited to their home. There we found several women, some were cooking and running the home, while one was working on a slipper violin. The man took his place on the floor and held a beautiful object shaped like a Canadian moccasin: it had been chipped from one block of wood with sure deft strokes. It was crudely finished and this was part of its charm. The fingerboard was of one piece with the sound box. There were four strings and a bridge, set at an angle, and four large adjusting wooden stops. The sound box had vellum stretched across it and this was fastened firmly to the sides with brass headed nails which gave a gleam and a pattern to the instrument and set off the red paint that decorated the cut edge.

The bow was of a willow sapling with string rather than hair. This was rubbed in resin. It was tightened by simply twisting the string over and round one end of the willow branch. The child held the instrument in his left hand with the slipper about waist high, and the finger board to his shoulder and played again and again the few strains of the one tune which he knew, while the boy's father and his sister worked as real craftsmen do, with measured movements, no waste of energy, no false moves. They had no pattern from which to work. Nothing was marked out upon the wood. They carved by eye and from experience, and they created small works of art.

As evening drew in, the square gradually became deserted; the pink/red of the buildings darkened and even the beautiful golden door ceased to shine. The silhouette of the palace of the fifty-five windows towered over the temples. King Bhupatindra, dressed formally in a tailored tunic with his gold cap and distinctive feather keeps his kneeling vigil from his ample gold cushion at the top of his pillar, ever watching this palace which he built. Bhadgaon slept.

At first light Bhadgaon came to life again, as it must have done for six hundred years or more, to the sounds of a drum, clarinet, triangle and cymbals. The morning procession to the temple with gifts of flowers and food, with suitable musical accompaniment came smartly through the old gateway on to a square and made its jaunty way to the temple. One hour later the procession was repeated. Everyone was astir. Women were laying their bright red chillies out to dry on honey coloured rice mats. They chose the steps of the pink stone fountains, or the cobbles of the streets, or wherever they could find a space near to their homes, from which they could keep an eye on their harvest. Other women and girls were ceaselessly walking up and down the narrow ways between the houses with the freshly spun cotton thread, wool or hemp and twisting it around metal posts that were fixed in the ground at measured distances from each other. They were preparing the warp for the looms which could be found in most houses and could be heard going clickety-clack as the sheds were adjusted and the shuttles were flung to and fro.

We drove back to Khatmandu in the late evening, and spent a further few days there, which enabled us to explore some medieval streets behind the Embassy and visit the museum, which revealed a good deal of armour, rifles, shields, spears etc. and some poor portraits and some fine carving. Early terracotta, later bronze and gilded bronze etc. The site for the museum was lovely, it lay near a temple and monastery. Behind the USA Embassy we found an old Buddhist monastery originally built for celibate monks, but presently occupied by a number of families. A group of children were playing a good game, a cross between billiards and shove halfpenny; a square board with a hole at each corner and a ridge all around had 'draughtsmen' in the middle and a white disc to be shot at them. When one of the 'men' went down a hole, another turn was given. This game was being played with a girl and an older boy, while young boys were quietly sitting on the ground round the board. A mother, in the shade under a tripod, was washing and oiling her baby, while another was washing clothes. Life was all about us. Shades of the celibate monks and their ordered contemplative life!

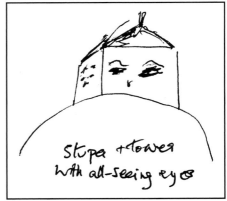

We watched the ceremony of the hubble-bubble pipe; one man blew through a hollow pipe and encouraged a little dish of charcoal to burst into a flame; and then other men inhaled from the pipe in turn. Four men were sitting there ready to enjoy this ceremony together; and another group was across the road doing the same thing – but what do they suck? I do not know.

We came back through the market, by the great stupa with the all-seeing eyes on each of its sides, and among the small temples and little grottoes children were flying kites. Others were sitting about, and old men were walking, all was quite uninhibited and natural. There were signs of whitewashing of houses at some time of the year, with wax in coloured spots. We saw much kissing by the public of some of the gods that were here.

The area was surrounded by lovely timber and warm red brick houses with red roofs that have heavily carved windows with variations of lattice-work 'flowers' and tiny doorways with carved friezes. The artisans were working in the half-dark making jewellery, repairing bikes, machining clothes, machine embroidering saris, gold on scarlet for Rs.125, while others were sitting cross-legged all day among fruit or cigarettes and sweets or groceries, in an area only about 6ft by 4ft.

We watched potters at work, a stick was used to spin a great flat stone, with a large lump of clay centred on it. With deft and skilled use of the improvised wheel, the centred lump was shaped into small egg cups for oil for lights for the festival of light. The potter made so many so quickly, while the stone was kept turning. Then he moved it round and round again with his stout stick and made another 20 cups, and on he went. They were not fired but put on wooden trays to dry in the sun.

We left Kathmandu about 11.15 am on Saturday 11th August 1973, and went to the first toll and then left the India road for the Pokhara road, and followed a noisy busy river to Gandat. The road was good, following the curves of the river, and where its valley widened out, it was flanked with terracing where crops of rice, maize and some cotton grew. Often the sheer rock hung over the road and landslides were common. Squads of road men and women and boys with shovels and long-handled barrows and bare hands cleared the clay mud and great boulders, and left just enough room for one car to get through. The ferns formed lovely patterns in the crevices of the rocks which often were golden shot with blue.

 The houses varied considerably, from wattle, leaf and grass *(illus.)* to daub and wattle with 'grass' roofs, to mud brick with one side painted a terracotta; while some others were of dry stone with stone roofs and some of these were two storeys high. We went through Nagdhunga and Khanikhola, bigger villages, and passed some small collections of hutments until we reached Aajuri where the Chinese who were building the road live, and here we stayed for the night. The cicadas and bullfrogs made a great row. The little shops were lit with oil lamps. One man squatting on the floor on the bare earth was ironing with a charcoal heated iron, others were sitting in their shops or restaurants with the burnished metal mugs and vessels hanging on the wall. A generator made electricity for the Chinese who were guarded by soldiers.

Next morning we found the village up and busy by 5-ish as we drove off over a fine suspension bridge and up on to the crest of a hill, where we breakfasted to the sound of water. The houses changed again and even the cowsheds were of two storeys, with cows below and fodder above. Houses too were of two or three storeys, with overhanging roofs. Some areas supported dwarf bandy-legged men and abject poverty while others had boys in shirts and long trousers, and books and an air of prosperity. We had to sign books at Damauli and at Dumre and Muglin, where we saw a notice talking of lakes, near to Pokhara.

At Pokhara we found the tourist office, and the main bazaar, where women were in velvet tops, dark green perhaps, and sari skirts and great cummerbunds, with heavy bead jewellery, and noses pierced, yet hair unkempt. Streets were narrow; and had lattice work as at Kathmandu and Patan. Chillies and grain were out to dry, and plenty of corn on the cob was in evidence.

We found our way down to the lake, from where we thought we might be able to see the 29,000 ft. Mt. Guarisankar, or Mt. Everest as we call her, which tops the range of mountains known in Himalayan as the abode of snows, but she is too far to the East to be seen from Pokhara. Clouds were lifting revealing a lovely green lake, blue in its wider part, and we experienced the peace of the lake. Later we saw women arrive with home-made oars, who got into the home–made boats and paddled across the still water to a temple on an island, leaving a faint ripple behind them. The women were shy as shy and dodged away from any camera. We were invited to tea in a Nepali house, and the following morning we walked around the lake and found a cluster of houses, from which a ten year old boy with a boat offered, for Rs.1 each, to paddle us off to the next promontory.

His boat was a very narrow canoe which rocked hideously – furthermore, it was wet and had traces of scales of fish. The boy was competent and paddled us through the water lilies, and some other flowers to the further promontory; and after a while we became used to the rocking motion. The return walk through the paddy fields was quite something; at first we tried to keep our feet dry, but by the end we were happily fording rivers that moved fast with water that came up to our knees; this was most refreshing.

We met the boat boy again, who had sung to us and acted as our host, and now we were invited into one of the tiny huts built of plaited grass walls and roofed with mud and grass. There we watched women spinning from cotton, which was roughly carded, and then spun so evenly and finely. A most attractive girl was one of the spinners, but she could not bring herself to have her photograph taken. We passed a man with a ploughing buffalo, and a team of women putting the seedlings into the freshly ploughed furrow, and then moving up for the next row. We passed another line of women who were tying maize plants up into little stooks.

We passed the cottages where washing and de-lousing of clothes was going on, alongside the drying of chilli and grain. In every household was a baby having much attention lavished on it. The houses, mostly of two storeys, had an open verandah on which most things were done. Each house had its half-basket 'crate' with a brass top, which is commonly used to carry fish, corn on the cob or just provisions (illus.). Such a shape was also used with a strap across the forehead, for carrying water, wood, or grass. We found everything very expensive here, until we went to Fishtail Lodge for ice, which was given us.

We were up early to experience the lovely display of the high fish-tail mountain among other snow- covered mountains of the Anapurna range, which are only visible between 5.30–7.30am. We had a superb view of these sunlit snow-capped mountains, marvellous and majestic; they came and went behind the cloud shadows displaying pure white snow, and glaciers with serrated edges, handsome, massive and towering over all, giving another dimension to the peaceful lake side. We took the moped to Martinez and then walked along a good grey road, crossed a narrow swinging bamboo bridge, and watched fishermen throwing a circular net and wading thigh high in the fast moving water. A man on a horse was led through the water by a fisherman. Prayer flags were up. The cup of tea prepared for us in the canteen was an experience: water in a flat pan was put in the wooden box area of the stove to boil so that the wood fumes flavoured the water, to which 'dust' tea was added. This produced a most peculiar flavour.

We went to watch the carpet weavers – oh how lovely, one or two girls and lads sit to a loom; there are strong white warp threads, and carpets are started with several rows of white weft, then the wool dyed the most marvellous colours, mustard yellow, blues, red and natural shades, soft green and dark blue were used. A sort of knitting needle was woven in and out, and the coloured wool was knotted round it. This was cut with a sharp knife and trimmed with scissors, after it had

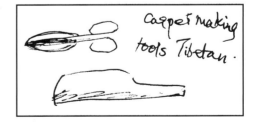

been beaten into place with one of two wooden tools. The women and lads sang as they worked, and were pleased to see visitors, hoping to sell to them the little things they had by them. 'Square' heads prevail; the girls were wearing long dark tunics with a coloured girdle and a coloured shirt.

We went to the canteen for luncheon, it was remarkably cool, in the wood and stone building with a corrugated iron roof, and shuttered openings for windows – chickens were much in evidence. We ordered meat mien, and got spaghetti cooked in fish oil and plastered with tomato sauce, and some hard pieces of almost inedible meat. The whole thing tasted of stale fish!

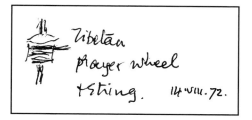

There was a fine old toothless Tibetan man, with a prayer wheel which he constantly kept turning, with the ball on a string flying round. He wore, in spite of the temperature, splendid Tibetan boots up to his knees, made of black, red and natural coloured cloth; the foot seemed small. We bought a carpet each for Rs.740 i.e. £28.10s.0d from a lovely selection, 3ft by 6ft and had them brought to *Peregrine* for R.1 which gave us time to get the money. We walked back and stopped a bit in the Nepali village to hear a man playing a slipper violin, while other men were playing cards. Women were washing and washing up, chicken and pigs were about, and their local baskets were in evidence. Villages here seemed much cleaner than around Kathmandu. The local people are Auruag; and wear a great variety of dress. Women often have heir hair plaited, with red pom-poms worked in. Some have aprons over dark skirts, some wear lovely hand woven skirts with wide striped triangles, while some wear saris.

After a rest to get over our ten mile trek past paddy fields we went off on the moped again, and saw a Brahmin dressed up for a festival. He was always surrounded by boys putting yellow thread on their wrists, daubing colour on their foreheads, and giving him frangipani flowers.

When we awoke at 5.30am next day to witness again the great display of mountains of the Anapurna range, we were aware of many people crossing the lake to the temple; we heard and saw the dancers of the festival, including three 'scarecrows' who were prepared on upturned baskets with a cross bar and dangling pieces of material, and a wisp of black hair. These clothes were worn by boys. Then a dance leader, a man in a red turban with flowing hair and dark glasses appeared. He wore a white tunic and trousers with gold thread and a scarf across his chest, and he carried a walking stick. Then came three men dressed in magenta blue and red saris with velvet tops, glasses and wigs with flowers in them, doing an agrarian folk dance, which was both spirited and graceful. Then a boy in a squashy hat with a drum, who danced with the others, then a most amusing small boy in trousers and blouse with a scarf tied round his head, who cavorted about. In the evening he was yet funnier, with a straw stook on his head. Older men played two drums and cymbals, and kept up the same beat and rhythm for ages. Most solemn in their role. Finally, we saw the procession of dancers and musicians leave for the city, accompanied by a throng of boys.

Preparations for the Minister who was to visit included the erection of a red and blue paper enclosure We drove on down a country road, where, after a chat with a Hindu shopkeeper, we were prepared by him for death! We put up my hammock by the lake and settled down. As it became dark, along came the procession, lit by bright paraffin lamps, first the drummers, cymbals, dancers and then the three tall scarecrows. They danced down by the boathouse, and the three boys in saris and the two small boys, one with straw hair and the other with a headscarf, aped the dancers. One boy had on a small trilby hat and beat a drum; he danced, while one boy in white, the leader, stood aside. After some time the tall scarecrows were put in the boats, that had been cleaned and moored to the right of the boathouse, and the dancers, the band and the devout joined them, and over they went to the temple with gold thread wound around their wrists. In the morning we had seen a man chained, and dyed a lurid red all over, going through the streets, resembling, we judged, the devil chained. He had a goodly gathering of small boys round him. Two other men had parts to play with our dancers, one man who offered water and another who offered grain – they went silently over to the temple in their lit boats, but the noise of drumming and cymbals was kept up all night.

At about 6.00am the following day the procession returned from the temple on the island; the dancing girls danced their way up to the village, one of them with a drum, and made the bus that had collected some German trekkers wait for them! We heard the drums and cymbals disappearing down towards the fishery, and the remoter part of the village. What a lovely start to the day.

We were soon climbing up and into the mountains; the landslides were not so severe as on the Pokhara road. We passed some lovely houses rounded at the ends at Thulgigi like those in the Yucatan, mud on wattle but painted a bright brown. The houses varied a good deal from bamboo slats and plaited walls to two storey daub and wattle and even a few were built of stone. Mostly they had grass roofs but now and then split stone or corrugated iron was used.

We thought of staying at Dlumre but felt the people there were hostile, so we stopped miles from anywhere and looked down on terraced fields and a lovely long footbridge. People were so busy, and all was most peaceful until this peace was shattered by boys who came out of school and started swarming on *Peregrine*. Here at Dlumre, where we walked down the main street, *Peregrine* was attacked and the rear lights were ripped open and two bulbs stolen. Such a nuisance, the back lights will have to be changed. We drove on and were kindly received at Ramdi, where we stayed by the river. We sampled this water and found it was quite grey, and the sediment was grey sludge. It is amazing to think these villagers wash in it and drink this cloudy stuff!

Smart well dressed men drew up near us; perhaps they own the well-built stone house with 'split' stone roof and beautifully moulded windows that lie between us and the river. Many goats and kids collected and took shelter in the hut with the road men and their wheelbarrows during the middle hours of the day. Four pretty girls and an urchin boy came along when we were brewing supper and giggled at us, then tried climbing the ladder at the back to have a good look in. We prepared a home-made backgammon board in a book and made dice from candle ends. A fisherman strolled by on the far side carrying a round fishing net on a stick, and some walkers cautiously crossed the gorge on a narrow dark bridge up stream to the shining new road bridge built to take the buses etc. A girl washed a lovely magenta sari and laid it out on the stones to dry. Everything was slow, peaceful, deliberate and in its own way satisfactory. The little shops sold local fruits, guavas, bananas and lemons, and the usual grains and spices. Life seemed very simple. I saw no one going in nor out of the military camp. This seemed to be a sort of 'forgotten' village – out of time..

From Ramdi we went up into the mountains again, and found plenty of landslides, with less being done about them. I have never mentioned the wonderful butterflies which abound in the paddy fields; several kinds are large, one was dark green almost to black, with one bright blue patch on each upper wing. One was black with a white border, one had reddish brown on its underside, and then there were the small ones – a bright yellow, or almost white or reddish brown. There may be few birds in Nepal, but there certainly were butterflies, big, beautiful, and often unexpected. At Ramdi check post small shops were waiting for bread; as we drove on up into the mountains, we had some wonderful views of terraced paddy fields with a bridge at the bottom. After Tansen we reached Butawal, and on to Sauranji checkpost and the border. They were so slow on both sides. Each border was near the other, with similar little stalls. We walked to and fro, no-one was about, so we drove through. Later we learnt that the border was 'shut' on Sundays!

INDIA (LUCKNOW—DELHI—AMRITSAR)

One road was shut because of the monsoon rains, so we had to reverse, but fortunately we found the PWD bungalow and were allowed to drive in on to the grass, in the shade of tall trees, and by a hedge. Six men watched our every move, and came and went, and a youth tried to have a conducted tour! We ate outside and spent a very hot night.

We made a leisurely start the next day, and left after thanking the nice PWD Roads Engineer, and the distinguished older man in charge of the establishment. We got pretty stuck in the market place again, and had to reverse where the intersection of roads crossed. There was much to avoid – a fruit man hoped I would knock his basket. Eventually I managed to turn, while rickshaw bells twittered all the time. We got out on to the highway, and drove through the paddy fields, and thronged villages where market stalls, buses, and people were tightly packed along the road. Bricks by the side of the road indicated future building. Donkeys were in evidence again, often with their front legs tightly hobbled, so their movement was awkward. One or two ponies were about, some were drawing ploughs.

The early morning light was lovely, Lucknow looked splendid from the river, with its domes and minarets and its lovely waterfront, displaying much Moghul influence. We reached Lucknow in the early afternoon and drove *Peregrine* past the lighted temples en route for a bungalow, and saw a bus and lorry which were embedded in each other. A man from the dry cleaners helped us to find the way to 'our' bungalow, and off we went for miles through the city. All temples were lighted, because the Hindus were celebrating Krishna's birthday: by another small temple we found a narrow lane and the bungalow, which was without any comfort. It had a central room with sofa, two armchairs and table; the room to the right spoke of a store for glasses, plates etc. and the room to the left a playroom for the grandchildren. Beds etc. were on the verandah, and there the cooking was done. The room was high, it would have made two storeys at home; blue paint was daubed across the ceiling, all seemed amateurish and unfresh and uncared for, yet the daughter-in-law was so polite and nice and ate so little for supper. A son waited on us, but did not eat with us. Espresso coffee and water came first with sweets; much later rice, beans and potatoes in tomato sauce; later still, water. When we came back to *Peregrine* we found she had 'lost' her windscreen wipers, five bulbs were missing or broken and one holder gone. I was fed up – it will cost Rs.25 to repair the damage. Still, we had a lovely night sleeping on the roof of the bungalow.

We were told of the difficulties of partition and independence; Pakistan was compensated by only one third of its total value, but the bird-like Barrister who popped into our friend's flat and sat cross-legged on a chair said he was grateful to the British for the pattern of law and the constitution, but a Member of the Secretariat looked in in the morning and was most offensive and abusive of the British; I challenged him, and he quieted down, and later invited us to tea. We walked in extreme heat to *Peregrine* and took her to an electrical workshop for replacements. It became apparent that we had to stand the entire loss of 30R.

At Avreluja we stopped for assistance in repairing the dripping household water tap, and I forgot to raise my mosquito screen and H. went across to deal with hers, and in the few seconds while we were stopped, my good Polaroid glasses were stolen – ugh, one's faith in human nature was shaken. Out on the road again, we drove on through Etawah, and there joined a convoy of Army trucks. We took a road to Firazabad – traditionally thought to be Krishna's birthplace, and there found signs of festivities and green arches from the day before that seemed a bit jaded, but there was much music, and preparations for dancing, western style. We had not then read India on $25 a day, and did not know of the ruins of the Moghul palace of the place; and although the sun was setting and dead in my eyes, making driving difficult, we pressed on for Agra, where we espied water tanks aloft on a new concrete building and drove towards it in the dusk and gathering darkness, to learn that we had chosen a leper hospital! We were given permission to stay by a young Japanese, who spoke to the Director on our behalf. We spoke to some poor lepers, inmates of the hospital, who stayed behind a wall, and we were directed on to concrete near the garages. We saw the sun set over the Taj Mahal . Just as I was going naked into the shower, we were challenged by soldiers with spears; they had halberds and looked seventeenth century. I protested that we had permission from the Director to stay and eventually they became less insistent. I really dislike the uncontrolled crowds, the young men in uniforms, and the little boys and young men who throng *Peregrine* when we stop, and those who delight in taking anything from us.

We awoke at 5.00am to a lovely sunrise, and were just packing up to go, when the Director's wife arrived in haste and thrust a basket into my hands, murmuring 'bread'. When we looked, she had packed bread, butter, bananas and chocolate for us and had written a charming note on a paper plate. I shall cherish that. She and her husband were just off to Japan by air; she signed my book and told me they were Japanese leper research workers and had 30 in-patients and 30,000 out-patients. The Government wishes them to do more research and to spend less time with the patients, but this was not their plan. They (the Japanese) provide the money and the staff for the Hospital as part of the SE Asia research programme. How gracious, thoughtful and kind of them to give us the goodies – my faith in human nature has returned.

 What a wonderful experience to drive through the red Moghul gateway of the Taj Mahal into the well laid out square with four gateways. To the left up some steps, are the remains of shops and dwellings. We went straight on out towards the Red Fort, and half left to a lovely park on a hill, and found to the right, the archway to the Taj Mahal. From the shade of this archway it is possible to see three or four entrances, each flanked by a slender column with chevron designs in black, and a gilded noon sign atop. The flat area has eight tall pillars between this doorway and the shorter thin pillars, decorated with chevrons. The noon sign surmounts the dome and 64 open petals of a lotus flower fall down from this central point and making play of 8, 16, and 64, embodying symmetry and regularity, much as 9 is the central unifying theme of the Chinese Temple of Heaven . The mausoleum with its great dome was built by Shah Jehan in restrained good taste, as a fitting tomb for his adored wife, Queen Mumtaz Mahal, and his baby who lies beside her. The colour on the main doorway, includes a Persian design of flowers, with black lines as chevrons or delineating some of the rectangles. The reflection in the water of the 'parklands' in the rectangle that has three sides pink/red, with the fourth side of the Taj in white marble, stands in all its splendour.

From the sublime to the practical – we visited the Tourist Centre, with the hope of getting the water leak stopped, and the lights covered, and the front light repaired. By chance, a boy on a bike said he could cover the lights etc. He did a very amateurish job, but it should deter would–be thieves. It was interesting to learn that only Rs.150 per month is paid to a local woman, who has for five years been a chambermaid, working from 6.00am to 2.00pm on six days per week. Her husband, an engineer, is paid Rs.250 per month. They pay Rs.40 for renting their miserable part of an old bungalow, once used by three Britishers and now let in lots to seven families. Older flats are let from Rs.25 to Rs.30. They have one married daughter of 17 who minds the house and two boys, so they have very little margin. They seem to own between them just two bikes, yet hope to be able to send the older boy to Australia, to join some other members of the family. They are Christian, and because they are Anglo-Indian, they reckon they are discriminated against, and unless trained in some skilled job, it is hard for them to get a decent and well paid job. The family in the middle had done better. They had two daughters, one a teacher 'confined' to teaching in

English medium schools, where pay is generally less than in the Government schools, and the next one is training to be a teacher. The mother worked across the road at the telephone exchange, and the husband had a job too. Round the corner was a privately owned small auto repair place, and the mother a very toothy woman, had six children and all go to school. How do they manage?

We decided to visit Fatipur Sikri and drove off, but were stopped by a nice man who had read my article in his Femina! He led us to a petrol station and to an ice factory, and gave us his sister's address at Srinagar, then returned to the Agra club where he has lived for 20 years. He wished he had known that we were about, as he would have liked to have acted as host to us. How kind. We drove out to Fatipur Sikri after a last careful look at the Taj, with its white domed building reflected in the water and shining out against the blue sky.

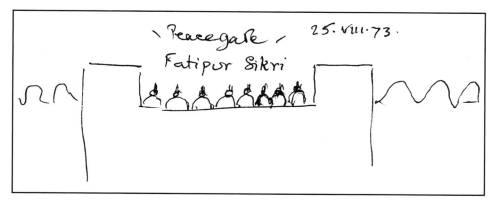

Near Fatipur Sikri we met a man and some boys with performing bears. Later we had to drive the moped into a bus centre, for protection from the boys and children, before attempting the steep hill to the 64ft Peace Gate of Fatipur. There we met a dago with dyed orange hair and moustache who said he was an official guide, and gratuitously told us a good deal. We entered by the Peace Gate, then went up a great flight of steps and found the impressive stabling for about 200 horses, and Palaces and Harems, all in red sandstone which took on colours varying from blue through sand colours to red. The walk ways and cut marble windows led to the pagoda type building with half the number of pillars in each of the three tiers.

The ornamented gateway leads to the sacred area where Christi's tomb in white marble stands for all time as a memorial to him who 'gave Akbar's wife a son'. As a result in the 16th century the palaces and whole set-up was built; and was much visited in Shakespeare's time; these visitors, spellbound, wrote of its beauty. It rises up from the only hill for miles around, between two rivers, tributaries of the Yamuna and Chambal, and commands views on all sides. It has the usual Moghul lightness, the small oriel windows, the pavilions, the courtyards, and the typical wall on three sides with a 'false' lake on the fourth side. Great areas are enclosed with cloisters, surrounding a bathing pool and fish pond. It must have been grand when first inhabited, with its carved buildings, and no expense spared. But probably because of lack of water, it was only occupied for 50 years or so. We had chosen a very hot day, and we were, therefore, not enthusiastic viewers. We returned to *Peregrine* and met the men with performing bears, poor things, in all this heat.

After a hot night, we were ready to go but we found that someone had fiddled with the mirrors, and had pulled a fitting away from the support, but with the brute force of a bystander, we managed to fix in a tapping screw, and the whole became firm and good. However, this took one hour. The weather looked heavy and overcast, and down came the rain, and we were running very low in petrol and had no cash! At Dalwal, we were directed to a Holiday Inn, and managed somehow to cash £5, and to have a good chat with the man who ran an hotel in Kathmandu and told us of the ancient underground road which ran from an iron grid in the courtyard at Fatipur Sikri right through to the Taj, though this is not thought to be extant now.

On reaching Delhi I recognised the farm of friends and without warning, we just walked in and were welcomed with a meal, bath, laundry facilities and drink, and a lovely bed. My Femina article had been appreciated.

We went off on the moped to see the Parliament Buildings, Red Fort, Old Delhi, Embassies, Connaught Place, and found it very hot. We bought a frangipani for our hosts at a nursery, and returned exhausted. A hot and frustrating day, but we were refreshed by a gin and lime and lovely dinner. The next day was taken up by efforts to obtain a pass for Pakistan, but following extensive enquiries, we found that no pass was necessary for our onward journey. As night was falling, we tried to stay in the YWCA or YMCA or anywhere, but in the end had to be content with parking in a by-road. Helen said a man mounted our ladder in the night and blew his whistle; I heard nothing.

After completing various tasks in Delhi we drove off, and in the gloaming found the Mercury Rubber Plant, where three senior men met us, and invited us to stay and to visit the factory. After showing us round, they invited us upstairs to sit on charpoys (four-legged beds) and to listen to the news in English. Then we supped with them, and were pressed to drink a glass of milk, which we refused. They arranged for a fan to be rigged up outside *Peregrine* and for cool air to be blown in for us all night.

There was some confusion over the time in the morning, because my watch seemed to be gaining an hour in each 24 hours.. We refused breakfast with them, as we found everyone was becoming too free and even climbing in, so we drove off and found a shady corner and had a nice breakfast on our own., before finding the tree-lined NH1 road into the Punjab, which led us to Amritsar and a dak bungalow for the night.

It was very hot but a young Sikh came at 6.30pm to escort us on our moped to the Golden Temple. He led us on his Honda, through narrow crowded roads, through high narrow red gateways amidst cows, rickshaws, and a few cars, bikes and mopeds and many people on foot. Eventually we reached an open space and there through an archway caught sight of the Golden Temple. We parked our bikes, removed our shoes, covered our heads and dipped our feet in filthy water, and slipped in through the arch and down slippery marble steps that had mercifully been scored - though one old Sikh, all in white, was evidently afraid of falling. The sun was setting, a lovely orange pink, and the Golden Temple, with its delicate yet firm symbol of the Sikhs, stood out against the setting sun, under a beautiful quiet steely blue sky broken with white clouds.

It is a rectangular building surmounted with a central dome and four smaller domes set on pillars; its facade is broken by a projecting 'awning' below which were windows and below this again the main doorway, with an inscription above it sculpted in gold. On either side Persian or Moghul designs were depicted in coloured marble. The ground is all marble, smooth and polished by the many bare feet that pass that way. Many men and women stop to kiss the floor or touch the step with their fingers and then press their eyes. Many bring an offering of food which is mixed into a general lot and then a little of this is handed back between chapatties to the needy.

We heard the solemn chanting, music or reading which goes on for most of the 24 hours but from 11.00pm to 3.00 or 4.00am the holy book is shut because it is believed that there were 10 Gurus who started the Sikh Movement, and the holy book is the 11th Guru. Each day the book is opened at random and the first line on the page is the sacred message for the day. The book contains writings from Hindu, Buddhist, Muslim and Christian scriptures; and symbolically the four gateways were also each to represent one of those great religions. The holy books are lovely manuscripts on vellum; the main one, downstairs, is under a golden canopy with rich gold tassels. The reader sits on one side, musicians are to his right and the faithful, men and women, to his left. The thronging pilgrims come in facing him and can receive food as they go by.

The whole area is richly ornamented with finely painted and patterned walls, with mirrors, set in beaten gold. The marble floor is clean and in good repair, and the walls are now mostly covered with glass to preserve the fine paintings. The whole usually stands surrounded with water, but it has to be cleaned out every 15 years, and this was being done now. Some fanatical Sikhs collect the mud and plaster their houses with it, or even eat it. Some women bathe in the water, because of a story of a husband leper who was dipped by his wife in the water, and was cured. Men bathe near the spot too.

Near the main entrance to the causeway is the Sikh symbol, between an orange and yellow pole, and nearby the government house where Sikh decisions are made. Here a treasury of weapons is on view, though the jewels are not shown. Everywhere men and women sit or stand in contemplation or prayer, or join in with the chanting. Those who claim to be direct descendants of the first ten Gurus wear a sort of blue mitre, a blue tunic with belt and white trousers, and a sash from their right shoulder; they are both proud and fanatical. We walked back on the well polished marble, and noted that the white intersections are marked with black strips and the outer perimeter is in a black and white design. We recovered our shoes and drove back to *Peregrine*.

The next day we were collected by Monie to go to the Sikh museum, and there found terrible pictures of bloody battles, but not very good art. However, there were two nice Moghul miniatures. Monie took us to visit his home. His Mother, a teacher, cannot speak English, his middle sister and university students were very shy, and did not appear, but the 15 year old sister is clever, charming and so pretty, and wishes to be a doctor. She sat up so straight on the bed, understood English readily, for she learns in this medium at her convent school, and kept her mother informed and was generally bright and alert – she should make a most competent and sensitive doctor.

We made arrangements to leave *Peregrine* safely locked up by the Bank in Amritsar, while we went of to Kashmir by bus. We were introduced to a delightful lady bank manager, the first in a State Bank, before taking a wooden rickshaw to the bus station. We found the going very hard and bumpy and relentless on one's backside. We bought return tickets to Kashmir via Jammu at 6.50Rs each, and were given seats 20 and 21. The bus was in and we found our seats. No deluxe coach this, but a scruffy dirty country bus with short backs to the seats and iron bars atop the back. The bus filled up. Passengers bought fruit, sweets and filled their water bottles. Very promptly we were off on NH1 that now deteriorated into a pot-holed narrow road. We swayed and bumped and became bruised and battered. Our driver lost no time and drove through the sunset and gloaming.

KASHMIR

We crossed rivers and passed much pampas grass, sugar cane, and grain and cattle to reach Jamu, which was in high fiesta mood because of the foundation of Sikhism through marriage. A fair with a big dipper and swings was heavily patronised. Food stalls were everywhere with cakes and sweets and fried things, as well as rice, and fruit of every sort. Everywhere men were in coloured turbans, red, green, orange, white, blue etc. There were a few 'originals' about with pikes and scimitars. Almost no women were to be seen. On we went into the darkness until a shattering noise indicated that the prop shaft had become uncoupled. We stopped and tried to get going again, and crept to the side of the road. Mercifully another bus came along, and we were all transferred to it The seats were a little higher and softer. On we went to Jammu, where we were all bundled out again, and transferred to yet another bus, one with hard seats and with that bar that just cuts one's back.

We drove into Jammu, getting what sleep we could, and arrived at 12.30am. A kind man drove us and a man to the dak bungalow for the night. We were shown into a dirty room with no lock, but found comfy beds and slept until 5.30am. What a day!

We staggered up and bought tickets for the deluxe coach to Srinagar, and found it left at 6.30am not 6.00am, so we had time for an omelette and coffee, a good starter. The deluxe had longer backs to the seats, which was a mercy, but we were at the very back with no foot-rests. A nice young boy was next to me, with his new wife, who thought she had flu: also a nice family, with a capable father, girl and baby boy with a bungible face, and an amusing but exhausted fat mum. Also a strange man in a tomato- coloured shirt, who kept getting out of the bus, and changing his place. The journey seemed interminable. We were driven to a garage to fill the bus with petrol, and there we were hit by another bus, but no-one paid any attention!

We kept stopping for snacks etc. Our journey soon took us to a mountain pass, coming down to a river valley at Ramdan. We were surrounded by terraced mountain ranges, but they never came up to the standards and beauty of those in Nepal. We went through the Jaiwabas tunnel and then dropped to the plains again – saw some evidence of flooding, broken roads, bridges, culverts etc. We took this part of the journey slowly and arrived at Srinagar about 7.30pm. We found the tourist resthouse filthy, and settled for a houseboat at Rs.15 per night; and there we slept well even if it was dank and dirty.

On the morrow we saw falcons as we explored the area and we met a factory owner who invited us to his boat and offered us accommodation for Rs.10: the boat was moored in the widest part of the fast-flowing river, and was airy and spacious, so we decided to move. I was quite sorry to make excuses to our first hosts, and to move away, as they had done what they could for us, and I had slept and eaten well there, but it was dank, and in a backwater, where slops were dropping into the water and were not washed away, so perhaps it was for the best.

At our new abode we drank Persian tea with herbs and saffron, brewed up by the owner's old father who, though towards 90 years, does the cooking and charged Rs.5 for a well-prepared and well-cooked vegetable supper for us.

Srinagar with its waterways and houseboats is unique – we learnt that this came about when a wave of immigrants wished to settle in the area, but were not given leave to buy land; and so established themselves in house boats along the waterways. We were taken to the lakes and floating gardens in a local shakari, by a tall and distinguished boatman in a black cap, loose white tunic and trousers; his shakari was an old and battered warrior, a sort of punt, with yellow and red spots, and an ancient canopy with 'spring seats' (in places) covered with red and white material.

We set off towards our first port, and there an extra man joined us, with a good strong pole, and we were swung right towards a lock-gate, through which the water was pouring at a great rate. A rope was attached to a canopy strut and the extra man nipped forward to hand it to a landsman who pulled us through the lock; but the stream was too rapid for us to turn the corner. Another man joined in and pushed, but we were beaten by the force of water in spite of the ropes and a man's force along the lockside. So we got into the midstream and allowed the force of the water to take us, but not before we had got another stronger and taller man as a substitute for one of the others. We repeated our assault on the incoming waters, managed to make a wider sweep, and got round, into the arms of men in another boat. Tiny fish jumped along the locksides.

Leaving the 'extras' behind we paddled or poled our way past many a houseboat and saw many kingfishers alongside the local folk, who sit on the bare floors of their simple painted boats, equipped with sliding panels, but with no partitions. Those to let were more elaborate, with sitting rooms, internal panelling and sliding doors and 'sanitary fittings'. Some were moored near land where chicken and sheep graze. Local shops were often on stilts. There were many creeks, and everywhere there were moorings. Our boatman took us a nice way, with the sun behind us, past willows and through water-lily beds. Trade does not seem to be very good, so constantly one was bothered to hire a boat. Small and larger kingfishers abound, fishing away alongside. Boys and men who were fishing with rods were everywhere, but we never saw a fish landed. The calm, the green, the peace and the rhythmic noise of the paddles and the reflections were most enjoyable. We arrived back about two and a half hours later, our boatman having had little chats with many friends as we paddled by – probably telling them how he lost his hat, and of his attempt to 'clear' the lock. We returned to our houseboat via the Srinagar Club, where we were given lovely clear sparkling drinking water, so unlike the brown murky stuff we were offered in the boat.

We went to Golmarg in a comfortable bus which eventually left at 9.20am and took us out down a poplar- lined road, past apple orchards and rice fields, here men and women were harvesting rice. They seem to start from a corner of the field and to lie the harvested rice down, always with the cut side to the road, and the grain to the field. The regularity of it had an especial charm. In the evening some of the bundles were tied in the middle and carefully stacked; always the grain was put to grain and stalks to stalks. The farmers usually seemed to wear dun coloured loose tunics and trousers and white skull caps, the Mohammedan women in the fields wore wide loose coloured tunics with sleeves that have a draw string, and trousers tied fairly tight at the ankle. They tackled great weights in the fields but in the towns, and when of better families, they were all in purdah and wore purdah cloaks of black, white or brown. Sometimes they were transparent, and sometimes their faces were not covered, but they could be at a moment's notice. The cloaks were often patterned and quilted.

The great wide valley was fed by a river that has tumbled down over great grey smooth stones, and covered a wide area with them. The river appeared small, but within the past two weeks it had burst its banks and caused flooding. Away in the distance were some sandstone hills, rising to about 300 ft. from the valley, having been folded and glaciated like the mountains near San Francisco. The usual cattle, sheep and hens slowed us up from time to time, but the ubiquitous water buffalo were missing.

We reached Talmarg and saw the peasants close to as they herded their cattle, and passed us on the road to Gulmarg. Some peasants looked like walking haystacks. At Talmarg, a fire had swept through all the little shops and left them in heaps of rubble on both sides of the road – it was thought that a cooking spark had set light to everything, but after two days much was still smouldering, and it had not been possible to recover anything. Besieged by touts as we got off the bus, we went to the tourist office and hired a helper and two ponies. Our helper was a square short man who once had owned his own horses – he was a real syce. The owner of the ponies was tall, spare, in a grey woolly coat over tunic and trousers, and with a blanket thrown over his shoulder. The boy who accompanied us was in dirty striped cotton trousers and a striped tunic and bare feet; he said nothing but carried a willow switch. The owner had a short strong whip and tickled the horses' legs with it.

We climbed up a rough path, with at first, pine trees growing from grassy banks and a few wild flowers, red sorrel, purple orchid, bright blue star flowers and a kind of heather lingering on. The best time for the wild flowers we learnt is June. The rest place was by the tent where tea was served and hard green apples were available.

Then on and up to Gulmarg where the British had built a grey stone 'Victorian' church surrounded by meadows of flowers, and chalets were sprinkled around amid the fir trees, leaving space for an 18 hole golf course with ski slopes around the edge. There was no road in those days, but now a road has been built. The army was in evidence to keep a tight watch on the border, fearing an influx of Pakistanis, or trouble between the Kashmiris and the Indians.

Back in our houseboat the next day we witnessed four men poling a heavy houseboat against the fast- moving stream to a special chant. They had difficulty in making headway or even holding their own against the tide, but with a concerted effort off they went.

We were invited to the old city to see a 'factory' where the ceilings were so low that we could not stand up in the room. We were shown to them up a dirty staircase amidst dirt and squalor to the looms, which were fixed cheek by jowl. Men and boys were at work on them, knotting and cutting with lovely old knives that were curved and twisted. The patterns were fine and traditional, 22 knots to the inch, and were written out on paper in numbers on long strips and hung over the looms. The boys worked so quickly and yet were ready to exchange ideas. No schooling was arranged for them as they sat on the floor and worked. The knots were pressed down with a wooden block with comb-like metal prongs. It appeared to be sweated labour and one felt that the joy of creation was missing.

We visited some silversmiths in their little shops, making oval silver cases and putting a jade polished stone at the top, for sale at £30. I wondered about the jade being genuine; the silver was adulterated, I should judge. Then we walked along narrow muddy lanes, wet with puddles and open drains, picking our way and minding the cows as well, and got to a filthy open space filled with rubbish, to a 'spring' at the bottom of green and stagnant water, said to be going to be reclaimed when an extension to the factory was built. We went in to meet the woodcarvers, who were packing their tubs and boxes. I saw no tools, and alas no work was being done. We went to see Jesus' tomb, with a supporting pamphlet to 'prove' that he died naturally in Kashmir, a great prophet. We heard weavers and looms but were not shown them. We went on to a warehouse and saw mats, beads, lotus lampstands, robes and tea-cosies and materials with crude colours and designs. Very much the work for export, rather than real craftsmans' models.

Our return to Amritsar was to be by an early 'de-luxe bus' in which we had seats by the front door with plenty of leg room, and it was to be in a bus that would fulfil its promise at last. The ripe paddy fields gave place to hills with a sprinkling of trees, then a crowded village where we stopped in a queue for we were told of landslides and a possible delay of up to four hours. After nearly two hours we set off; at first, all the traffic was going our way, none was coming towards us, but we were soon stopped, and crawled past trucks. Arguments blew up between the many bus drivers and the many carriers as to whom should have pride of place, the buses generally seemed to win. The day went on like this, stopping at unlikely places for food and stopping for landslides, until towards 5.00pm when we reached Batote. Here the bus driver and the fat man in the grey striped white shirt left us and after about an hour, we learnt that they were in Court bailing out a conductor who yesterday had got into a fight and had been arrested. They returned at last, well pleased with themselves and accompanied by an elderly short-sighted 'barrister' who never spoke, and several Sikhs who were in good spirits. Presumably they had got the man off. We continued our journey!

It was now growing dark and we had found nothing to drink all day and had just eaten apples to keep going. More mountains, and the advent of a man who strangely sat among the gears, and had his arm around our driver! On and on we went, and then we stopped by a single restaurant where surprisingly we got good milky Nescafé, but we still had two or more hours to go before reaching Jammu.

Jammu at last, dirty and deserted, but meat was being cooked on skewers over a charcoal fire by a smart boy who served us with great ceremony, and also washed the glasses and prepared more meat on skewers. And there were beds in a tourist hotel for us.

Up for the 6.30am bus to Amritsar, and heard a woman with a lovely voice singing, and saw from our taxi old beggars and children. At the bus station, there were sleeping forms everywhere, and cows had wandered in and left their 'cards'. We set off in a dreadful bone-shaker with scant room. The bus was full yet now and then we received perhaps 25 more standing passengers. It was driven by Jehu himself. We passed everything and were never passed. The land at first was open and stony with much pampas, and thus not able to be cultivated, then gradually we observed more intensive farming and denser populations. Towns were crowded, the Sikh turban was much in evidence again.

We arrived in Amritsar in the rain and reclaimed *Peregrine*, who was hot, but mercifully intact, and after making the necessary preparations we got off the next day to the India/Pakistan border, where we endured long formalities with a silly little man who was confused by *Peregrine* and my moped.

RETURN TO PAKISTAN

Eventually free of the Indian Customs, we crossed into Pakistan. Here, car formalities were processed by a most efficient Muslim woman, the mother of ten children, five boys and five girls, who had held the job for 22 years! We had arrived just as the border was shutting, 4.00pm in India, 3.30pm in Pakistan. We drove along a narrow road through two or three little towns to Lahore. There was evidence of flooding still, especially under bridges and under the railway. We looked for the British Council building, and got sent to the British Consulate. We were introduced to a local doctor, who led us to the Hospital and said we might park outside his house. A really good spot. His wife and son and daughter were there, and we were established by a small market garden and given butter and milk and, even more importantly, we were given addresses of friends to visit in the Murree Hills.

A trip round Lahore on the moped introduced us to conditions and developments in this part of Pakistan; for example, we saw numbers of cars on the road of every kind, British, Japanese, German etc. A number of motorbike rickshaws but no pedal rickshaws. Very many shops selling TV sets, transistor radios and motorbikes. We learnt that there were TV stations at Lahore, Karachi and Rawalpindi, and colour will be on the way soon. Workers, as well as the educated, have TV sets. We found the people courteous but as in India, limited—so ready to say things were not possible because of the rules—for example, we were not able anywhere to exchange Indian to Pakistani rupees.

Our Doctor friend and family took us off to visit their in laws, where we found a large woman propped on a couch with a granddaughter asleep beside her, and her son doing the honours. We sat in a passage with a fan going, and saw signs that a wall had been knocked down and a larger window put in. At right angles to this, carpets were rolled up and left along another passage, which was flanked with chairs giving the impression of a warehouse. After some time we were invited to supper and had a delicious meal. No one ate in great quantity and, unlike our Arab friends, all ate with knife and fork. A civilised and tasty performance. Granny turned out to be a charmer, worried about a son in law, a Pakistani Naval Captain (with an English wife) who is a prisoner— probably in India—then we heard that our Doctor's brother, so dear to him, had been killed in the '71 war; it was easy to see how the feeling of hatred for India, of which they had never felt a part, was still a real thing. So like the conditions in Ireland. A son produced a marvellous fishing rod, which was approved of by our host.

We met a 'go-getter' woman in her 30's who had just won the competition for design of the new uniform for air stewardesses for the DC10 to be put into operation in March; this brought her Rs. 10,000 and two round the world air tickets. She has two girls who go to school in Murree, and she designs the costumes for the films.

We went to visit Mohammed's family: Mum was neat and spare and efficient, the mother of seven, four girls and three boys, her husband, the physician, had a beard and glasses and a quick walk. One boy was in the Pakistani Air Force, one in railways; one girl of 24 was a medical student in her second year: and there were twins of 15 and Mohammed and a younger sister. The medical student was good looking and vivacious, and never stopped talking, showing us embroidered clothes, and telling us of a Mohammedan Pakistan wedding – a vivacious bore! The twins were solid, the shorter one was both musical and artistic.

We ate semolina with beaten silver on it and rice pudding. The railway brother produced endless photographs. An exhausting evening, but Mum was a winner. The bearded physician father was both amusing and busy; green trousers and tunic, with a thin head covering made by the younger twin, who also made the coat for the doll with glass pieces set in Mogul type designs. The tunics come from Baluchistan, and had apron pockets and were of natural linen with red cross designs.

The following day we visited the Badshahi mosque, part of which was built by Shah Jehan in 1631. We mounted the great sweep up of wide steps from an open square, with a garden in the middle, to an arch surmounted with 'icing meringues' and turrets at all four corners, and a great enclosure of white marble picked out in black, with a fountain in the middle, and the mosque beyond. We did not go in because of the fuss of shoes and tunics, but visited the fort which was about to shut, and saw the mosaics on the wall depicting elephants at play, jousting with horse and rider, horses jousting, and some strange camels. The colour was basically blue and blue and white, apart from the camels. Evidently elephants and horses were known and studied, and camels were rare, and therefore poorly depicted.

We only had time to drive round the fort, and learnt that until the 18th century, water from the River Ravi encircled it and added to its protection. We returned via the poorest markets along bad roads, with bullock carts, fruit and flies, women in burkas, bicycles, motorbike rickshaws, dust and cows and crowds, and reached the mall at last.

We were taken in a jeep the next day to the mosque and fort, and found the fort a very pleasant surprise. It stands in a large green area among grass and flowering shrubs. We worked our way around, and found the Jehan hall of mirrors, once the meeting room of the chiefs. Cut glass was set a few inches from a mirror wall so that a hundred reflections of anything, be it person or light was created. The parliament house led up from the green square where Jehan had had an open space covered. The king once sat in the middle, on a balcony which could be reached from the floor, flanked by two other balconies. Within this area, where now only foundations remain, there is evidence that once there were royal living quarters complete with a bath or ornamental water pool. One hundred yards away, the chiefs meeting place stood behind a wall which was decorated with pietra dura (hard stone) surrounding octagonal open rooms, and four 'fireplaces', which may have held papers, been secret stores, or even used for fires in winter. Niches where fountains played, among several more mirror rooms. A fountain must also have played in the middle of the square. Small decorated rooms were built at the side of the square, one side of which overlooked the Ravi river and the countryside.

The mosque stands in a central square, so hot that I burnt the soles of my feet! The mosque was oblong, with a central part supporting the pulpit from which a man could read and preach. Two-thirds were open on three sides so that a nice perspective of the mosque was apparent. We struggled up one of the minarets to the first stage, from which we got a good view of Lahore and of the mosque and saw how very flat the surrounding country was in every direction. We came down and walked in shade, and found the surrounding 'cloisters' once had had lovely marble floors; now the greater part had square red tiles. Opposite the mosque was water where the faithful were both washing and drinking.

Back to the waiting jeep and over a toll bridge where I was asked for one rupee in each direction.. We were shown the flood area, where crumbling brickwork was in evidence among the flooded fields, the result of broken bunds; and then we were taken to the tomb of a Mogul Raj and Rana, Jehan and his wife. This was shut to visitors, but we were allowed in, and saw an avenue of junipers leading to the tomb, which was set with pietra dura right across its facade. We saw trees of many sorts, but learned that earlier there had been flowering almond and cherry trees. It was a lovely park, with the first square surrounded by small rooms, and from the right a view of the tomb in a huge area of garden. The pair to this was on the other side, but since the prince died, no gardens have been laid out, and a railway line and road have been built.

Back to the toll bridge, en route to the museum, where we worked our way through the textiles, ivory inlaid boxes, Bukkara carpets etc. to the Sivas and Buddhas, and then hit upon some lovely Mogul miniatures and Chinese pots; but had to hurry off because of a pre-arranged luncheon.

The following day we joined our host by 7.30 am and we were driven west-southwest of Lahore to the ancient site of Harappa where there are seven layers of civilisation reaching back to 5,000BC. Harappa was a twin capital of the Indus river culture with Moendijaro, and they had their own brown/red pottery, samples of which I would later see displayed in the Kabul museum.

We drove along a good road where rice, cotton and sugar cane and maize were growing. At first it was along a lovely avenue of mimosa type trees known as tika whose bark is used for leather dyeing, . The wood is hard and used for furniture and implements. The spikes on the branches prevent the goats from eating them!

This road led to the local museum at Harappa, where we found fertility goddesses with extra round patches for eyes and breasts, so like the early Mexican Olmec ones – any connection? Pots in red/brown clay, with regular wavy lines, some triangular designs and all-over flower patterns, also horizontal lines and shapes made with string or rope, as in Crete. After a time in the museum, we set out to see the site, perhaps to see some of the early (5,000 BC) lower levels. Interestingly bricks were used here because no stone was available. Bricks were in different sizes and well shaped, and like modern bricks, baked hard. Many pots and bits of pots were lying around.

The first site was confused and confusing, but remains of storage jars were to be seen in situ, and we heard of human bones found in jars beyond a wall, with a drain hole. On and down to an area that must once have been a river bed, perhaps the Ravi. Then on (past a Mosque used by the new town Harappa) to the Granary – so like a Roman granary found near Hadrian's Wall; and then to the work area where many circles and the paths and rounded foundations were found.. A copper kiln has been found, with traces of copper on the wall. Copper, bronze and tin and alloys had been used at that early date.

In the blazing heat we returned to Lahore on a private road that flanks a canal: we found at each ten miles there was a rest house, and a weir and bridge were built at every two miles, and every mile had five guide stones. This road was hard gravel, with good shade, and with many birds, hoopoes, parakeets, mallards and lovely white birds of the wader variety, with black wings, and many another pretty bird, one with an orange-red undercarriage. A good deal of pampas edged the canal, and the fluffy off-white heads blew in the breeze.

The trees on our side generally formed a wood and kept us cool. We took a turn round Sahiwal and then went on along our canal route to the rest house, from which we were able to view the head waters, the floods and flood damage. We watched five punt type boats ferrying folk across the gap where the bund and road had been breached by the floods: horses and buses on the further side were lined up to take folk on their way. One man pulled or swam or walked dragging a boat with a huge metal box balanced across it. A busy scene. Back via gardens to another rest house for tea, before at last we set out for Lahore, driving very gingerly in the gloaming.

We had to leave our hosts the next day, and after our farewells set off for the Mangla dam.. We first called at the Rajar rest house on the upper Jehlum canal before crossing the Chenal river, which was quite a 'thing' for the floods on this river have been terrible. We found a Bailey Bridge, a bridge built on boats like our pontoon bridges, followed by a floating bridge, and we got across in single file. We were lucky, we only had to wait ten minutes or so, but we were plagued by every sort of seller, with sweets, fruit, cooked biscuits etc. and corn on the cob.

We followed up our introduction to meet an official of the Water & Power Administration, and heard that we were expected and should be well looked after – indeed we were, and we much enjoyed our visit to the great dam.

The dam was built by the Americans with financial aid from Great Britain, Canada, Germany, USA and New Zealand between 1962 and 1967. It was the largest dam in the world and had a nine arch spill-dam, with fish steps, that allows the water to feed the old river bed. The ten turbines in the main dam provide electricity. So far only one was working. Still electric trains run from Lahore to Karachi. This water filled a new canal which two miles downstream joins the old Jhelvin canal. During the floods all nine gates of the spill-dam were opened and a large area of land was flooded, but the dam held. It was the Chenal river and the Indus that did most damage; no count of loss of life has yet been made, but it is thought that several thousand perished, for sometimes whole villages were flooded. The folk were taken by surprise and unprepared. We had seen trees uprooted and marks on walls earlier. 100 square miles of land was flooded to give the headwaters for the dam, and 81,000 people had had to be resettled. The landowners were well compensated and given houses and money, but no one seemed to know how the poor had fared.

We walked up to the old fort, Mogul in origin it is thought, and looked out from two of the remaining turrets, and saw the lie of the land around. A well set out museum showed how the water enters the power house and turns the turbines. Many kinds of sandstone were bewilderingly laid out – hard, soft, dark and light, newer and older – what a lot there is to learn even just about sandstone. Next a case of remains of animals: the hip joint of an elephant etc. found when digging for the dam. Apparently no sign of human occupation was found, which to me was strange. Then an interesting cross section of the dam and tools, showing strainers etc. set into the concrete to show if anything is moving and giving way. We sat with the man who 'minds' the fort with a friend of his. The number of folk the government employs and servants to go with them is legion. The Civil Service must absorb one third of the population. Still perhaps it was better so than that they should be unemployed, because there was no unemployment money for anyone.

As we drove back on our moped we discovered that our next stop should be the Rawal Dam just by Pindi. Now came the rub – we had only one rupee and a low tank of petrol because all had been calculated from the Rawal Dam, and we were 75 miles from there. The kind man who had become a friend rang the banks who do not deal in travellers cheques, and he generously and chivalrously lent us 50 rupees, and rang Caltex at Dina to arrange for petrol for us.

With all this help we set off for Pindi and found the country was wild, jagged, with grass covered subsidence; in parts it appeared to be like the Arizona desert on a small scale, and in parts reflecting the hoodoos of Banff on a large scale. The strange broken eroded sandstone hills gave one a scene that I had never seen before. The road had often subsided. Sandstone is no base for a road, it is so vulnerable to the weather. Here and there Weyborne wrag conduits were apparent, with stones embedded in the sand. Sometimes an area was flattened and cultivated and appeared to be fertile. I wondered if great bulldozers would alter some of this landscape as land becomes more scarce.

We drove through the barren hills to Pindi and found it a teeming dirty place displaying many beggars, women in burkas, in purdah; lime barrows and limes on ice with squeezers at the ready; ox carts and tonga and Ford utility buses. A man was sitting under an awning repairing a halter. Carpet and brass shops abounded. We gave a lift to an elderly man with an interesting long shaped head and a broken arm, who in turn served us at the Rawal rest house.

An Assistant Superintendent turned up and kindly drove us to the Afghan Embassy for visas, which were not readily available. However after filling in two forms each we were given visas for 'transit only' Our escort drove us to the Iranian Embassy, where we were given brochures and suggestions for scenic routes through Iran. We were driven round Islamabad, and we must have seen every Embassy, the Secretariat, Ayub Khan's house, and the new residence for the President still under construction. We signed the book at our Embassy, and went to the British Council Library, where we read the Sunday papers and learned that poor Princess Anne had had a spill at the suicide jump and hurt her leg and had had to retire from the cross-country competition; and that hundreds of sailing boats were starting on a round the world trip from Spithead. Less about IRA bombs, thank goodness.

We must have driven every road in Islamabad, and seen houses of every kind, spacious foreign ones and tight unimaginative Pakistani flats etc. The Hospital had an arched roof to provide coolness inside. The hills surrounded the town on the north, and the trees and flowering shrubs adorned the four lane roads, giving a sense of greenery all around; spacious, self-conscious, international – and clean!

Armed with our passports we set off for Murree and found the road very twisty with a gradient of 1:18, *Peregrine* was in second gear most of the way, and growing hot. In spite of the growing dark we pressed on and spotted the Army Farm, with the motto *"Faith, Discipline and Unity"*. We drove in and were allowed to spend the night in the driveway, surrounded by pine trees, and were looked after by two night watchmen, one of whom had fallen from his bike and badly grazed his arm; mercifully, the chowkidar was all in one piece! We met a salesman with 'archaeological' pieces from sites, including a lovely figure, and a frieze that was fairly complete, and one or two figures that were in themselves beautiful; gold coins were lovely. He expected us to smuggle them through Customs, and make money at Spinks, in St James, Piccadilly! Strange that he should have shown them to us, they came from behind carpets and pouffes, before we handled them, and they were returned to their hiding places. They were said to be from Sanchi.

After a rather cold night in a built up area we found we were on a bus route; we saw boys in grey lined up for school, and men in black coats and astrakhan caps, and white or khaki trousers who carried fruit or wood or hay. August and September are the months for laying in a stock of hay for fodder for cattle, for soon the grasses will dry up, as the effects of the monsoon will have passed.

We were two miles from Murree and the President's house, where a special pass was officially required, but because of our invitation from friends in Lahore, we were allowed to proceed, through pine clad hills to 7,500 ft., and Kashmir Point. We found our hostess a gracious lady, both comfortable and assured, with a twinkle, but English was a bit of a strain for her. She was surrounded by her daughter in law with her young family, to whom we showed *Peregrine* before we left for Murree on the moped, down the steep hill to the Mall, which was free of traffic. Small cobbled alleyways and local produce shops flanked the main street for Kashmiri goods including trinkets, leather coats, walking sticks, material shops, some carpets, caps and baskets and restaurants. The hills were too steep for the moped to take us both, so Helen had a horse for part of the way. We visited the President's House at 3.30 or so, and found marvellous views of four ranges of hills, the furthest and highest was snow capped. We heard that the schools were not opening until 1st October this year because of the student strike. Most students do not wish to learn, they get exams postponed, so that those who wish to study find the exams cancelled and their futures compromised. Also schools were shut, because families wished to be at home to welcome the POWs who were due back from India on 25th September. Most school classes have over 60 students, and from all accounts in general the discipline is poor.

We enjoyed a lovely lazy morning by design. From our vantage point on a rock we soaked in the view; and saw five ranges of mountains in one direction and six in the other. We watched an overseer who did nothing but chat to a friend while a team of four worked – No. 1 had a long iron pole with a spiky end; with this he split the natural rock of the hill: No. 2 laboriously picked up a good sized bit and carried it on his shoulders that were mildly protected by a desert sheikh type head-dress above his tunic and baggy trousers, and dropped it over a wall. Nos. 3 and 4 each had hammers and a ring of metal in a handle, and they cracked down these pieces of rock into shingle sized pieces, and swept them aside with the ring tool.

We watched various riders on ponies, some girls from St Denys School attired in white trousers and blue tunics, and men and women astride ponies coming up and down to Murree; very little purdah to be seen about here. We sat out in the shade and wrote and gazed at the marvellous mountains, wooded on the south-east and more barren on the north-west. The houses were all of individual designs, most had corrugated roofs, the new ones were so shiny, while some of the older ones were painted, generally red but one was yellow. Spruce, fir and pine and the remains of a horse-chestnut tree were growing here, and Jinnah Street and the Mall of Murree were lined on one side with walnuts. Lovely apricot colours streaked across the sky as the sun set.

A casual stranger with a baby in a push chair offered to give us shoes because I admired hers; they were orange, and turned up at the end, and made in her village. She has invited us to coffee. How kind people are in this remote and restricted part of Pakistan.

In Murree Helen saw a man fill a sheepskin with water and go off to water his garden. Men wear skull caps of varying shapes and materials – a boy wore a green one with a yellow tree pattern, often gold ones were worn and sometimes fur ones; the gold or material ones often have turbans wound round them, some with cockades up one side and tails behind. . The chowkidar for the Netherlands Embassy who had served with the Argyll & Sutherland Highlanders took us under his wing and tried to get water for our tank, but *Peregrine* would not climb the hill so he offered us the use of the telephone, but the lines to Peshawar were down. He showed me over the Embassy House, opening each door with a great flourish. He wore a head-dress with cockade and tail, grey coat to the knees, a waistcoat and grey trousers – most smart. He had put coreopsis in jam-jars in several of the rooms, and had everything ready for the family's arrival, had aired the clothes out in the sun etc. There were four or five double bedrooms with bathrooms and two sitting rooms, simply furnished, with prints of Holland on the walls. Wonderful views from the windows that overlook the mountains The chowkidar's helper was a tall man with a moustache and black hair, in a white tunic and trousers; he minds a cow, and a most amusing young bull that bellows a good deal of the time

On a lovely day again, with soft air, sunshine and puffy clouds, the Argentine Ambassador, his wife and mother-in-law turned up in their car en route to the RC Church, the C of E is shut. We were in the wrong clothes to join them. Next the British Ambassador and his wife called upon us having heard of us from the Argentineans. They were charming and we had a great chat telling them of our experiences and learning of Afghanistan. They left at 11.30 to prepare for a luncheon party and we resumed our life.

Next two Pakistani men and a girl in a pink dress with 'necklace' and several horses and their attendants walked up … to our amazement they asked if they might photograph us in a group with them. This they did, and we were so dumbfounded that we neither asked for a copy nor learned why they wanted it.

The sun began to set, and the mountains became misty and mysterious again, the lights came on and in 30 minutes it was dark, and the twinkling lights took up their vigil again for the sun had made a horizontal red apricot streak against the sky, and it was misty below and duck egg blue above; and then the stars shone bright and uninterrupted in the sky.

We were invited to dinner at the Argentinean Embassy at 8.00pm, and arrived to find a distraught Grandma, because the Ambassador and his wife, her daughter, had not returned from their golf. She feared an accident or ambush. She is a marvellous little lady of 80 years of age, Italian, a linguist, two pots high, amusing, fluent and absolutely on the spot. She had despatched the chowkidar in a taxi to try to find the Ambassador and wife. It was dark, and she had not been able to contact anyone by telephone. I feared the Black September folk, or an accident and wondered if we would be having to drive to some hospital to find them. I rang the British Embassy but our Ambassador had left for Islamabad.

We waited while the old lady regaled us with stories. She can recognise Italian accents from North and South and even village to village. We were served with Madeira instead of sherry, it was delicious, and served with home made salty biscuits. At 9.00pm Maria burst in, full of life and health, followed by the Ambassador rather flummoxed, and we heard that the car had failed at an out-of-the-way spot, and they had had no lights and could not get them going. There were no telephones near, nor taxis, and they had just to stay there until eventually a taxi came along. Drinks again, then nuts and Italian salami. Then at 9.30 or so, dinner. What a meal, served with red wine, then brandy, while we enjoyed the warmth of this united family.

Next day, we set off for Peshawar in good time, and found a difficult turn for *Peregrine* at the bottom of the hill where the ponies collect, but on the third attempt we got round, and down the narrow winding steep road to Sunny Bank. The mountains looked marvellous in the early light, soft and velvety, craggy and vicious.

Women were reaping the maize by hand with bill-hooks. The restaurants were open and the chai pots were steaming, and cups prepared. Fruit stalls were bulging with apples, red green and gold, and vegetables straight from the fields were displayed for the day. Peasants were about, and boys in grey were going up the hill to school, and those in off-white were going down. Eventually we got down to the river valley, and climbed again, seeing that stretch of water held back by the Rawal dam, glinting in the sunshine. We came out of the mountains, through several villages, with the remains of a pseudo-Tudor Monastery, and saw signs of Mogul buildings. It was strange to see how many good stone buildings were in irretrievable disrepair.

Giant concrete blocks heralded Islamabad, and many white buildings housed folk from every part of the world, each holding on to his national customs, food, language and traditions. Past the honey farm to Rawal rest house for water and ice. There we had such a warm welcome from the old chowkidar who had previously served us; he would take nothing for this nor for our earlier stay. We found the Taxila Museum and saw Gandhara things, Buddhist bits from the time of Asoka, who made one of the three old capitals here his headquarters. We saw the small seals and ruby necklaces, bracelets in gold filigree, and buttons in six petal designs, and five buttons with a triangular piece sticking up, to be pushed through the material. I suspected the six petalled ones were for ornamenting the pall over the sarcophagus.

There was a showcase with lovely little carved animals, a seated monkey, an elephant in blue shiny material, and a lovely clear crystal lion. Various tools and goldsmiths ornaments, pots etc., and well shaped nails and iron needles, large and long. A Buddha in bronze and some other brass figurines. The pottery was of red clay: the shapes were not striking; but amid the large storage jars was an interesting stack of pottery rings, I wondered of their purpose and how they had been used.

The Gandhara black carvings were there, and I do so wonder if those we were shown were fakes or not, I think many were. Coins were well displayed, but none were as bright as those in Lahore! We felt we had not time for the sites which are scattered, and went on to Peshawar to the British Embassy house, where we had been expected, but earlier! The chowkidar was fetched, and we were let in, given a room each with air conditioning and fans which we found most acceptable after our long drive from the Murree Hills.

The chowkidar had been here for 26 years; his son worked here too, and his mother was 110. . He remembered HM the Queen and Prince Philip who were here in 1961, when a photograph was taken. This house then was the office and HQ for the British High Commissioner. We appreciated the good repro- Chippendale chairs, tables and sideboards, and the white and gold Minton china. The dining room had no outside walls nor windows, but some interesting prints, one of the Tower of London and one of the Royal Mint of 1830/1850 and one of St Paul's etc. from Southwark Bridge.

We were given a great send-off by the chowkidar and cook; the former was all dressed up for the occasion in gold skull cap, long tasselled turban hanging down his back and a clean shirt and trousers, unlike the cook who was in a very scruffy and dirty white jacket and trousers, and his grey astrakhan cap as usual. I added a few coins to the chowkidar's collection, and wished I had had more to give him.

We found much copper and brassware in the bazaar, and rather indifferent carpets and then drove down the Mall and out into the country where we passed Sudan-like adobe houses, with no windows and padlocked doors. 'Poor man's graves' of piles of stones, were dotted about, and grouped very near the houses. I felt we were on the wrong road, and Helen asked a man with a bike, who confirmed this; he was so nice and fluent in English, and volunteered to bike ahead of us; and he gave us splendid directions to the Khyber road, by the airfield and across a desert area.

We were on our way again on the Khyber road, through scrubby, desert country, and then through poor farmland with adobe type houses. We reached Jamrud after crossing a wide empty grey stony river bed and gazing at the Suleiman Range of mountains and the Khyber Pass. The approach is a bit like that of leaving the prairies for the Rockies. Some new and experimental buildings were, on the whole of good. design. We reached the gateway of Jamrud, a 'toy' fort with small cannons on top of its stone gateway; it was circular, with circular bastions, so like the forts with toy soldiers we played with as children. We paid 4 rupees for *Peregrine* and 1 each for ourselves, for the privilege of driving the pass, and off we set. The sedimentary sandstone rock was sand-coloured with a pinkish tinge, and was craggy and relentless. The gradient of the road was easy, and the road surface was pretty good. Remains of small fortifications and dwellings in and on the side of the hills were among about the four ranges of hills to be seen. One imagined marching troops in the valley and the snipers on the hill sides.

We met some boys with catapults and stones, reflecting one of the old means of defence. The valley widened out, and here fortified caravanserais were grouped on each side of the road. The natural stones washed smooth from years of the melting snows were piled upon each other to form a dry stone wall which was plastered on each side with the clay and dung of adobe mud, and topped with sharp stones.. The walls of the caravanserais must be 12ft to 20ft high. Great doors stand in one wall only, these were generally shut or a charpoys was across the opening, guarded even in broad daylight, and today when the threat of invasion is not great. I wondered what sign would be given for the inhabitants to return to their homes in an emergency.

Within the caravanserai were inner walls, with the entrances staggered. Trees grew inside, and perhaps 'iron rations' were kept? Where the valley opened out maize was growing, and one or two really green patches of cultivated crops were to be seen, such a contrast to the arid, hard unrelenting mountainsides.

We passed women in printed camises and shalwars; the camises had long sleeves and a rick-rack decoration around the neck, and the tops and trousers matched. They were walking bravely down the road or across the mountain slopes, almost hidden by their bundles of fodder tied into square cloths, winter food for the animals perhaps. I saw one house, earlier, having a roof put on, first the insulation of a layer of dried maize stalks and leaves was arranged, then the adobe and sometimes, as in the Murree hills, clods of earth, through which grass grows . The roofs were flat and water troughing of hollowed wood or galvanised tin emerged from one side of the building.

The loads the women were carrying were so great that it was not possible to see their faces, and only very little of them. The way to the top of Khyber – 3,500 ft. – takes one to Nandi Kotal, 29 miles from Jamrud. This we found a very busy and friendly place, with stalls displaying good flat baskets, mats, brass and copper jugs and every sort of thing for panniers and harness for donkeys on the Pass. We started our downward path, and saw a private car down to its gunwales striving to get up the pass with about 20 men aboard. What would the insurance companies or Ministry of Transport say?! Then we drove down the less spectacular wider valley side and on to Torkham and the border.

29th July 1973—26th September 1973
Mileage: Kathmandu—Khyber Pass (Torkham) 1,448

Self catering in Afghanistan!

Afghanistan—Route Map

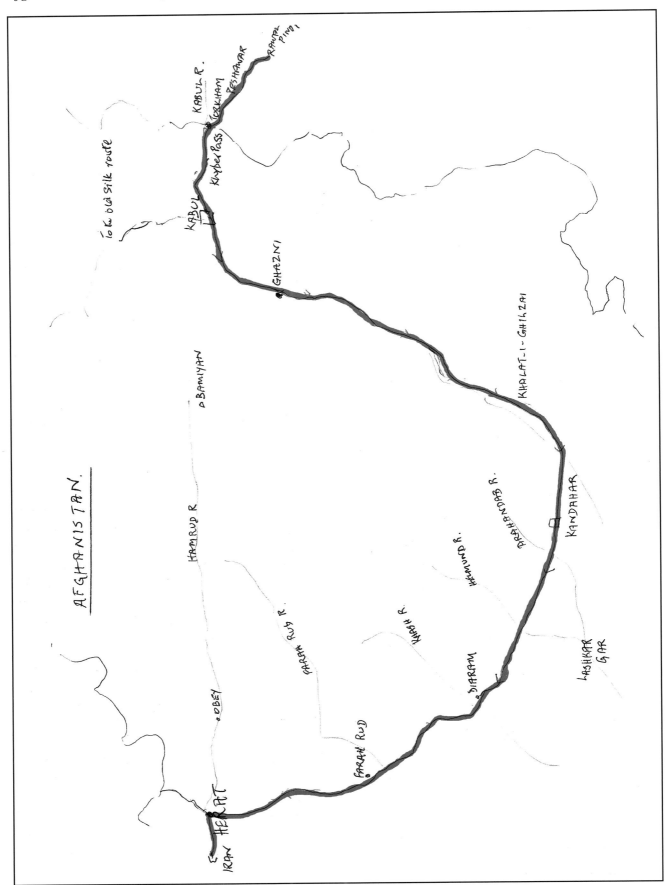

Chapter 7

AFGHANISTAN

The Pakistani Customs were pretty quick, but we had to show our passports three times before we crossed to Afghanistan, where amusing passport boys in grey were cracking jokes; then came the rub. First we had to have insurance for *Peregrine* in spite of the international one, this cost 450p and drained us of our Pakistani hundreds. Then many were getting visas, and we joined a scrum at the desk fit for a rugger field. Mercifully, it was established that we had our visa so an inexperienced boy was detailed to look after us, which entailed a good deal of writing in our passports. When this was over, I asked for a carnet for *Peregrine*, and found that they did not use them, but more was written in my passport and on a form. The moped caused confusion, but all was fixed at last, through the kind offices of a 'hippy' Iranian who was travelling with a French 'hippy' from Lyons. Driving was to be on the right hand side again.

On the Khyber Pass side we were stopped at a toll gate where 30p was demanded. We had only 10p left, and a few Pakistani coins, so we were threatened with a complete search of the vehicle by an irate man. I drove down to the passport check point and explained our predicament to the officer, who must have said something to the threatening man, for we were allowed through without payment.

On along tamarisk-bordered roads where near-desert conditions pertained, except where the land was irrigated and the citrus trees in plantations struggled for existence. Many pack horses or donkeys were to be seen, but few cars or lorries of any sort.

Between Jalallabad and Kabul, we stopped to watch a camel caravan laden with tents etc. and accompanied by whole families, making their way North. At once a bevy of boys, full of energy and devilment, came along and danced about. We were rescued by two elderly men who saw off the greater number of the children. We came across a small hydro-electric plant, and the dammed up river had wonderful reflections of the dark juniper trees and pink, grey and gold mountains, and the fluffy tamarisk trees. The weeds in the shallow parts were so lovely, both gold and green. This scene was enriched by a group of women and children dressed in red and orange colours, making a lovely peaceful pastoral picture; goats and sheep and sometimes cattle were to be seen by the water, but we only saw one buffalo. Black and white plovers seemed to have taken over from the cheeky yellow eyed starlings of India. In the valley, adobe villages huddled together, with not a tree to give shade nor to break the heat of the scorching sun; yet farmers tried to grow their maize.

We had reached the river valley, and were only about ten miles from Kabul, when *Peregrine* gave a snort and stopped; was it electrical or petrol failure? I found by getting shocks that it was not an electrical failure so I fiddled with the carburettor and supply pipe and off she went again. Just as we were rather pleased with ourselves, we heard a loud report and she stopped again. We coasted along a road towards an army training camp. No petrol was reaching the carburettor, though the indicator showed 2 or 3 gallons, so I thought the fuel pump must be faulty, but could not enquire of the local folk who only speak Afghan! Some soldiers eventually came along, the first a shy slow-witted man who wanted a lift. Then we met an officer, who made a show of helping but was devoid of ideas; then a young bullet-headed boy who was for action. He got into *Peregrine* and took off his squashy pill–box hat and put his despatch case on the table and blew and sucked furiously at the fuel supply pipe. The officer stopped two trucks; the first was useless but the second had a nice sensible elderly driver who established that we really were out of petrol!! Off I went on the moped trying at small villages to fill our can, but without success, and finally on reaching the outskirts of Kabul, changed our Indian 10 rupees for 60 Afghan p. and got petrol in a can, and also some for the moped. It was difficult to manage the can, and to add to everything, I burnt my right leg on the exhaust pipe when adjusting the tin! and my glasses blew off my nose! Boys rushed for them and threw stones at me, but a kind tall man picked them up, saw off the boys, and gave my specs to me. I drove off gratefully.

The sun was going down as I reached *Peregrine* and got the petrol into the tank through an improvised funnel, plastic bag in cardboard trough. Drove off to the garage where they were derisive, not helpful, and ready to cheat one at once. A supercilious young man spoke a little English and got the men to help a bit, but we made do with 2 litres of petrol, and got off to the centre of Kabul. We stopped at an imposing looking gateway with many soldiers to ask for help for parking, or the way to the British Embassy. We were rushed at with fixed bayonets and hustled on – later we found we were by the Royal Palace so recently taken over by the military when the King was expelled from the country.

So we beat a hasty retreat and made for the Kabul Hotel. The man there with tie in disarray and shirt collar open, short hair hardly brushed and parted in the middle, was hanging about awkwardly – drunk perhaps? – and was more unhelpful in a smarmy way. A Sikh passed by and asked if we wished to change money. We took 465p for 100 Pakistani rupees, and in this stronger position I walked off to another garage for petrol.. Men at this garage were really helpful, and even let me take the 5 litres in a can without payment. An older one–eyed man in a cap, and a spare younger close-cropped lad, both in brightish blue, helped us, and the sense of humour that we had found at Torkham appeared again.

They showed us a parking lot adjacent to their garage, and on the corner of the park, and we drove in. I chose a public open-air loo in the dark which was unfortunate. Here we were at 8.15pm and in the dark and feeling very cold. We awoke to a cold clear morning and lovely view of the mosque. And found one black sheep nibbling the grass while one man was cutting grass with a hand knife, and another was at Mohammedan prayer. Several were walking by with long coats over their cotton clothes. Several sleepers at the garage were entirely covered in woolly sleeping bags to offset the cold wind blowing from the mountains.

We found we were surrounded by crowds of men, some were gazing at us from a mound near 'our' park, while others, near the mosque, seemed to be gathering in great numbers – we were glad to notice that they were not armed. We learned how to reach the British Embassy and found it was housed in a lovely old palace some distance from the centre of Kabul towards Mazza Shariffe. There we were received most graciously by the Ambassador, who said he had been in Kabul for eight months during which time there had been three governments. The coup of ten weeks ago was carried out while the King was out of the country, by the young officers of the army, the Lieutenants and Captains with only about 200 troops and a few tanks and armoured cars. Only the son-in-law of the King put up any resistance, and his bodyguards fought with the troops. He is imprisoned and no-one knows what will happen to him. The rest of the royal family have been sent out of the country, apart from the President, who is of the royal family, and the Foreign Secretary, but neither of them has much power.

The Police were watched by the Army, and there was a rumour that the Air Force wished to bomb the Palace, now the HQ of the new regime. A great feeling of uncertainty, suspicion and rudderlessness pertained; people were very edgy, and no-one knows who was watching whom.. Although late we went off to find the Museum, and rode for miles down a tree-lined wide road in the shade and cold, only to find the Museum was shut and guarded by two soldiers. We returned by another route, and spotted some gardens near to a charming little tower. There we were roughly stopped by an armed soldier who threatened us with the butt of his rifle. Mercifully a gardener arrived and signalled, and we were allowed to go. We drove through a very primitive village and were glad of the moped's turn of speed. In these troubled times we witnessed a greengrocer who was giving away grapes as he had so many, but insisted that we should pay 5p for a bunch; and he would not let a beggar woman have even a few vine leaves.

We reached the gates of the British Embassy manned by smiling Ghurka soldiers, who saluted us as we came and went. After a disturbed night in the Embassy grounds, we made another visit to the renowned Museum of Kabul and found the Nouristan room with finely carved wooden pots, animals, and spoons; and also the Mungidak room with its alabaster, limestone and gold treasures of great antiquity, perhaps even from BC 4,000 to 2,000+. Among them was a (somewhat battered) golden goblet with a bull's head design upon it, and silver objects with similar raised work. Two bronze age sites at Mungidh and Morsai Suadai were found, about 20 km from Kandahar, they have yielded up great treasures, including Susa Mungidh II and Morasi II terracotta figurines, flint artefacts and stone seats. We saw some plain pottery and sundried bricks as at Harappa, while Morasi yielded a female figurine, steatite seal, copper tubing, goat horns, and a magnetic nodule among their cult objects.

In addition to these rooms the C19 objects from Chitral of the Kaffir's supreme deity and various secondary gods were displayed, along with wooden effigies carved to represent a dead person one year after death, for the soul to lodge in. These Indo-European people lived in wooden houses built on the steep mountain slopes and, unlike their neighbours, had red or blonde hair and blue or green eyes. Recently they have been forced to turn to Islam and the practice of ancestor worship has been stopped.

The Ambassador kindly invited us to luncheon, and was most surprised to learn that I already knew two of his other guests – one from the Sudan, and one from Runton Hill, the School I had run. Before we left this safe haven we were given much prized stores to augment our provisions.

We drove out into the desert as we left Kabul and saw craggy mountains ringing the horizon, and the pink and grey scrubby earth broken with mud houses of the same colour; and where there was water, the land was carefully tended in small terraced feddans, often surrounded and protected by poplars, interlarded with cypress and juniper trees.

We passed nomadic tents of stretched goatskin, and others, less picturesque, made of bits and pieces. Camels were much in evidence in caravans or just about the place eating. We stopped to watch a man directing a glinting stream, first into his prepared upper feddan, then when it was

Kabul Museum. The author made these images and notes 'on her knee' in situ.

Ak kupruk head

Bronze 1,200 BC   LURISTAN

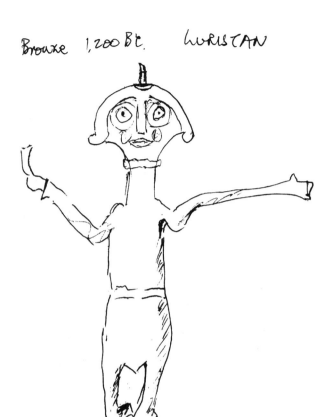

20,000 – 15,000 BC

A limestone pebble

These were fashion⁰
with a 'burr' or flint
tool of screw driver shape

Eyes possibly deepen⁰
with flint perforator
'app' with a wooden
tool.

'Chalice' / Fullol Hoard

c 2000 BC found in N.
on ` Lapi lazuli route

Mungidak

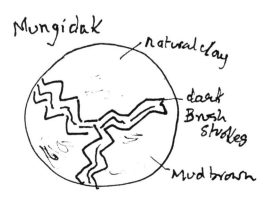

natural clay

dark
Brush
strokes

Mud brown

Kabul Museum. The author made these images and notes 'on her knee' in situ.

MUNGIDOK

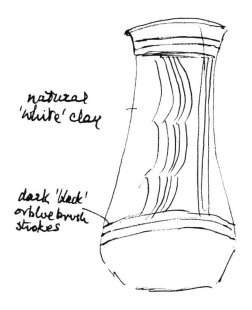

natural 'white' clay

dark 'black' or blue brush strokes

Terra cotta bowl, with back fill⁰ in solid stylis' animals.

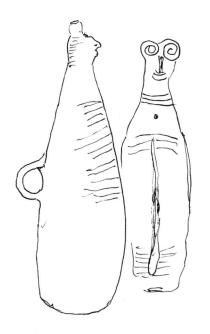

clay bottle.

LURISTAN. C 1,200 BC.

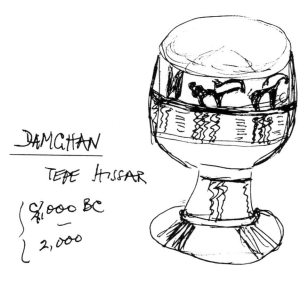

DAMGHAN

TEPE HISSAR

{ 4,000 BC
—
2,000

Kabul Museum. *The author made these images and notes 'on her knee' in situ.*

Most ancient Sculpture in
a round found in Afghanistan
limestone c. 2100 BC.

Wine tumblers.
in clay red & decorated in black.

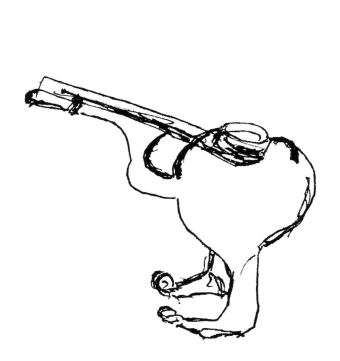

KALWRA Z (GILAN)
1,000 BC.

Kabul Museum. *The author made these images and notes 'on her knee' in situ.*

LURISTAN
1, 200 BC

Valley / Sai Hazara in
N. Afghanistan
2,000 BC.
Red clay
Black decoration
Wine goblet.

Grotesque Man
from SUSA.

1000 BC.

Kabul Museum. *The author made these images and notes 'on her knee' in situ.*

Carved in Ivory.

Griffin
ridden by
a Naked Lady.

Bearded Bull
c 2,000 BC

KALURAZ (GILAN)
1,000 BC.

Lion's
Frieze

Kabul Museum: The author made these images and notes 'on her knee' in situ.

Kabul Museum.

Nouristan Wooden things.

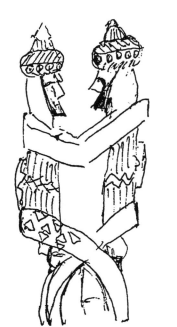

c18 Hero worship
figures.

'Tatrouk' of Nouristan

standing in water, to the next lower one. He had a long-handled spade with shoulders, and he managed it with great skill, bringing down clods of earth and opening and shutting the bunds.

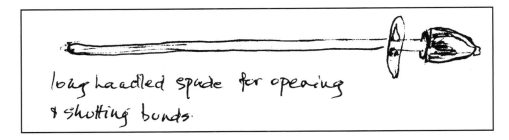

long handled spade for opening & shutting bunds.

We drove on through the Afghan desert, which was broken by streams and irrigation, and a river which nurtured trees and brought the desert to life – with crops of maize, rice, lavender and cotton that supplied a cotton ginning factory.

The road surface was good, but it was littered with the results of accidents – three dead horses, a smashed car and a bus across a drain, with another embedded in a house. Boys were returning from school, and a camel was silhouetted against the skyline. Ghazni was identifiable in a concentration of trees, with the remains of its second century minaret, once of 15 storeys, but now only half its original height, and topped with knobs and corrugated iron.

Our sightseeing walk was curtailed as a man was going round and round *Peregrine* just when I thought that I had spotted a basalt head in the mud, but I could not dig it up, and a soldier came towards us to hurry us off. They are so officious. The old city was ringed by a wall with Norman shaped bastions. We found a bazaar set up on each side of a wide grass middle to the road where men were selling hardware, material, fruit, etc. Finding a suitable safe place for the night was difficult – the Public Library had no guard at night and although a young man in grey police uniform at the Governor's house, and the chowkidar there were very friendly, we could not understand each other's language, so we had to park by the Ghazni Hotel. It was a very cold night, we put on warm clothes and got inside our canvas sleeping bags, and were still cold. The locals were all bundled up against the cold.

Wooden pronged spades

In the morning, nomads with a camel caravan and two sheep were working their way south across this Hindu Kush. We had to pay 100p road tax because of our six wheels. We saw, as we had yesterday, the freshly cut green grass piled into mounds, using their wooden pronged spades *(illus.)*. This was in readiness for a heavy 'sledge' of wire and wood, to be drawn round and round by a bullock, an oxen, a donkey or any handy animal, to reduce it to a finely cut mixture. It was then dried to a golden colour by the hot sun. This was then laden into a donkey sling and pushed down and tied up into a bundle, loaded on to the donkey and taken to the store for winter feed for the animals.

All the houses here were of adobe, and the general effect was rather drab. The mountains today at first looked like a posed photograph, then later they were a mere outline with a suggestion of mountains, while the foreground of desert scrub took over. We saw a family sitting in the middle of their melon field counting their crop of melons – men, women and children amidst striped green and yellow melons. Pumpkins and gourds as well as melons grow here, also olives and peaches, along the Tarnak River. This river winds along a stony, shaley bed much too wide for it at this time of the year.

We reached Kandahar and found the people here seemingly friendly, even if they were wishing to do one down. A local bookshop was doing business. Many of the buses come from Germany, and retained their 'D's on the back: the Americans are said to be helping with education and road building, while the British are doing something, but I am not sure what!! The day became hot, time to peel off one of two jerseys and the thick socks and boots, and at Kandahar I put on a sleeveless shirt and cotton trousers. We passed the mosque at 17:00hrs, prayer time, and found impressive rows of men at prayer; the Moslems do set us an example of discipline. It was warmer tonight, thank goodness, though we had prepared for a second really cold night!

The market in the early sun's light was so fresh and attractive, with open tongas in gay colours, polished brasses, and horses looking well fed. The fruit stalls were so attractively arranged, green apples and red pomegranates predominating. We found men whittling wood for knife handles, while others were beating tin for trays, and still others were grinding and sharpening knives on a stone kept moving by a boy who pulled a leather strap so far, and then let it run back, and then pulled it again. Meat was hanging up in the shops in the shade, and men were sitting among their dahl and soap-flakes and matches, and around them was chatter, debris and open drains. We came across beehive houses, or houses with ridged roofs built as insulators from the sun. We saw several sorts of dewponds which we had spotted since Kandahar and learnt in the evening that they were part of the ancient irrigation system for the desert. The mountain streams were tapped, and underground canals were dug, sometimes a few feet below the surface, and sometimes in deep underground canal systems. 'Wells' were sunk to these canals and along these lines fields were irrigated and cultivated.

We saw no moving caravans, but a number of 'bat' camps with camels roaming; perhaps caravans only move in the morning while the afternoons are reserved for cooking etc. We turned off for Lashkagar, along a hopelessly corrugated road, and wondered if we could continue. Stopped a lorry to ask if petrol was to be found there and a white bearded man with an intelligent face reassured us on this score, and another two confirmed it. So on we went for 30 miles or so and found a veritable oasis, USA run, with straight tarmac roads built on the grid system, with neat US staff houses and fenced gardens. We were allowed to become overnight members of their club and to buy a book of vouchers for food and drink. We met the man in charge, who promised to find us transport to visit the Ghazni desert sites in the morning. The bar was full of ladies playing bingo. A short and dark man in a pink shirt and his wife were compulsive players at one of the machines – always hoping for the jack-pot. They put in 5c a time – I learned that they were 1,600 down! Shades of Las Vegas! A man with a bad squint and a friendly wife were playing bingo. A long-faced Afghani at the bar was efficient. Mary, the manageress, from Alaska has been here with her small fair-haired child for two years. One wall was decorated with local 'hats' and shoes of the turned-up-toes variety; the whole was warm, clean and cosy.

Next day, we found the man in charge, who had contacted the Head of the USA Research contingent at Lashkagar, and he kindly provided a car and his driver, Ahmed John, and off we went to the 12th century citadel of the Ghaznavids, who wintered here and spent the summer at Ghazni. We saw the citadel atop a hill, but could not explore it because it was in the hands of the military.

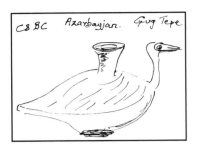

We drove out from the tree-lined asphalt roads into the desert and bounced over sandy banks and came upon a group of men and youths, a camel and a donkey, and a grinder like an over-sized coffee machine. This was driven by an engine housed in an adobe house, sheltered by plaited stalks of pampas, that gave a good shade and yet allowed air to pass through. Within it, nice friendly chaps were preparing the flour for the local bread 'narn'. On we went to the River Helmud, a widish fast flowing lovely blue river, with 'jungle' beyond and desert on our side. On a promontory the land was part of a ten square mile fortified area. Strangely, the Queen's bathwater came from the land, and went out to the river. We wandered through the living quarters of the palace, and found windows in old 'demon' tennis racquet shape, and sunbaked bricks arranged in chevron patterns, and late 'early English' arches, giving an interest and balance which was most attractive. Back to the car again, and to a tomb so like a miniature Agamemnon beehive tomb - I wondered if the builders had done a grand tour, and seen it? The windows, keyhole shaped, are reminiscent of Las Casas Grandes in Northern Mexico.

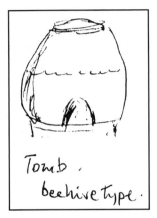

Tomb. beehive type.

On again to Qalibist and the citadel with a keep, on a hill that commanded a tremendous view from which we could see the extent of the modern farming on reclaimed land, where the plough turns up old coins and glassware. There were two shafts that we saw and a lovely four-storey well, shaped with arches on four sides, and passages running off from these arches. Some say that there may be an underground city here, for it was supplied with water which would be handy for a siege. Between 962 – 1156 the Ghazniids were destroyed by the Ghorids and then the Mongols destroyed them for destroying's sake, sacking towns and killing every living thing, men, women, children, cats, dogs, donkeys, hens – most revengeful and sadistic. We were hoodwinked by men selling `finds from the farms' and I bought a decorated stolid horse and a Gweko coin. I was pleased with my finds until in the evening when we met some archaeologists who said that they were clever copies, i.e. fakes. We returned via a very new looking arch of baked bricks that had been much renovated, some traces of blue/green colouring or white tiling. We took the desert road, threading our way through old city walls, and even parts of houses or palaces along the waterfront; then inland into the desert, en route to the admin block to thank the head of the USA research unit – such a nice, capable, quiet confident man, with his finger on all that goes on, before meeting an architect and an archaeologist and two others who were working for Trousdale of the Smithsonian, and excavating in the desert. They had finds from the first century AD to 13th/14th centuries AD including a Buddhist one – was this Ashokan? It would have been grand to have had a day exploring with them.

We chose the canal route back to the main road en route for Iran, and nearly got stuck in a river which we had to cross, because mud had built up on the concrete. However, we reached Girisha where we saw narn being baked; the proved balls were kneaded and pulled into a long round fish-like shape, and marks were made with the fingers; then they were slapped on to sand filled asbestos bags and pressed upon the walls of the oven that was heated by wood that burns about 6 to 8 ft. below the floor. The top of the oven has a round tin concave 'lid' at floor level, and one man sat near enough to be able to reach over and 'fix' the narn to the wall, while another man at a cooler spot shaped and prepared the narn. A third man sat at the end of a well-used board, and received the baked bread, and stood it on end on a shelf or stacked it for sale. A boy or two may also be employed. It took about 15 to 20 minutes to bake a loaf, which was no more than the good milled brown flour and water and lovely to eat, and it will toast well too. We first watched the process at Lashkagar and were glad to see it again at Girisha, where we bought a lovely hot loaf.

Just short of Diaram we ran out of petrol and men in the lorry most kindly gave us one gallon or so from a large open tin, and then drove off. We reached Diaram and a toll gate, where our tickets were eventually found under the mat after a search!

We drove on to real desert, followed by dark rugged mountains. We stopped at the top of a hill with six ranges of mountains before us, lavender blue through blue to black, and also where the sun hit them, pink, sandy colour. *Peregrine* would not start. We were anxious about our supply of petrol, so pushed her, and she covered nearly five miles free-wheeling. I jumped out to push again; this was a dangerous but necessary expedient which nearly ended in disaster when *Peregrine* outran me and I only just got back into the driving seat in time. *Peregrine* ran out of petrol about five miles short of Farah Rud. Mercifully I was able to go on my moped and bring back 6 litres in a can, which enabled us to reach the splendid hotel area for the night.

We were desperately short of currency, and hearing activity next door, we entered and found the Governor of the Province of Farah Rud who was having a meeting with a General, an active man in a fawn anorak, and four or five doleful, awkward-looking youths, while men were sitting along one wall. The Governor said we might borrow 500 Afs. From the Police and pay the Police in Herat. This sounded splendid and so simple, but the General in the Police Station had gathered the folk from the garage and Hotel around him, and had heard that Helen had 20 marks; so after giving me 500 Afs. He demanded them back again. He had two interpreters, one a policeman and the other a youngish man with an ornate gold beaded cap and white shirt and baggy trousers. The garage man was much in evidence. We were so incensed at our treatment that we returned to the Governor, who now held to the 20 marks, but said that the rate of exchange was to be 28 not 15. To think of the 200% profit made by that man yesterday! The man from the garage was sent for. He nearly fainted to hear at what rate the exchange was to be, and had to hold on to the wall to steady himself. We returned to the garage, and just as we began the transaction, two men from the USA arrived in an Afghan tour car with a driver. They quickly became involved in the transactions and graciously lent us 500 Afs. the amount to cover our drive to Herat. We showed them round *Peregrine* and found that they were from north of San Francisco and had relatives at Woodside, where I had friends. We found them so helpful, delightful and considerate.

This part of our journey in the high mountain ranges of Afghanistan was further complicated by the lack of information on the whereabouts and infrequency of garages and Banks, and our inability to speak or understand the language.

The road went on over the mountain pass as if it would never reach the top. There were very few people or signs of life, and little on the road – just a few goats and donkeys occasionally, and later 'bat tent' camps and camels. We stopped in a village for narn and to look at the gearbox, which had thrown some oil. While Helen was outside the door, I saw a hand taking the hammer, only later to discover that the hammer and the larger ring spanner had gone – what a loss!

Because our supply of petrol was still very low, I stopped a petrol van and got the man to let us have four litres of petrol, in exchange for 10 Afs. and 2 Pakistani coins and a packet of cigarettes. Several men and a boy clustered round and one man sat in front of the car. When they saw we had no more money, aghast they stood back, and we drove on. The petrol was dirty, and *Peregrine* was not pulling her best, but we reached the top of the pass 1,772 metres eventually, and shortly we were able to coast down to Herat for perhaps six to eight miles. This enabled us to reach the centre of the town and a garage where a man undid the gear box and pronounced that we needed oil. Nice

German and Afghan and Persian folk in a GB car led us to the Niagara Hotel grounds for the night, and told us that they were en route to Nepal with a Tibetan 'friend' and member of the Tibetan Society in London.

We drove on and passed the Jami minarets, and saw, perhaps, the bases of the windmills that it is thought antedated the Chinese, British and European windmills. We heard it was still 78 miles or so to the Iranian customs, along an exposed desert road.

At the Customs, a little man in a blue suit was making a Kuwaiti man turn out the whole of his car, including his spare wheel, and then tapped the doors etc. He came into *Peregrine* and looked around, and did not even check my cameras etc. – and we were through! A nice young USA couple, he a lawyer and she studying jewellery, had two tin boxes on the roof of their car, filled with things they had bought at Herat; and they were required to pay 30,000 Afs. for them. So they decided to return to Herat. We came on, but were stopped at the border because we had no police stamp. I returned on the moped and had a bright chat with a dour man; gave *Peregrine's* number and net weight, and we were allowed through.

The soldier on the gate stood by and watched us struggle to return the moped into *Peregrine* and then came in and looked round for what he wanted. He looked at *'In Britain'* which, when he had got out, we gave it to him to look at. He would not open the gate for us, but mercifully, a lorry came from Iran and took his attention. He returned the book, and let us through. The uncouth power these youths display because they are in uniform, was alarming.

We found at the Iran Customs that it was 20 kms to Taibad and the nearest Bank and petrol! Could *Peregrine* manage this? First, we were ushered into quarantine, and given two capsules to take in case we were cholera carriers – what a nerve! We returned to *Peregrine* to take them with our own water, and pantomimed this without eating them. Then our passports were dealt with by a sick-looking man, and on to get the carnet done. We were given a huge and lovely pomegranate and had much chat; my moped was entered in my passport, no carnet because it was not on the road – I hope this will be OK at the other end?

"Beehive' roof top for insulation.

With bated breath we drove out of a narrow gate, and into the desert again. There were many signs telling us how may kilometres to Taibad, petrol and food. There was a time change so we put our clocks back one hour. We were in Persia and driving Westwards on a desert road to Torbat Iam, a neat small town with adobe dwellings in groups, with chimneys through their beehive roofs. Many poplars were grown for shade and wind protectors around the edges of the larger houses. Graves were on mounds. I wondered what treasures might be buried there?

26th September 1973—8th October 1973
Mileage: Khyber Pass (Torkham)—Iran (Taibad) 985

A page from the Author's Diary: her sketches were mainly produced in this way 'on the spot'

Afghanistan—Route Map

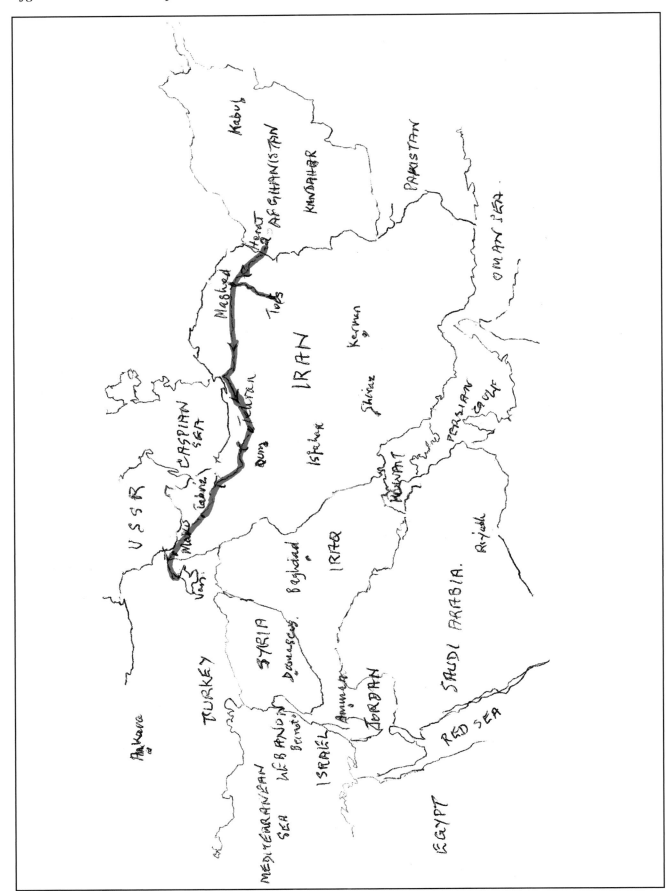

Chapter 8

I R A N

We have left the wild remote mountainous Afghanistan, where we had to stop a petrol delivery vehicle, en route, to enable us to continue driving, rather than coasting up and down the mountains. We have left the bitter cold and have reached Mashad, Iran's second largest and most holy city, where Shi'ite Muslims meet. Here there is a great golden domed shrine over Imam Reza's tomb, where the Gower Shah mosque and the tomb of Nadir Shah stand. Mashad boasts an university and a British Council HQ. It stands at a junction of roads, one of which leads to Naishabur, the home of the great and famous poet, astronomer and mathematician Omar Khayyam, translated into English by Edward Fitzgerald in 1902, while another road branches off to the ancient city of Toos, the birthplace of the honoured national poet Ferdowsi, whose statue marks the North end of the Avenue of his name in Tehran.

We found our way to the Asian Highway to Tehran, which we learnt was soon to be a four lane road leading along a wide desert valley through small villages supported by irrigated land, where adobe peasant houses were fringed with trees, and where cotton, sugar beet and maize crops were worked in smallish fields. These fields were enclosed by bunds, and one was being dug as we went by – the heavy clay soil was being dug by one man, while another pulled it up into position by ropes in a rhythmic swinging motion to form the bund mound and furrow.

A journey of this length must sometimes be met with difficulties, and my faithful but elderly fire tender *Peregrine* was showing signs of fatigue after nearly 22,000 miles in many and varied hostile environments; and this was compounded by our shortage of money. We found our way to the British Council, and learnt from them of *Peregrine's* second caravanserai with skilled mechanics, one who dealt with the gear box, while another oiled the engine and adjusted the carburettor.

We next turned our attention to improving our finances – I had hoped to find a temporary teaching job, but this was not to be; but I earned a little by giving a talk on my diarist great uncle Frank, and by giving two high class cookery demonstrations to some wives of the British dons at the University. Driving the moped in Mashad was an experience. Boys on motor bikes or bicycles ride at one, and taxis pass and stop suddenly in front of one, cars, boys and people come on one from all angles and the traffic moves fast.

Mashad was our introduction to Iran, and it demonstrated the contrasts to be found throughout the country, such as nice residential areas and smart shops alongside the small trading shops that sell a jumble of things. The pride of the people in their Persian history which goes back, it boasted, over 2,500 years to Cyrus, their great king of Persia. (At a later date, I visited Persepolis and experienced something of the power of Persia, and saw the carvings of the varied people who came to pay their tribute to him.) We found the present day Iranians, unlike the wild Afghans, sophisticated, but, with a few exceptions, without the natural courtesy we had enjoyed in Pakistan.

Rested, refreshed and replenished after a few days in Mashad, we found our way to the Asian highway to Tehran. The sugar beet was being harvested by rows of men and women with coloured head coverings, who were cutting off the green tops and preparing the beet for the lorries or carts which would take them to the sugar factory.

Our route was on the Asian Highway via Quchan, and we found the smaller hand tilled fields were giving way to larger fields cultivated by tractors and growing sugar beet for a nearby factory, as well as cotton and grain which had already been harvested. We found a woman washing clothes in a small pool of water that had not yet evaporated, and we wondered about a conical building, which might have been one of the old ice 'houses' though how ice could be made and stored in the desert conditions remains a mystery.

At Dasht while *Peregrine* was again being repaired we found that the only water supply for the village was dispensed from a brass tap, and our 'turn' at the tap was constantly interrupted to enable the 'locals' to fill a saucepan, or drinking container, or a blue plastic bucket, and also to wash, for it was the hour of prayer. A long distance driver washed to the elbows and most devoutly prayed beside us, uninhibited and undisturbed by the bustle and noise of the garage and the three little imps of seven years old or so who were darting about like mosquitoes. We drove on as the sun was setting below the mountains, and the full moon appeared, silver, silent and supreme; and we turned off to Gonbad-e-Qabus, a town on the Gorgon river, and established ourselves for the night: but we had attracted the attention of three youths and some men, resulting in a visit from a policeman, who indicated without a word of English, that we would be safer nearer to the police station, and we were led there.

This must have been in the centre of the village as all was astir in the early morning – a morning that nearly spelt disaster for us. It was Jumma, petrol was not available nor could we change money, and I had dropped the keys of *Peregrine* irretrievably down a hole. We were locked out of the seemingly impregnable *Peregrine* with little hope of getting in to find the other set of keys. Nothing daunted, we asked for help and were lent a display stand from a shop, and I climbed up and tried the kitchen window, but found it too well snibbed: then the driver's window – no go – then to the final possible window which had a broken screen. The stiff window obligingly gave, the screen came down and thankfully I scrambled in and with the spare keys unlocked the doors. Another close shave.

We drove through large and well tended cotton fields. The valley stood between narrow sandstone hills of reddish, brownish, greyish rock each shading into the other. The river was just a trickle of water as it threaded its way through the grey smooth stones in the shaley, sandy, wide riverbed.

We reached Quchan and turned into its main street, bought petrol and to my horror and dismay I saw that the gearbox was dripping oil. I got underneath to tighten up the nuts, and such a nice well-covered man with two fingers bandaged in rags took the spanner from me, and really got to work, turning the nuts a further quarter or half turn. He called for a 'ringy' spanner. Mine had been stolen, but we were just outside a shop that sold them and one was lent. He then said the axle and gearbox should be greased, and he would do it for 100 rials. We agreed 50 rials and the shopkeeper dropped his price for the spanner from 120 to 50 rials at which price we bought it.

We headed towards the Caspian Sea, the largest inland sea in the world, which we heard was gradually evaporating and being reduced in size. The hard sandy shore was studded with shells. Again a vigilant policeman asked us for our safety to spend the night near the local restaurant, but this turned out to be an unfortunate venue for a drunken soldier had with difficulty to be restrained, and there was much coming and going through the night, with reinforcements including an officer and a soldier with a loaded rifle. Calm was restored and in the morning the proprietor was praised for his part in the proceedings. Relieved, we walked on the hard sand by the Caspian.

As we left, there were smokey blue mountains on our left, and the land flat and sloping away to our right. The maple trees of Mashad had given way to birch trees and now a good number of poplars studded the horizon in every direction. The pinky green of the desert became a scrubby green, and as we topped another ridge, the hills became greener again, so as we neared Gorgan we had the dark green firs and pines and dull green cotton trees with their white wisps and pinkish look from the pods, once the cotton had been picked, and the grey-green of the tobacco plant with its cluster of off-white flowers and the bright green of the corn on the cob. Then the cropped corn, whitish when bleached by the sun, and golden where just cropped: and sometimes the skyline was broken with the winnowing, and the harvesting, but none so spirited as the first group we had seen. We had passed folk collecting the wheat stalks in hand bundles to be taken to be reaped. They looked so like Millais' gleaners, or a Breughal painting. The sheafs so regular and so carefully handled. It is lovely to see some of these old crafts being practised instead of a soulless combine harvester.

At Gorgan we tried to change money at the airport – which was shown on the map –and found it was for local export from farms only! Therefore since we had no money we looked for an hotel, and after walking through a municipal building, we spotted the 'Miami', and there we persuaded the manager to part with 1,620 rial for £10. Armed with this we put in 100 litres of petrol and headed for Sari, where we found signs of expansion and westernisation following the development of the Asian highway. The centre of the town had concrete or brick built houses and well laid out roads, while the outskirts were muddy and the houses were made of adobe. Sometimes new two storey houses with balconies were to be seen within the old adobe walls.

We found the road to Farahabad and the Caspian but were turned about by locals, partly because we were off the Asian Highway and partly because it had the wrong name! So we went due North to the Caspian on a good road flanked by farms and looking so like the South of Holland, with poplar trees and flat polder country. The sun was a red ball as we arrived, and we walked by the sea, picking up shells which were in great profusion; and we found an amusingly shaped piece of wood. We saw many birds, two or three cows, a flock of sheep and goats and also a horse. Small families came in cars and jeeps and the children bathed in the nude. Men usually kept on their dark trousers and had bare tops. I saw no women bathing.

On our drive to Babol and Babolsar we passed arable farms and one field was studded with mud huts with pitched roofs. These were used, we learnt, for storing the straw and hay stacks, a sensible precaution against the heavy rainfall in this area . We saw rice, barley, wheat, maize with lovely mauve wild flowers edging the road. At Babol a roundabout was planted in clumps with petunias etc., a most refreshing sight. Soon we should see tea on the hills. Many limes and citrus fruit were for sale in the shops, also melons, tomatoes and apples, and radishes of outsize proportions, and pomegranates galore.

We found our way across the bridge to an important caviar factory, and were given a most comprehensive tour by a guide, who was proud of this 80 year old factory and of the trade it did with the UK and others. He looked so smart in a blue flowered shirt and neat grey striped trousers, unlike the working clothes of the fishermen, in their long rubber boots with woolly tops, cotton coats and cotton trousers, woolly caps with ear flaps and gloves. He led us first to a fishpond, where examples of the different caviar fishes were swimming around in the shade of a corrugated awning. Beluga is the big fellow, Ossetra the small one, and Serruge the particularly long nosed one. The large caviar is the 'best' we heard, and the white caviar was kept for royalty. After the pond,, we went to the museum and there saw some of the white fish such as carp and herring, as well as tinca tinca, siherus and jakole. He pointed out that from a fish farm, the river is kept stocked with young fish that swim out into the Caspian. Eighty different kinds of fish swim in this inland sea.

We were shown the spotlessly clean preparation room, tiled with blue, and a spacious refrigeration room, and a deep freeze. Caviar is stored in barrels. Finally we were shown the flat-bottomed boats that were made of hard black chenar wood, rowed with four pairs of oars, or sailed under a single sail, which transported the barrels to markets.

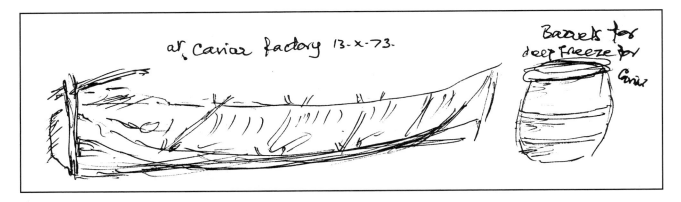

We left and went to the coast, where we found a lovely deserted beach with about six men shovelling up grain that had been spread out on the carpark to dry in the sun. They used wooden curved long-handled spades and a Spanish type basket, and they sewed the tops of the sacks with local thread. We had passed good grain growing fields that had been harvested, and this grain was drying everywhere, on the roads, paths, and roofs, before being stacked in great heaps by the owner's house. Many houses were thatched, but many new precarious looking and ugly buildings were going up near the coast: it reminded me of Seaford.

The shore of the Caspian is of hard sand so cars drive on it before reaching soft sand, then sand dunes, then polder with small bamboo edged fields either growing with pampas like flowers or cut and threaded together to form boundaries. Going South we soon came to the Alborz range of mountains, the western tip of the Himalayan range, and at first the mountains were wooded with deciduous trees, round and lovely in the morning light, surrounding small white-washed cottages built of wood, and then covered with adobe and thatched. We again noticed that villages were becoming more prosperous here, with buildings of modern brick standing within their adobe walled areas, and allowing the old adobe house to be a store, or to fall down.

We were caught in a scurry of heavy rain just south of Mahmudabad, the farmers were all reaching for their sheets of plastic. No one put on any extra clothing and no umbrellas were to be seen – so unlike India. Suddenly the 'next' range of mountains was bare of trees, and we settled down to drive along a stony river bed by a small busy river hurrying down to the Caspian. Wherever there was moisture and soil poplars were planted and their leaves turning green and gold shimmered in the bright sun. The sky became cloudless and the way became steeper, but on and up we went through tunnels built to protect travellers from falling stones. Even so, one good sized boulder hit us at the back and made a dent.

We pressed on and up this long hill in second gear and were just able to reach the top, with its views of a wide fertile valley on our left and sandstone mountains to our right. We coasted down in fine style and cooled off, but not all are so lucky. Two separate cranes were raising two smashed cars from the depths below, and a third car in the valley. Their driving leaves much to be desired! Villages clung to the sides of the mountains where there was soil, and a mineral water factory benefited from the lovely gushing water from the bare mountainside. But *Peregrine* had had enough, and spluttered and stopped. In spite of fiddling with the carburettor and making adjustments, *Peregrine* was not moving. We looked in the engine and found the outlet manifold was red hot. Alarmed, we opened everything and waited: later we sponged *Peregrine's* petrol pump and carburettor down with cold water and adjusted the carburettor. We got going, but *Peregrine* was still protesting, and night was falling, so I left her and walked through the tunnel in the dark, torch in hand, so see how much further we would have to climb. Mercifully at the other end of the tunnel was a cottage in which was a man to whom I had spoken earlier, when he had been winching up a car along the road. He told me that the cottage was a stop for lorry drivers, where narn, Pepsi and tea were sold. I was given a narn, and accompanied by a mechanic and at first the woman of the house with a lantern, we returned to *Peregrine*. The man fiddled knowledgeably with *Peregrine* and soon had her going . We drove to the cottage and parked for the night.

The cottage had one main room and one other, both with mud floors. It was furnished with a long built-up bench against the further wall on which a frail old man with shaved grey-white hair was propped on cushions, hubble bubble at his side; and a fat woman was sitting near him and eating from a tin bowl. A pretty young girl in black and white trousers and a camise was sitting down while the active woman in brightly coloured clothes was serving 'Pepsi' from the icebox, and ice, and also attending to a wood fire for cooking on the verandah outside the room. We gave the man a packet of 'Craven A' for his pains and he and his pretty wife settled themselves for a good smoke. The Pepsi bottles were grouped round a supporting pillar, and a built-up shelf on the left served as a table. Through in the other room was another built-up shelf on which was a narn folded in three and kept in a cloth. There was no other furniture, and just a striped cotton rug on the floor where the woman was eating. When we awoke next morning we found we were facing a sheer sandstone rock on the roadside with a group of trees growing in the south-east facing valley, and on the other side a young copse of walnuts, and then the earth sheered away, and a road led far into the mountains, ridge upon ridge. The roof of the house was like so many, with clods of earth and adobe, supported by poplar poles, with bamboo stems and leaves arranged as insulation.

We left our refuge and overnight friends in the mountains and shortly saw signs of Tehran, a great sprawling modern city, the capital city of Iran since 1794. Like so many developing towns Tehran is a real mixture of buildings and roads. Coming from the East we arrived at the North end of Tehran's main street, the Avenida Ferdowsi (Persia's revered national poet) and we found our way to the British Embassy, which lies at the South end of this important street, though when it was built it was beyond the Northern borders of the town. We drove in and parked near to the Ambassador's house, in a spacious park, and signed the book, and made enquiries for the Consul, in the hope of earning money for our onward journey. A very nice and polite security officer asked us how we had got into the grounds, and why we were parking for so long. He told us that 'squibs' had gone off in the grounds, and that the Ambassador was very busy because of the Middle East war, and because the BBC had visited Iran, and produced a most forthright and non-diplomatic documentary; worse still, when they knew some offence was given to the Iranians, they justified themselves by quoting and naming those interviewed. Much 'patching up' was now necessary at this end. Furthermore, and more immediately, there were reports of snow in Turkey in November, though it is to be hoped that the main roads will be kept open. I had much anti-freeze put into *Peregrine* in readiness.

We found our way to the British Council, and were allowed to park in the well planned grounds for the whole of our three week stay. During this time in Tehran we were introduced to Iranians and British, from whom we learnt of the ancient and recent history of the country. We were initiated into the history of Archimenides when Persia extended from Asia Minor through Syria and Palestine and Babylon, and across the Iranian plateau later to be conquered by Alexander the Great. We learnt of the Sassanids in the seventh century AD, and of the nine centuries of Mongul rule, and then of the Safavid power until the Qujar dynasty that ruled Tehran from 1796 AD.

Tehran Museum.

Bas Relief ~ Treasury   Darius seated receiving tribute money   C2,600 BC

We learnt that wealthy and influential Iranians were buying land to the North of Tehran in the lower reaches of the mountains and so pushing Tehran's boundaries North, perhaps eight miles or so, from several years earlier, when the British Embassy was beyond the Northern boundaries of the town . The contrasts between the rich Iranian elite and the farming communities were striking; the former are building themselves spacious houses in the foothills of the mountains to the North of Tehran and drive themselves in large cars to the centre of the city. Here, the amazing one-way traffic system runs North to South <u>until</u> 12 noon—and <u>from</u> 12 noon South to North! This adds to the difficulties of driving in Tehran, especially around noon! The farmers bring their produce to the market in the Southern area of the city, or—one farmer I saw, walked his 8 to 10 geese to the centre, lining them up to cross the road, dodging the traffic, en route for sale to the poulterer—an amazing sight! Many of the older and narrower roads have ganats (waterways) alongside them, and cars often have to be pulled from them.

We were invited to a Persian luncheon which was a happy experience. Turkish coffee was an appetiser, then a nice tablecloth was laid on the floor, where rice, chicken, pickle, dates, salad, dahl, and tomatoes were all laid out. We were invited to sit on mattresses, but everyone else sat cross-legged on carpets and without shoes. Our host went off to fetch round honey things then we ate fruit, and drank tea in the sitting room.

We tried to see Zochonay, in the Zurkhaneh (House of Strength). This is kind of wrestling to rhythmic chants, and is an example of ancient Persian sports, but because it was Jumma all was shut. It was not only Jumma, but the 20th day of Ramadan, commemorated as the day of the death of the Prophet Mohammed. Flags were flying at half mast and everything was shut. We gazed at Persian carpets behind closed shop fronts, and luckily found one tiny open shop run by a little old lady; it was about 6 ft. by 6 ft. by 6 ft.. We asked for butter although the shelves looked pretty bare and rather scruffy, it was produced from a deep freeze! Then eggs, none to be seen, but she went behind her little counter and up came five good sized eggs. Then bread, and lo and behold she crossed her shop and from under a sack offered a new crunchy loaf. This was indeed corn in Egypt. We learnt as we paid this little grey-haired competent lady that she was Russian and not a Mohammedan. What a blessing for us that she was there in her open shop. We returned through the small opening in the firmly shut high gates of the British Council to *Peregrine* in our secure garden.

Next day, we were off to the museum which has lovely early exhibits from Luristan, and others with a feeling of the Hittites and a plan of Persepolis, with a wall from the treasury in bas relief of Darius, Xerxes, Archimenides *(illus. p.144)* and also Chinese plates and pots, celadon bowls and blue and white in large plates and bowls. A beautiful Persian bowl with three birds portrayed in dark to black or off-white parchment colour. The lines of the birds were so free, and the legs hooked on to the line of the belly, with a small intense bird at the bottom of the bowl. At the bazaar we found much trash, mass produced tin goods, shoes, and modern plastic goods. Very little local craft. This was in contrast to exhibits at the covered bazaar where the lovely carpets have their own appeal. During our three weeks in Tehran I was able to replenish my resources by giving cookery demonstrations to ex-pats and English lessons to an Iranian diplomat, and by teaching in a mixed school, where I tried to get my final class at the school to act charades. This last session ended with a handshake from the boys and embraces with the girls, and a gift of slippers and an appreciative note that shewed they had enjoyed learning English 'by new methods'!

Having earned the necessary money, we made *Peregrine* ready for our onward journey, and set off North-west for Tabriz. We left warm Tehran under grey skies, past the Shahyad memorial arch *(illus.)* erected in 1971 in honour of the 2,500th anniversary of Cyrus, King of Persia who in the sixth century BC sat in state in the ancient city of Persepolis to receive tribute from emissaries from the many nations which he had united into his monotheistic Median empire. He, with representatives of these nationalities are so splendidly portrayed in carvings up the flight of steps to the State Apartments which I saw on a subsequent visit. We were soon in the desert, and among small ribbon development villages, where as usual, when fields were irrigated they were green and fertile. We saw the remains of many thoroughly smashed cars and lorries.

We went through Gazvin after collecting blue stones, and reached Zanjan by 1715, and heard the Imam at the mosque. We asked police where we could stay, and were told of a park at the end of the city. We drove along a valley between mountains which went a lovely gold-red colour in the sunset, throwing lights and shadows, while the mountains by the setting sun were a lovely purple blue, and there we found a quiet road behind these gardens, and turned in.

The next morning there was ice on the water standing in the road, warning us of things to come. *Peregrine* was slow to start, however we soon left Zanjan, finding ourselves by a riverbed with mountains fairly close. Poplars and willows were thick at the water's edge, the poplars were golden with a green fringe of leaves and silver stems, the willows were almost olive green by contrast. Sheep, goats and cows grazed under the trees where they were planted more thinly and the slopes of the mountains had strip farming. The river twisted and turned and over and over again we were met with lovely pastoral scenes, with gold, green and silver trees and sand colours in them, and the blue stone mountains like those in Tehran. Some of the mountains were covered in green shale, and others were reddish-brown. We were routed round a mountain instead of through a tunnel and this mountain had lovely colours in it, where water ran down, some patches were green and some grey, and some tomato coloured. Further on, the sandstone mountains had layers of chalk in them giving the effect of horizontal white stripes of varying thicknesses. The light and shade and shapes were so varied and full of interest. Then small volcanic shapes appeared, followed by copses of poplars.

We saw snow on oncoming lorries and soon we ran into it. It was thick and freezing and all of the mountains and fields were covered in snow as far as the eye could see, but we were told that the roads in Turkey were kept open all the year round, and that really bad weather should not start before the end of November. It became dark, then the sun and blue sky appeared and made a lovely contrast. We reached Tabriz and set about looking for an oil stove; we found the exchange part of the Bank was shut until tomorrow, but bought a stove for 240 rials. We found a garage for more anti-freeze, and three great tins were poured in . We drove on to a soldiers' complex and parked *Peregrine* in the officers' car park. Sergeants tried to get us to move, but a young officer said we might stay. The sergeant returned and remonstrated, then came a Captain, and finally we were allowed to stay. Three dogs came and barked, and the sentries chatted on their duty rounds.

We still had to nurse *Peregrine*, for I found the red mountains to our right were steep and snow covered at the top and had green trees at the foot, and beehive houses were about, most attractive under the blue sky. Mountains on each side, then a valley and poplar trees looked so beautiful in the sunshine. Then desert, and very flat land on every side, then intensively farmed land, fringed with walled plots with fruit and poplars, villages of adobe huts nestling on the South side of hills. Many sheep, goats and camels were about, and women were to be seen in brightly coloured clothes, or were washing in the rivers in the cold bleak wind, and with snow all around them.

We reached the mountain pass and suddenly ran into dense fog; eventually lower down the hill the fog cleared. We passed an overturned lorry with a driver covered with a cloth. When asked if we could tow the lorry from the carriageway we declined. We passed red and brown rocky land, snow covered and barren, with craggy rocks: a deep cut gorge with great boulders lying around. Is this an earthquake area perhaps?

We reached Makoo and found it small and strange. Houses seemed to be hanging from the side of a steep rock which shelters the town on the North and North-east side, along steep and narrow roads. It was primitive and remote, and in these conditions travellers rely on each other – two people told us about the condition of the roads in Turkey. News of the war was vague. USA and Russian supplies were said to be pouring in, while Great Britain and other countries were in a 'tizzy' regarding selling armaments to the warring countries, and to the other Arab countries. President Nixon said Israel must be supported in order to remain an independent state, so we were keeping an eye on developments, for there appears to be a fear of escalation in this volatile situation, with the possible participation of the great powers, and the use of nuclear arms.

Our last night in Iran was spent near to the foothills of the snow covered Russian mountains, with Mt. Ararat of Noah's Ark fame seemingly hanging in the mist.

8th October 1973—7th November 1973
Mileage: Iran—Turkey. Total 1,272

Alexander the Great

The Tomb of Alexander the Great in Northern Greece

Cyrus King of Persia c 559-529 BC, of the stock of Achaemenides, the dynasty of the Persian kings, founded his great empire with his capital Persepolis that stretched from the Mediterranean to the Hindu Cush. During his reign he adopted Zoroastrianism and a conciliatory approach to differing religions. He allowed the Jews to return to Jerusalem, with their beliefs, thereby earning the titles of 'The Shepherd' and 'The Anointed of Jehovah'.

Darius I c 548-486 BC, a Persian by birth, established Zoroastrianism as the organised religion of the Persian Empire. With his capital at Susa, his empire stretched from the Bosphorus to the Caucasus and the Indus. He was succeeded by Darius II who died c 405 BC, then Darius III who died c 330 BC.

Alexander the Great c 356-323 BC, a pupil of Aristotle, was son, heir and successor to Philip II King of Macedonia. He defeated the Persians led by Darius III and freed the Greeks from their subservience in cities in the Persian empire (Egypt, Syria and Mesopotamia) and restored to them their native institutions.

In c 331 BC he founded and established Alexandria and carried his conquests eastwards as far as the Punjab where he introduced Greek colonies: thereby spreading the Greek language and civilisation to the eastern world and becoming ruler over the largest empire known. He married Stateira, a daughter of Darius III at Susa on his return journey westwards. He had further plans for expansion, but these were never fulfilled on account of his sudden unexplained death 11 days after attending a banquet.

Turkey—Route Map

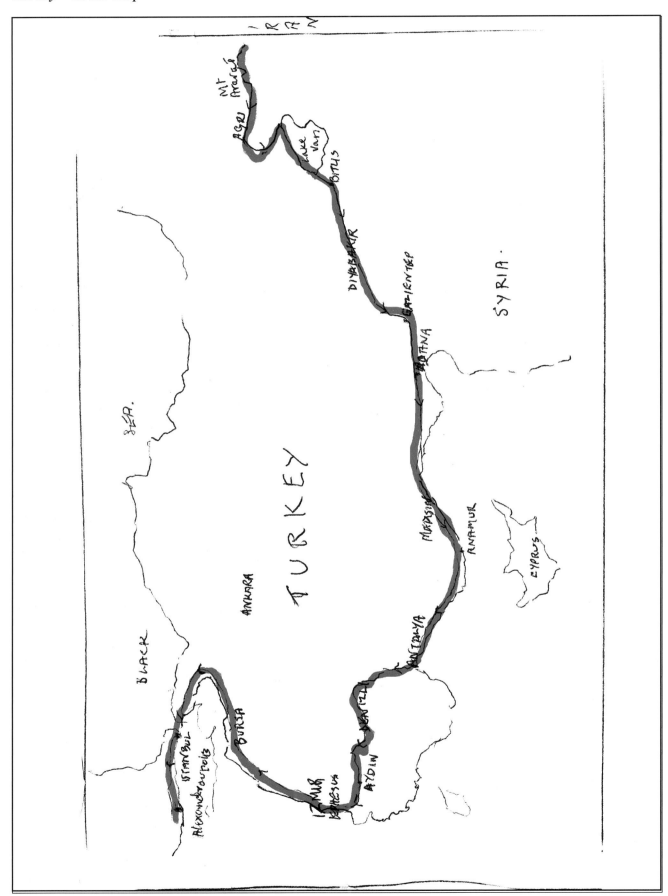

Chapter 9

TURKEY

We spent our last very cold night in Iran, with frozen water, near to lovely Mount Ararat, of Noah's ark fame. She was snow covered. We took our place among the great long queue of truckers and overlanders and badly smashed cars in the crowded Customs area, but on neither side did the officials look at anything. Amazingly we were through the Customs in one hour! Tourists on buses were busy clicking their cameras as we passed Mount Ararat and the lovely snow covered imperious mountains. The Turkish road was poor with only tarmac on the central piece, and petrol was in short supply. None was to be found at the bare little village of Dequbaya, nor at either garage in Taslicay itself, a dark little village with the villagers moving about, set in snow clad mountains with snow frozen trees, and houses grouped together. Donkeys were busy carrying wood and hay and even drawing a plough; oxen were also ploughing part of the snow-covered earth. Few women were to be seen, but some were washing in streams amidst the snow, clad in two layers (at least) of gaily coloured cotton, or in velvet with white wimples, which they sometimes pulled over their mouths and noses, for warmth or purdah? The sun was brilliant and the sky blue until about 3.30 when this gave way to mist and fog and freezing conditions.

We were glad to reach Agri and to find a garage where we filled up with petrol and parked *Peregrine*. It was very cold indeed when we took a turn in the village, and found several men eating freshly baked bread and drinking tea. All was very dark as the electricity had failed and there was little or no water. We got to bed in the extreme cold, and Helen woke me to listen to strange noises. In the morning we found the pipes had broken loose from the kitchen taps, the gaz had frozen, so had the automatic loo. Mercifully the little oil stove worked..

Both our watches had stopped in the freezing conditions but I had remained warm in my sleeping bag. We got up and I found the gas heater and lit that. The small gaz cooker worked so that we were able to have breakfast. Then to the serious business of getting *Peregrine* started. The oil had frozen in the engine. A French-speaking brother of the garage man visited us. Each man had a broad face, big moustache and big frame. They said for 50 lire they would get *Peregrine* going. I tried 30 lire and we settled for 40 lire. They arrived with a great pan of lighted charcoal and two tins, and they stood the charcoal pan on the tins and smoke filled *Peregrine* as the flames licked the sump and curled up the engine. In half an hour or so *Peregrine* was going, ticking over happily. What drastic treatment! The garage man drove *Peregrine* round the garage, pronounced the engine good, but the clutch and gearbox poor. Furthermore they said we needed chains. They checked the differential and gearbox and found satisfactory levels of oil in both; and off we went to Van, without chains on the icy roads.

We drove down the Merat Suye River valley where the river was frozen in its stiller parts, and the thistles and other plants were dressed in frozen snow. Yesterday we had seen a wood with snow in stripes down the trunks of the trees. Today there were fewer trees. The south facing slopes were terraced while the north facing slopes were barren. Now and then little hamlets nestled in sheltered corners. We left the river valley and made our way over and around the mountains to Patnos where we tried to get water from the garage, but since there was no electricity, the pumps were not working and there was no water. We saw boys with jerry-cans on yokes, and also women with pails, fetching water from a river. The temperature was very cold and great winds blew, but still the women washed in the streams in their brightly coloured dresses and white head coverings. We found a pump, and nearby a young woman in a blue dress was washing in what looked like hot water because it was warmer than the snow and was steaming in the sun! A grey fox crossed our path and stood at a safe distance watching us; I wondered what he could find to eat in those wild and barren mountains.

Shepherds led sheep and goats with a few donkeys from the hills towards the trees and villages from 3.25 pm or so, and were heralded by sea gulls that had flown north. Nature put on a wonderful spectacle for us as we reached the shores of Lake Van; the lake was calm and blue and had lovely reflections of the mountains in it, but more was to come.

Erna, a little point just east of Ercis, was surrounded by poplars and had a few houses and a cemetery, marked by single upright stones. We continued round the north shores of the east side of the lake and up into the mountains on the south-east side where the tiniest rainbow patch was in the sky, then as the sun began to sink, their peaks glowed pink. Great feathery clouds golden and ethereal, (quite like a Turner) greeted us then the sun sank lower and the sky reddened to a lovely scarlet crimson, powerful and fierce and threw its reflection into the lake which was a narrower strip just there. On our left the sky was a soft lavender mauve which reached through crimson to the deep focal setting sun, and ran off golden and red on our right. The mountains on our right were sharp and craggy in silhouette while on our left they were almost horizontal to the ground and covered with a generous coating of snow. We looked to left and right and were never disappointed. The splendour, grandeur and brilliance, the softness and featheryness, the intensity of it all was really marvellous, and the silver full moon was up to see it too.

In contrast, Helen thought she smelt fire and we found that part of the outlet manifold was red hot! We tried to tighten the controls but found the spanner was missing, as are the moped's keys and the water padlock and now my biro. Anyhow, we made our way into Van and spotted a great high garage greasing shed, and we asked if we might pull in there, and were graciously told in English that we might. *Peregrine* was attended to, and we were visited by the patron who, spellbound, sat on the back of my seat and took in the situation with us over a glass of vodka.

In the lovely sunny morning we had noticed the tracks of sheep and other animals by the side of the road and across the mountains – from whence had they come, yet where could they be going? We also saw the local women in hand-knitted white woollen stockings and coloured baggy trousers, and over this a red flannel petticoat and a plain or patterned one, or a green or blue velvet skirt striped with silver. Heads were covered in white wimples edged with green red or yellow stitching and their velvet sleeveless jackets were worn over plain or patterned blouses. Extra shawls might be thrown over and around the head and shoulders.

We needed to see about the outlet manifold, which we had found red hot again last evening. We were shown to a most efficient garage by a small boy. A young man at once knew what we needed, a new outlet manifold gasket. This we produced from our supplies, and in a few minutes all was fixed. Then he noticed a fracture in the outlet manifold which needed skilled and serious welding. Our nice curly-headed boy led me with the manifold to a specialist welder, who heated the whole manifold over a gas flame, then with a blow lamp soldered and welded it. At 17:00 all was finished but it was too late to re-establish it in the car. So we were stuck in the mud and melting snow while the men scrubbed up ready to leave at 17:30 on the dot. Already, men were playing backgammon in the local men's club while others were at billiards and yet others were in the restaurant.

We had to adjust our watches to new time, 05:30 when we heard folk about in the area; they made more noise than the cinema emptying at 23:00 the night before, and there were only about three women, the rest men, youths and boys already in their dark suits. Men opened up the garage at 06:30 and lit the fires inside and got ready for their elders to arrive at 07:00. 'Our' boy was bright and intelligent, with a sensitive face and a good command of the situation when on the job, in spite of being dressed as he was in torn trousers and an old greasy jacket frayed at the edges.

We breakfasted in *Peregrine* and stumped off to the museum. Still our curly-headed boy did not attend to *Peregrine* but to the front axle of a green police car. At 0840 he came and started, then the patron, unshaven and with his left eye more often shut than open, took over. By 0930 *Peregrine* was put together again, and off we went on a trial run. He adjusted the flow of petrol to the petrol pump, and *Peregrine* feels much happier and more powerful. The mechanic was greatly teased by his friends and employer on our return as I drove him to his garage. He says the noise at 40 mph is shock absorber noise. I wonder?

At 1130 we got off to Gervas. It was lovely – a vast circle of mountains in light and shade, with a view of the lake, including the sheep in the village by a pile of poplar poles. Then began a chapter of accidents. First the white ice container fell to the floor and broke its lid; then strange sharp noises followed by a bang caused by the exhaust which had burnt its way through the asbestos, and the spare wheel, and the inner tube had gone, and the tyre was burning. We moved it round after surveying it ruefully and drove on. Fortunately we decided to have another look to be sure the wind had not rekindled the burnt tyre, and found it was burning in another place. We decided to pull it up on to the roof, but it was extremely heavy. Two shepherds appeared from nowhere, and in a trice the tyre was up. Helen and I lashed it down and on we went to Gervas, where we hoped to find a boat to take us to the west of Lake Van, to Akdamar. The sun was lovely, the lake green and the blue mountains were snow covered. A lovely group of reeds was growing on the bank by the lake. The boat we were told would cost us 10 lire. When we got there they said 75 lire! No one went to the isle when we found it too expensive. A shapeless old woman was washing by the shore dressed in a white jersey and baggy trousers and with much on underneath. We found this old woman's cottage, with both the back door and the larder locked, but she had food stored in lovely brown 'biscuit fired' pots of various shapes, much as they must have been for years, and sold us what we needed.

We were accompanied back to *Peregrine* where men pointed out a right rear outer wheel puncture. Now we have no spares and one badly damaged outer covering. The local boy was splendid, and kept a lunatic dark haired man in a blue coat at bay. While a man messed about with the air pump etc., the boy mended the puncture and restored the punctured wheel to the spare rack and tightened the nuts on all the wheels. Off we went and saw the full moon with its gold and silver path on the lake, then on up the Bitlis Sinali, 1557 metres, a long climb, and the manifold was red hot again. The mountains were lovely in silver moonlight, with odd light in the valley. A solitary man was walking with two flocks of sheep, and only a few lorries and buses passed; there was very little sign of life. We saw conical dry stone buildings which were covered with adobe clay. Are they winter primitive fridges or store houses? The houses generally were flat roofed with piles of hay neatly stacked on top of the poplar poles that span the walls for the roof, with dung for internal firing pressed into rounds and often adorning the walls.

We were up in fairly good time after a good night, and bought petrol from a nice man who kept the boys at bay. We went to the port and looked over a ship and walked around the point. We reached the water's edge and found marble and the shiny obsidian that is used locally for its hard cutting properties. It was sunny and warm, and the snow was melting. We drove off into the snow-covered mountains and gradually there was less snow. Groups of poplars, then a river valley and a back road. A man and pony caught up with us, and was very annoyed that we had no cigarettes nor anything to give him. Mirrors broke loose, and we stopped to adjust them atop a hill with barren khaki sandstone rock formations stretching for miles.

We wound up and down the mountains, with tobacco growing in the valleys looking brown and forlorn. The road was really awful, but we enjoyed the waterfalls and a beautiful river, and saw square adobe houses with wooden 'Regency' window frames but no glass. Often clusters of these houses were atop the mountains, and some nestled on the lower peaks. Women in their brightly coloured full skirts were working with the men with goldy yellow turbans and baggy trousers, the crotch of which being almost at knee height. The view of the low peaked mountains in khaki green seemed endless. It became dark as we reach Diyarbakir, the ancient city on the banks of the Tigris, surrounded still by its imposing black basalt walls, second only in interest to the Great Wall of China. We estimated that the walls were perhaps still 60 ft. high and 8 – 10 ft. wide, with bastions or towers that stood at regular intervals.

We found one of the five monumental gateways, with a lovely Greek keystone in the key position above a 'shell' arch and a number of stones with bas reliefs of pictures of cats or tigers or birds, much in the Persian style. We saw texts in cuneiform and in Greek and Latin script, including an inscription revealing that Severus Septimus built the atrium and repaired the walls. Masons' marks and 'swastikas' featured, along with Roman brickwork, while the great tower was built in stripes of black basalt and yellow sandstone, standing out among the older similarly striped houses.

We were on the road, after shopping, by 1230, and away over the barren hills to Siverek, *Peregrine* was going well on the good road, though it was wet and raining. Some of the land was very stony with rocks bursting through: then lovely red soil, like Devonshire's, and huge ploughed fields, vineyards and busy villages.

As we had arrived in the dark, in the morning we were glad to find that we were in the old square, with a stone-built building on the corner with five arches and iron barred windows. A narrow lane revealed oriel windows and carved wooden windows opening on three sides of the lathe and plaster walls lining the stone-flagged roads. We were followed by children as we walked around. There was a wheelbarrow in the middle of the square with posts for its awning and a charcoal stove where vegetables were fried and put in narn, and sold to the youths and boys. A man came with lovely thick, well-made rush or pampas carpets 6 ft. square and 6 ft. x 10 ft. Long avenues of trees lead back to the main road. We saw an orderly queue of children, boys and girls, at the narn shop. By 0645 hardware, meat, material and vegetable shops were all prepared and open.

We passed olive groves, then olive, pistachio and walnut trees; then orange orchards and found men with oranges for sale in plastic bags, straight from the trees. Next came vines, cotton plants, some yet to be picked, then ground nuts. There were family gatherings in parts of the fields, where the nuts were laid out to dry. Also red things … chillies, perhaps. We stopped for water in the village. The tap did not work, but a young man organised boys to draw from the well for us. We gave him a lift to Adana, and we climbed the Taurus mountains and had superb views of the plains below stretching for miles.

We saw various curtain wall citadels on hill-tops, notably Gazientep, which we learned had been founded in the sixth century and rebuilt in the eleventh and twelfth centuries, and was currently being restored again.

We pressed on through Adana to Mersin, and on to the Mediterranean coast. It was interesting for me to recognise the many changes that had taken place along this coastal route. In 1965 I had driven from West to East: the road was then under construction, and I had had to wait for half an hour on one occasion for a bank and hedge to be removed before I could proceed on the gravel and dirt track road, and now in 1973 this was a four-lane tarmac road! Moreover many of the Graeco/Roman sites have been or were being restored and were now tourist attractions for guided tours, whereas in 1965 few were established with guides or even entry tickets! The climate seemed to be like that of California and persimmons were for sale and were decorating many a barrow. We were among the cotton and ground nut pickers, who had erected their tents on rough wooden frames and covered them with some hand-woven tarred coarse material or with plastic sheeting. We were told by a nice young man that we might stay near to his uncle's house, and to ask for anything that we might need.

In the morning we were near a field of groundnuts and saw sheep being escorted down a road, their many black feet were fast moving: their legs were so thin and delicate and their hoofs so soft that they passed almost noiselessly. They had horns and their flanks were covered with an extra coating, and they had broad flat tails for water storage, we learnt. Tractors painted blue or red were drawing carts with the family and shopping on board, including babes asleep, strapped to their mother's backs. Weights were carried on the back around here even if it was necessary to bend nearly double. Baggy trousers and cardigans seem to be the rig, with a white head scarf tied under the chin.

The land was fertile and flat from the foothills of the mountains out to the sea, cattle were grazing, little wooden framed 'tents' covered in polythene were dotted about and a patch of bright lime green broke the pattern of red brown earth and stubbly grass. The children coughed as they went to school or to their work. A black overall with white collar and white bows in the girls' hair was the local school uniform over trousers or stockings, so French looking. Small children with switches accompanied their fathers and the cattle. Voices carried and echoed from the mountains. All was busy but not rushed. The birds were speaking, and a bee had come into *Peregrine*. A truly rural scene.

The doctor cousin of our farmer host arrived, and told us that he had trained at Great Ormond Street Hospital in London, and locally had built a hospital with 75 beds, and a road that served 40 villages that enabled the villagers to be driven to the plains for winter, and to the mountains for the summer, instead of making the trek over several days with their camels. In consequence, those heavy dromedary camels were becoming fewer and fewer and will soon leave the scene altogether. We were given oranges, lemons and groundnuts, and we showed the doctor, the farmer and an architect brother over *Peregrine*. We were given breakfast, including hot milk from the house, and then, when we called there for water, and invited the ladies into *Peregrine*, we were shown their home.

We visited the ruins of Aspendos and scrambled onto a gallery platform and looked down at the 20,000 seats of the theatre, and the fine back stage wall with its two rows of 'palladian' doors and windows, the central steps down to the half moon orchestra with the spot for the altar still visible. After a good look over the wall again we walked through fir trees among the lily bulbs, other bulbs, small purple orchids, yellow flowers, a fine holly shrub, and the herbs. We peeped into the theatre from the ground floor level, and then went off to Perge. This we found in the throes of excavation with many capitals, pillars, and parts of sculptures lying around marked with numbers. We first went to the stadium said to have held 25,000 and found the arches like those at Jerash, and then went into the theatre. This was most elaborate with marble carved sarcophagus type seats with backs, the stage, and a beautiful doorway in marble decorated with diamond and lozenge shaped carvings. Similar treasures were being unearthed on the left side of the stage, such as a lovely little corner carving of a young boy supporting old age. We found more seat backs with open work marble for the senators. There were fifty tiers up to the 'dress circle' then forty-eight up to the 'gods' and several carved stones with Roman lettering or Greek characters. From the top we had a marvellous view of the Agora, the remains of the triumphal arch, pillars, the stadium with the mountains in the background and cotton fields all around before going on to Antalya, a lively bustling place.

We went via Denizle to Pamukkale, where there was a petrified waterfall and a great display of 'Mappin Terraces' much as those in Yellowstone Park, but here they curled and had left small 'walls' like a field awaiting irrigation, and stalactites and stalagmites were apparent. We found extensive unexcavated remains of a Greek site once known as Hieropolis, and saw some sculptures in the Gymnasium still in the hands of Italian archaeologists. We saw the Agora with its restored marble pillars and the very recognisable Greek theatre.

Turkey had so many Greek and Roman remains to care for, such as those we visited at Geyre and Aphrodisias, where olive trees, pomegranate trees, and poplars were growing in a valley by the river. A little bridge had a warm welcome notice to travellers, who were invited to rest and revitalise by the bridge and the stream. Among the fields we saw the walls of Aphrodisias, where a man and a woman and a donkey were working. We walked to the site along the Roman flagstones, between pillars with Corinthian capitals leading to the marble propylae steps, and from there looked for the temple of Aphrodite with its marble steps, so white, that led to the remains of a marble doorway with patterned lozenge and diamond shapes. These pillars were fluted, and had Ionic capitals. At the further end there was a lovely seated lion, with mane and tail, like an Egyptian lion.

We crossed a harvest field to an immense stadium with seating for 25,000: it was oval at both ends. Part of the wall remained with noticeable carved stones let in courses, with half size stones breaking the line, with the occasional stone vertical instead of horizontal. Was the circle we found on a stone with eight segments a mason's mark or a secret sign, of perhaps a freemason? We saw two Byzantine houses, one with a mosaic floor covered with sand for protection – fairly coarse tessera in blue, black and white. We found a Byzantine palace with black and white flooring. The white marble floor had hexagonal tiles with black diamonds at the corners. We uncovered three lots of mosaics in black and white, with blue and red figures of eight as a border, then an older design with a red centre and a border of triangles, with some blue and white, while the third had a rather indistinct interlacing design.

The apse of the palace was faced with marble and had the black and white floor leading through an arch to the private bathroom, marble faced, with a stove and the old drain pipes in situ. The two holes for drain pipes were like those at Knossos, larger at one end and narrower at the other, so that the water is forced through it.

The finish of the superb white marble Odeon, complete with its orchestra, has grand seats at the top and narrow regular steps decorated with lion's leg carvings. The stone pillars of the small Romanesque cold bath contrasted with the brickwork of the sudatorium, and the hypocausts and the hot bath that displayed the fine Greek inscription across it. The sweating chamber had its seat and now a pomegranate tree in the corner. The chief custodian joined us, and gave us some of the fruit. He had a moustache, blue eyes, and was a stocky figure in cap and dark blue suit, rather an amorous type, but found us pomegranates and herbs which refreshed us before we crossed the Agora, adorned with a Medusa's head and a bull's head, and found poplars gold with silver stems, growing among the pillars and lintels of the south end of the Agora. From there we went to the Acropolis and the theatre which holds 15,000. It was in a good state of preservation with eight or ten pillars back stage, and the back curtain wall behind them. We walked down the hill to the car park, complete with a water tap and lovely chenar trees giving shade, and found the sculptures and the museum, and saw a disused mosque with crudely coloured paintings. From there we had a pleasant view of the 'modern' village life, with houses that have red/brown and well weathered tiled roofs. The whole site was full of interest and detail and of a very high standard.

We went on to Nazilli, with olives along the old road and maples, pomegranates and poplars by the river. Then on to Aydin and found a nice old man who spoke Italian, and sold us vegetables and olives, and gave us chillies. A nice group of boys wondered what nationality we might be, and a boy with a limp who had worked in the tourist information centre last year, accompanied us to a shop, which helped us.

We went to Ephesus and the contrast between my 1965 visit and this visit was most apparent. In 1965 I drove into the site and down the Roman way towards the sea, with very few people about, while in 1973 car parking was controlled, tourists were in parties, and tickets were required at a site gate, both for visitors and for a camera! Furthermore, much reclamation work had been going on and I noticed that the amphitheatre had been built up, and the foyer steps have been found and reinstated. The Greek Agora was open with erected pillars, and the library was being rebuilt with 'Palladian' arches and overhanging areas supported on pillars. Later we learned steps will be provided. It will be a grand affair. The old Greek road to the sacred way bears on up past Hadrian's Temple and Trajan's fountain, which is also among the bigger buildings. Much reclamation work has been done behind these buildings, small roads that run at right angles to the top of the sacred way have been opened up, while the houses for richer Ephesians were now apparent. Excavations at the top of the hill were in hand, and work was being done on the Greek town hall. The Odeon looked a pretty poor thing after the exquisite one at Aphrodisias. In front of Trajan's bath now were houses with a marble road, and then the State Agora or market place. A reservoir was behind this, and pipes of varying sizes come from here, and were to be found all over the site.

In line with the reservoir we found some Byzantine houses in good repair, with internal walls painted and sometimes over painted. Sham marble at the bottom, with stencilled rigid floral designs in the bathrooms and rear rooms, but two lovely birds and a lively deer over a fireplace lower down in a living room. Floors covered with tessera and marble were now covered by a modern roof to preserve them while reed mats covered the paintings. We climbed down and in and really felt we were in a private house. Bathroom, fountain room, niche for Diana, and other rooms leading one from another. Green and a soft red were the predominant colours, with the birds and the deer in black. We found some more stones with circles upon them, divided into four, six and sometimes eight. We also found a peacock on a step at the top of the North side of the amphitheatre. We found signs of fish, the sign of a Christian, and PX. We found a marble slab with two large holes, and a space for something that must have slipped into those holes and rested there … an exciting time to experience a little of the thrill of archaeology before rebuilding occurs, and to imagine life in this important centre about 2,000 years ago from the evidence that is as yet undisturbed and in situ.

We went down the Roman road to the sea end and found that no new digging had gone on there. Rather the reverse, the grass had taken over, and no tessera were to be seen along the sidewalk: but the bull drinking troughs were there, and the little fountain and the bird on the column. We grubbed about a good deal and I found a pot handle with Greek writing on it, and Helen found a pawn, and we both found little bits of Roman glass. We returned to *Peregrine* and drove away up the hill and stopped by the stadium, which we found by accident. In the museum there we saw two great figures of Diana (the Goddess of Fertility) and of Artemis one in marble and the other in stone and with an extra 'crown'. How symbolic she is, with the signs of the zodiac and six sets of three different animals down her front, and two lions on each arm. She was beautiful yet forbidding, firm and unrelenting, standing there against a backcloth of blue. There were also mosaics, some bas relief and a bronze statue of Artemis, and a delightful boy on a dolphin, forever holding high his right arm, and just keeping his balance on the dolphin who, with curved tail, was in full motion. Socrates was depicted in bronze as a venerable cheery type, with beard and side whiskers!

On to Izmir to see about the car and to fill up with radiator and household water. Such a nice merchant seaman engineer was introduced to me, and he was quickly able to grasp our problem, and in a garage in a narrow lane efficient men removed *Peregrine's* inner cylinder and found the rubber gasket had perished. They skilfully cut another from thick rubber, reassembled it and fitted it, and would not receive ought but thanks. We wined the engineer, filled up with water, and went on our way to Izmir and parked by a pier and monument, with the permission of the police, and awoke next morning to the Imam's voice.

We found that Izmir was not expecting frosts yet, so drove on onwards Pergamum, round the bay and over the mountains, and down through vine and sugar beet country, and on to Asklipyon, which I noted had been considerably excavated since 1965. This Greek site was once a medical centre where the sick were psychologically assisted in their recovery as they walked along a subterranean passage to the tone of encouraging voices from above, and where blood disorders were expertly diagnosed and treated. New remains here are largely of Roman origin. There were olives and walnuts as Asklipyon neared, and the bazaar road had been excavated and pillars erected, showing signs of the small shops emerging from the grassy banks.

On such a pretty corner of Bergama, we found a Byzantine church ruin and a lovely octagonal building with cupola and glass lantern. We went on and up to the acropolis which has been much excavated by Germans. We parked *Peregrine* by a village tap and walked up the steep grassy hill, entered by the boys' gymnasium, then the city gymnasium, with remains of many pillars and beautiful pedestals, and we found six wash basins in marble. There were lovely shrubs growing from the old stones.

There were a number of Roman rooms at one end, part of a temple and at the other end, the washrooms. On a higher temple area, we were told that rites were performed especially for the women of Pergamum. We reached the walls of the citadel and went in; the temple area and the great deep amphitheatre were somewhat overgrown; but nearby we found the temple area and the royal palaces on the NE and NW of the citadel walls. The road went on and up, and there was more yet to be discovered. The recurring marks on the stones differed from those of Ephesus, as did the masons' marks from the gymnasium section.

We enjoyed again the grand view of the fertile plain and the ranges of mountains reaching back for miles. The sun set while we were there.

We had a poor start in the rain to Balikesir on a dreadful dirt road. The mirrors dropped off, we slithered in mud, the drawer dropped out of the desk, and it was bitterly cold. The tarmac road we had been promised did not materialise. We saw the children being driven to school in trailers behind tractors. We went through agricultural villages, including one distinguished one, and on round the lake to Bursa; there we got on to a better road and stopped sliding in the mud.

At Bursa we saw some of the old houses that were now being pulled down and replaced by concrete flats. We passed many sugar beet lorries rather than the cotton lorries of yesterday, many

Ephesus

The Main Street

Roman Arch

Hadrians Temple

The Basilica

Turkey and Italy

Arches at Pergamum

Farmer's Wife near Pergamum, South Coast (W)

Sarcophagus at Aphrodisias

St. Clare's Church—Assissi

Selcuk and Istanbul

Fatima Mosque—from University Tower

Selcuk—Basilica St. John

Santa Sofia

Roman Aquaduct

Reflections

Those Wonderful Vernal Falls →
Yosemite Park, California

Safely home in 'one piece'!
complete with many lovely
and unforgettable memories.

were lined up all along the road waiting their turn at the factory. Olive trees were showing a fringe of new growth and the brighter green leaves gave the trees a look of velvet; we passed walnut and olive, peach, cherry trees, cotton fields, and many men and a few women ploughing in a biting wind, but the sun was lovely and hot. We saw lambs in a field with daisies and dandelions out – in November!

We reached the Sea of Marmara, blue and beautiful, but next morning, we awoke to rain, then snow. The traffic was heavy, and a bus from Austria was trying to overtake everyone. Later we saw it had skidded off the very slippery road. Mercifully still the right way up. Just short of Istanbul the snow turned to rain, then stopped, and the sun came out and lit up the Bosphorus for us as we crossed on the splendid new suspension bridge.

We parked in the suburbs, with the Church of Santa Sofia and the Blue Mosque in the distance. There was a very cold biting wind and flurries of snow as we drove to the Police HQ, and were allowed to park there amidst trees, with a lovely view of the sea and such splendid peace and quiet.

We awoke to a grey cold morning, and set off to the Tourist Information office, and were provided with maps of Turkey and Istanbul, and books on Turkey and Bursa. A helpful man directed us to the Zicaret or trade bank, where we changed our dollars for lire, and armed with this wealth we made our way to Santa Sofia. It had been cleaned up, the Constantine crowning area was roped off and the mosaics were difficult to see without field glasses, they are so far away. But the saints on the North side of the clerestorey are distinguished and good.

We went on to Topkapi and in the treasury we saw the fine bow and arrow holders; and the gilded arbour of Sultan Ibrahim, and the tiles of Izmik lined the circumcision room. The china in the kitchens was superb: Chinese bowls in celadon and blue and white and lovely mustard yellow. The kitchens were interesting too, with their chimneys and brick fires and their huge pits and trays, spits and ladles, equipment for 500 meals daily and 4,000 for festivals!

Next day the sunrise was gold, red and deep blue, with a high wind and the sky changing every second. We went into the Blue Mosque, and on to the Archaeological Museum and found Alexander the Great's sarcophagus on the ground floor, with pictures of battles between the Persians and Greeks on one side, and a lion hunt on the other. Alexander was shown in a corner, with broken hand and foot – when whole, he must have had a bow and arrows. This sarcophagus, originally coloured, had beautifully carved lions at the corners. We saw oil lamps and pots and small finds from various sites, and rows of Roman heads, also bronze life sized figures of Zeus and Poseidon, and a head of Janus with two faces, one looking into the past and one into the future.

There was a lovely dawn the next morning, pink and gold stealing across the sky. The Bosphorus was still rough with spray and a keen wind. Ships were chopping about, and steamers were having to manoeuvre against the wind. We took the coast road around the walls, and out into the intensively farmed land, where we heard farmers get two or even three crops a year. Horses were pulling single furrow ploughs, but tractors were also ploughing. Seed was sown by broadcasting, donkey sacks were slung over a shoulder and seed thrown from the front white bag; or seeds were released from the tractors, with a man standing on the back. Also at the same time, there were signs of harvesting and winnowing using a lovely long wooden fork. This appeared a most satisfying performance. Boys were in charge of smallish flocks of sheep, white with thick coats – all hurrying along.

Much colour washed reinforced concrete surrounded the new houses, motels and camp sites, prepared for the summer tourists. A set of four lovely bridges that used to carry the old road may now be seen to advantage from the new road. We shopped in Tekirdag, and reached the customs by 1725 and were through both by 1800: no one looked at anything.

Greece rewarded us with a peaceful sunset with a glowing peach blush which spread over miles of flat country. When the sun went down it was both cold and dark and this seemed to reflect our personal situation, for although on Monday 26th November we had reached Adrianapolis on our way home from a world trip and all was peaceful on the border, at the Customs as we crossed to Greece from Turkey we heard on our radio that there was shooting in Athens in Omonia Square, and that the streets were being patrolled by armoured cars and tanks. This news, on top of the recent reports of the Middle Eastern war, and the resulting rises in the price of oil and petrol, caused us to feel cut off from home in a way which we had not experienced even when were in far off Nepal or wild Afghanistan.

Our plans and arrangements which had until now worked out well were going astray. We were in any case short of money and *Peregrine* covered only 10 miles to the gallon at best. Petrol had been 15p per gallon in Iran and Turkey and now we learned it was 60p. per gallon. Life was not going to be easy. We counted up our stores and our remaining £s sterling and USA $s, and calculated that Athens, where we have friends, was over 1,000 miles away, and we were due there in two days' time...could we make it?

7th November 1973—25th November 1973
Mileage: Turkey—Greece. Total 2,351

Chapter 10

GREECE

We were in Greece and we awoke to the sounds of cocks crowing, pigs grunting, and turkeys chortling on the roof and warily watching us. The village church with a small dome, whitewashed and seemingly cared for, had a great stork's nest on top of the dome, large and tidy for once. Cyprus trees, black and straight, surrounded a cemetery on the hillside and shed a lovely calm all around. The young couple who are teachers in an infants' school were soon off in their fawn VW and we were left with the delightful delicate farm cart. A white pig was led out to the field, a stake was put in and his bowl of food put down; the pig fell to with a will and kept returning to the bowl in the hope of finding more. He was overjoyed when a hot second helping was brought him! A turkey cock with tail in a fan was in command of eight lady turkeys and ruled them with a flick of his red gullet, keeping them in a ring round him, while he strutted wherever he liked. Shades of Animal Farm and of the male domination in this part of the world!!

Our onward journey took us past tall poplars growing in groups and making elegant delicate patterns and designs amidst the fields, some of which showed evidence of strip farming. Up a great hill and then down to the beautiful and historic Kavala with its Byzantine castle dominating all from the acropolis. We found the fine aqueduct superficially looking Roman, like the Pont du Gard, but according to the guide book it is C17! As we drove up the pine clad hill with an old monastery in a commanding position on the top, we came upon running water at a fountain provided by the Romanians of Kavala for passers by. We filled our tank and kettle.

We left the plains and climbed to a good height and looked down on the fertile agricultural plain, and soon reached Thessaloniki and most fortunately reached Aristotelou Square and the British Council Building. We called in to find out about conditions in Athens after the coup, and saw a Greek, a doddery old man who reluctantly left his typewriter, spoke indifferent English and churlishly asked us if we had noticed unrest in Thessaloniki. He told us the Greek Bank could get us money in a day or two, and he was generally unhelpful. Oh for the British Consul in these parts!

We thought to sell the moped, and so cleaned it up and wrote a ticket for sale, trying for Dr.6,000 as new ones fetch Dr.9,000. We found a man who wished to buy it and followed him to Customs. He was a 40 year old, in tight fitting jeans and jacket, unshaven, but lithe and on the spot. Alas, the Customs said it was unlawful to buy or sell? so that was that. Meantime we were too late for the Bank. But we did manage to drop in to S. Sophia and saw its lovely dome, and martyrs, and a Christus, before going on to S. Georgius, the rotunda church, for which we had to pay Dr.5. Constantine used it as a chapel and Theodosius caused the lovely mosaics to be used to decorate it. All around the central clerestory Roman houses were depicted with 'preachers' in toga, chasubles in purple and white, and traces in the apse of the risen Christ with the twelve disciples, birds and bread in baskets and leaves decorate two of the other altars' domes, and a geometric design is over the opening. The whole building is built in brick with tall and elegant walls supporting the Roman arches, the curve on the inside and the curve of the arches and the dome o'er topping all presents a fine balance, and a most satisfying piece of architecture. Spaces in the supporting walls break an otherwise overlong plain wall. Each altar had a marble low screen with carved birds, crosses or representational carving. Lovely. We found postcards of the church of Saint Nicholas with the twelve martyrs and its wall paintings or frescoes. The sun shone, and we had skuds of rain. We needed money, and so tried to sell a movie film but none of the five shops wanted to have it; then we tried to sell a tape, but no luck.

On we went to Larissa, where we had to pay Dr.20 toll, and again Dr.15 to get from Larissa to Lamia. Money was running very low, and we will have to wire for some from Lamia tomorrow.

We saw Mount Olympus was snow covered and wild, with soft grey and white clouds half shielding her from human sight. The colour of the trees, often poplars, was golden and glorious. A new moon appeared, and an evening star, as we passed Olympus and drove up the vale of Tembe.

Next morning we checked our petrol and judged we could reach Lamia, and off we went, through olive groves with their new growth making the trees look like velvet with dark and light sheen. Lovely peeps of the blue sea and across the Pagassitina Bay to the broken coastline of Evia. We reached Lamia at 1015 or so, and found the folk friendly. A lame man moved his invalid motor and ushered us to a good parking spot just by an orange tree, with an orange looking in through our window!

The square was white and dotted with these bright trees. We visited the Bank Manager who said we should ring or telegraph London and await a telex reply, to have money sent from Athens. The manager was grey-haired and graciously lent his telephone for the Athens call. He was housed in a raised glass box behind a great desk, and customers acknowledged him, or waited to speak with him, and the employees constantly referred to him, but he found he could do nothing for us.

The petrol was holding up well, which was lucky, as we had no money; so we drove on through vines, peach groves, olive trees and arable farm land, with red earth, until 1300, when we turned off to Atlanta through olive groves and reached the Bank at Bis. We were told that it was officially closed, but we were ushered to the Manager's box and I put our problem to him, and produced a cheque book and card and my passport. The Manager was young with sandy red hair and a moustache, and had a rather obstreperous assistant who spoke more English than he. We waited to hear our fate. The Manager said 'You are British'? and I replied 'Indeed yes' then a nod between the two men, a playful smile from the Manager, and he most kindly offered us Dr. 500. I offered surety for the money, but surety was not considered necessary, as we were British. So I agreed to restore the sum to him on the morrow, and he jotted down my name from my British passport, and the assistant wrote me the name and address of the Manager in English, and he gave me his card for insertion in my visitors book.

Our faith in human nature restored, we went to the olive groves and celebrated by having tea, and watched the pickers, and saw a nice old man with grey hair and blue laughing eyes piling olive branches on his donkey, while his wife was sitting on another donkey with panniers of olives. They were so busy they did not at first notice us, and when the wife and donkeys went on, he came to examine *Peregrine*. It was sporadically raining, and rained hard as we sped on our way down the National road to the toll booth, where we were asked for Dr.4 Helen persisted that we only had 20cs and we were given a Dr.20 ticket! We drove on to Thive and there bought petrol Dr.450 and found our way to Kifissia and our host for the night. Our host and hostess gave us a great welcome, provided a delicious meal and we talked till 02:30 am!

Our hostess brought orange juice next morning, and lent me her car so that I could drive to the Bank and send off Dr.500 to the Bank at Bis, since her husband had now lent me funds. Helen mercifully came with me, as we several times got lost, but eventually found the Bank and how to drive the Renault, and with the aid of a garage man, where to find the windscreen wipers, for it was pouring with rain.

We visited the National Archaeological Gallery and enjoyed the Mycaenaean room, which had been rearranged: and found the jockey had been mounted on a huge horse, and was far less impressive for he seemed too small, and can no longer be seen so well, for the horse was at eye level and above. *(Illus: Jockey from earlier record)*. We particularly enjoyed a temporary exhibition of finds from an island that probably had a volcanic eruption, an earthquake and a tidal wave, which, coming so soon one after the other or even almost simultaneously, destroyed the civilisation at one blow. Was this a story of Atlantis, the land between Turkey and Greece which sank, leaving just the mountain tops as islands?

The amount of gold in the Mycaenae gallery is tremendous; the bullcups, the cream jug, the funerary coverings, the masks, and suits for royal babies, the belts, sword hilt decorations, jewellery rings and chains of leaves for jewellery, the tiny buttons and so much more. Then fragments of the warrior pot with helmeted soldiers, staves in hands. Oh that the rest might be found! The lovely restrained brass figure of Apollo from the Piraeus, the first large bronze to be hollow, C6 BC, I think. Then Poseidon, strong and active, bearded and nude, and the stele of the three floodlit in a corner.

We discussed alternative ways of getting home because of the petrol crisis, perhaps on a ferry across the Adriatic etc.? Lorna kindly put through a call to Lloyds for me, and the Manager has agreed to forward £126, though my account has little in it.

Silencer problems had to be sorted out, and I found that a nut was required to support the exhaust pipe. A garage man fished about and found a nut and soon fixed it. He was a dour heavy fair-haired slow-moving man, who changed to a dirty overall jacket for the job. I asked him 'How much'? and he replied Dr.100. I imagined he meant 100 lepta and got out the purse. He looked at me pityingly and fumbled for a Dr.50 note. Even this meant the job was 17s.6d. or so for one nut. So I still looked incredulous and produced a Dr.5 bit, 3s6d. or so, and he then said he would receive nothing. Do the Greeks think women are quite without any monetary ability?

We left *Peregrine* by the park, and went off to the Acropolis: on and up, we passed the lovely temple of the winds, and a newly excavated corner of the Roman Agora, the small Byzantine Church and the ancient agora with its newly erected stoa, where the row of small cottages used to be. We looked again at the lovely North marble door of the Erectheum, and enjoyed Mount Lycabettus, the temple of Jupiter, Hadrian's Gate, the 'new' stadium, the temple of Dionysius, and the Odeon with Atlas supporting the stage.

We gazed at the mountains and the sea with an aircraft carrier and ships, grey and dark in the glinting sea, and at the islands and the smoke rising with the light behind it, and at the roofs of the older houses with their dun red coloured tiles, and at the bright little restaurants on the roof tops. It became cloudy, cold and blustery and we made for the museum, only to be told it was shut; so we returned to our hosts.

We awoke on 1st December to a clear sky and steady sunshine, and got busy cleaning *Peregrine* and filling up with water, and tried to find our route and petrol from the Touring Club of Greece. News from England included very expensive goods and petrol coupons, and houses in London wildly expensive to buy, £100,000 for small houses with tiny rooms and sloping roofs. We took an active part in making new plans for our onward journey, for we learned that not only is petrol very expensive but in very short supply, with restrictions of 200 miles per car per month in the UK. Moreover, there was snow as far South as Larissa and chains must be used for driving in Northern Greece. Furthermore, Egypt had broken off talks with Israel because she said Israel had not kept her side of the cease fire bargain. The Watergate affair was even more unsavoury, and twelve of the President's staff have now been indicted for criminal offences. The power of the President was weakened by all this and his relations with congress were less firm. Accusations were levelled at the secretary concerning the erased 18ft. of tape. All most distressing. North Vietnam had infiltrated into South Vietnamese waters, and high-jacking had become a disease. In England, coal miners were on strike, along with brewery drivers. Electricity was rationed and there were cuts each day causing traffic light problems.

We helped to prepare for a day out at Daphne and Ratsarrari. Percy was up earlier than was his custom! We found a nice young man and dark haired German type woman in charge of Daphne. Free entry today. The impact of these C12 mosaics was as strong as ever. The Pantocreator in the dome, book in left hand and intelligent sensitive face, with short beard and dark moustache, and the crucifix against a gold background had free flowing blood from the chest wound and stigmata to counteract the theory that our Lord did not die on the cross, that was current at the time. The hand movements in the doubting Thomas scene of Our Lord with the 11 disciples.

The lovely nativity scene shone out, with the virgin in her gold Byzantine 'dream bag', the babe in a gold-lined crib, St. Joseph sitting a little apart, in front on the right. The shepherds were crowding in from outside back right, while the angels were watching and protecting from gold flooded hills and plains on the left, the ox and ass were close to the crib with heads only, but they were there to work and carry and wait for the cross, and the ride into Jerusalem. Our Lord was depicted for once oversized, because of His dominating power on His earthly triumphal passage towards the Jewish capital and stronghold. There were several fragments of priests in white with gold on black crosses on their stoles and the betrayal by Judas with the soldier, the disorganised crowd, the jealous avaricious old men contrasting with the calm of the Christus, already strengthened and assured through his close relationship with the Father.

The lovely baptism scene of the naked Christus standing waist deep in the clear blue water that passes across his body, with St. John the Baptist stopping his work with the Jews from Jerusalem for a minute to give his full attention to the Christus. The unobtrusive dove and the symbol of the angels above this. The story was bursting through the Byzantine specifications for the decoration of churches. The somewhat indistinct wall paintings are to be found on the lower walls of the church and in the narrow chapels that flank the main altar. It is a gem of a church. The building itself is complete and satisfying, and outside the cloisters and the castellated wall contrast with the tall cypress tree. Alas, it was cloudy with soft rain, so the colours were less bright than they can be.

Off and through Athens with the Parthenon just merging into the sky. Few cars were on the road because of the petrol economy, only those with even numbers may be out today. We drove to sacred Mount Hymetos, famous for its herbs, wild flowers, trees, and the old times, and up and up a very narrow road which was stiff with parked and moving cars in spite of the overcast sky and the rain. The Wildlife Society has become interested in reafforestation of the area and others in preserving the lovely wall painting in the church of circa C16 C17, including the especially lovely painting of the Palm Sunday ride on a 'green' donkey. Percy gave me a book on the monastery and the wild flowers with lovely pictures. So with those books there could be more to write of the plane trees, the ram's head, the spring behind the marble panel worn by the many who have drunk at the fountain, the bath, the cloisters, the bread oven and the refectory with the low entry arch for the monks who in humility bowed under it as they entered for food. We enjoyed the smell of the herbs, the wild cyclamen, the wild cucumber at Daphne, the rain, the steps and walks, the promise of the other churches and ruins to be rediscovered on the side of this hill sacred to Zeus. The view of the rigid new university buildings, coherent and utilitarian, make a big contrast to the sheer beauty and balance, peace and tranquillity of Kisriani where Socrates sat and thought.

Awoke at 0500 and heard the 0600 news. An overcast morning with rain in the night, but it looks more hopeful for today. I heard that my £126 had arrived, so we packed and got *Peregrine* ready, and I gave an Anthuria plant with dark green leaves and an orange waxy flower, with the hope of more to follow, to Lorna, who had so kindly filled our larder. Off we went at 1100 and bought Dr.1,000 of petrol and left *Peregrine* at the garage and went by bus to get our boat tickets.

After further repairs to *Peregrine* and gaz for heating and cooking we took the old road to Corinth. We saw the canal after we had stopped off the road by a river that opened into the sea just east of Corinth. Drove into Corinth and stopped by a restaurant right on the water, before going off on the moped to AcroCorinth. The moped did well, taking both of us, then one of us, then just itself — guided with me on foot. The top of the mountain was shrouded in cloud. Corinth on the Gulf of Corinth was lit in brilliant sunshine with the sea so blue and so clear, every pebble and its colours shining through the water with great clarity.

The country was planted with olives, vines, orange and lemon trees and small cypress trees around the new network of roads that have sprung up. Thyme and sage and sweet smelling herbs surrounded the mountains. Some of the mountains were rugged and bare with outcroppings of rock, while the land to the North was rolling and fertile, with mixed farming. The five and a half Doric columns were still standing, and further digging had exposed ships' planking and the Agora. We went round the site on our journey up the hill. A low hotel restaurant had been built outside the site, and a long 'barn' inside the first gate which alas, prevented one seeing the second gate from the first. They are well designed and built of the old stones, still the view is spoilt: the marble and granite stones and pillars now horizontal form the steep path once used by donkeys and ponies. Such lovely rocks were to be seen on the way to the top, including one patch near the top of deep brown and nearly red, green, khaki, and light brown, all within ten yards or so.

We visited the little Byzantine chapel painted so white on the outside with its Consecration Cross on the South wall, and a lovely Byzantine slab let sideways into the wall. This church was still used, it has lovely stones on the floor, and a collection of indifferent icons and pictures of clergy, yet it is a dear little church. We went up to the ancient walls and looked down on the great sweep of land, the road and the blue gulf of Corinth and the houses of New Corinth pinked in the evening sunlight. The top of the mountain was covered in cloud, and so there was no advantage in going further. We found remains of a place of worship with marble pillars on its East side. One of these was interesting, with a very faint inscription marked on it, but overgrown with lichen and difficult to read. There was evidence of living dwellings in rows on a rather narrow road. As we returned we admired the pillars inset in the walls for strengthening the gateways, and the triple wall of defence.

From Acra Corinth we looked down on olive trees like grey-green balls on stalks, on vineyards, on factories, on oil storage tanks, and nearer at hand on two butterflies who were gold brown in colour, and having such fun with each other, and seeing that a larger admiral or tortoiseshell did not appropriate their pitch in the temple atop the mountain. Men and women sang in the valley, and the sound wafted clearly to the top, so also did the noise of traffic on the new National Way. A lone fair-haired German boy in jeans with yellow sailing mac came and sat by the pillar and gazed at the superb view. The walls are said to be the finest in Greece, ten feet high and built often from the sheer rock, of stone with tiles let in. The Venetians, the last owners, destroyed all the old buildings. I wonder if anything will be discovered if they dig? We met three Greek girls cutting the young dandelions to cook as a vegetable, said to be very good for the stomach. We collected mint and a strange tree-type herb with mauve flowers. A noisy quartet and child filled the ancient site with chat. It may always have been a noisy place, for all sound seems to be trapped within the walls.

We drove down on the moped and were among the small whitewashed houses with their vines, geraniums, oranges and olives so typical of the Peloponese, and found such friendly folk here. We enjoyed the snow-capped mountains visible from AcroCorinth and also the snow on the mountains North of the Corinth Gulf. The pink light of the sunset reminded me of the wondrous sunset near Lake Van, especially because the Gulf was such a lovely blue.

A gale was getting up in the morning, and soon great waves were splashing over the quay side. We moved and got head on into the wind and saw the spray from waves 15-20ft high as they hit the boulders. The church behind us was lit up in three tiers with the light pouring out of the red and green slit windows. The sky was midnight blue, and the sea dark streaky grey with much movement.

We found no police on the route as we drove along the old coast road to Patras, rather than the new National Toll Road. We went through pleasant small villages where men and women were collecting olives, oranges, lemons and grapefruit. The citrus fruits were put into coloured plastic containers, blue, orange and yellow, and stacked by the side of the road. Gone here are the full skirted women with their head scarves. There seemed to be many more folk around and the cottages were built in a plot of land which generally had a well-laden orange or tangerine tree by the front door. Bamboos fringed the road and sometimes there were eucalyptus or gum trees, or date palms, and where the rocky mountain protruded, there were just a few olives and firs. So often branches of the olive trees were cut off and the olives collected from them. We saw just a few donkeys carrying the branches, straw etc. Water seemed to be 'laid on' for there were few pumps or taps and no-one was to be seen carrying water.

For some miles we had been very near the South coast of Northern Greece and could see snow-capped mountains, though we missed the mediaeval forts: but we mounted the twelve flights of sixteen steps to the Acropolis of Patras, where there was a locked Frankish castle. Patras has some lovely houses and squares, one with two fountains and 'winged' lions at its base and Pan at its top. In the museum a nice mosaic frieze of wrestling men, and above, rather 'wooden' women attired in red-browns, black and white. Many heads and some small sarcophagi. We saw the opera house and other good Palladian type buildings, now dwarfed by the tall concrete flats and offices, but there was a wonderful view from the top of the mountain of the Gulf of Corinth, with a nearby town decorated with lights for Christmas, silhouetted against the mountains of Northern Greece.

We waited for ages, and the ship came in at 1035 or so, and we did not board her until 0130. Great numbers of cars and articulated TIRs came off, and then the queue started driving on. A sudden rush for the exit, police and Customs, which seemed to be a mere formality, perhaps because it was after midnight before we boarded the 'Mediterranean Sea'. This boarding was enlivened by the antics of a drunken TIR driver and a stupid policeman: a briefcase was thrown to the floor by the green sweatered driver, who next threw out the mats from the car, and got underneath the truck. The Captain, Purser and a senior Customs man with other folk came to see what was what. We drove on board and left them to sort things out.

As we got into position, water rushed out of the pipes from both bulkheads, and we thought we should need Wellingtons to wade ashore! The torrent stopped and the water drained away and we were escorted into a lift to the Purser's office, where we left our passports in exchange for a slip of paper, and were shown to our cabin. This trip is costing us £90 but saving us about £80 and the drive over snow-covered mountains. We were able to land in Corfu and walked to the fine Orthodox church, with its dome in splints. It is dedicated to St. Andrew who traditionally brought Christianity to the island.

I had tried to open my window when I awoke, forgetting that I was in the upper bunk of the 'Mediterranean Sea'. We visited the dark green carpeted bridge and found a tall bored Second Officer in a dark blue polo neck sweater, and later we met the Paymaster Captain, a multi-lingual man who though guarded in his remarks, did let fall that the Greeks had hoped 'things' that is, the state of inflation and the control of their lives would be better after the coup, but 'things' were worse. It seemed the shopkeepers, expecting a rise in prices, were holding on to their goods and everyone was hoping to make money as prices were rising.

After two days at sea we landed at Ancona and a brilliant sky and sun greeted us. We learnt first that we should put our watches back one hour, and then that driving was not permitted because it was a festal day, neither would it be on the morrow, because it was a non-driving Sunday. Our hopes of getting to Ravenna were dashed. We went for a walk, passing the old port gates, up to the late C17 cathedral which was under repair. We found lovely C17 squares and houses in the Palladian style, some also under repair: we were told that there had been an earthquake here within the past three years. We found it so strange to hear no cars moving, with only buses and bikes and roller skates on the road.

On Monday 10th December we set off along the road by the sea and found great breakers coming in: we were in intensively farmed market gardening country with cabbages, brussels sprouts, and strawberries and persimmons which were growing by the houses. Plastic sheeting was in use to protect the vines and plants against the prevailing winds. We stopped at Classe, and saw again that lovely old church with the good Shepherd story so beautifully carried out, with sheep walking up the great round arch, and sheep in rows in the apse with groups of plants and flowers and the Christos in chasuble in the centre. Alas, it was in the hands of restorers, but it was good to see something of its glory, including four evangelists and the pantheistic cross at the top of the arch. There is a dignity and beauty of this great old church, with its roofed and arched campanile and its walls built of handmade mellow pale fawn/red bricks.

On to Ravenna and darted in and out of several buildings, St. Appollonare Nueva, to see again the procession of 21 women, behind the active three wise men each with a crown, and with especially gorgeous stockings. Their movement had both urgency and reverence as they approached the Madonna and child, flanked by four angels. The South wall has its procession, 24 men in chasubles with crowns leaving an ornate castle with curtained loggias, to offer themselves and their service to the seated Christos, flanked by four angels.

On we darted and by chance took a good route through lovely colonnaded and arched squares, with buildings painted yellow ochre or old rose. All so very dignified and complete. We found St. Francis' church and a plaque telling us that Byron and English friends had given money for the restoration of the square. This church was small and intimate and had the feel of one that had been continuously used. Three men were making intensive preparations for a Christmas crib, with a screened off platform. Candles were burning at altars and two women moved about. Then to the Duomo with its fine pulpit carved in marble with seven sets of birds and animals. Doves, deer, quails, and at the bottom, fish. We found ourselves by the Baptistry at 1650–chiuso at 1700! Rang the bell at No.2. We were met by a large and powerful housekeeper woman who said 'No go'! But a nice slight younger woman in a black coat and dressed to go home, had the key, and we paid 100 lire for the light, and 50 lire each and were in for five minutes! There was the Christ in the water with an old and naked man, with a satisfied John the Baptist pouring water over Christ, and the dove in position. A really lovely and revealing mosaic, which included the twelve apostles surrounding the central figure. The light clicked off. Our kind guide was raring to go, and well satisfied, we returned to *Peregrine* and drove off to Ferrara for the night.

We heard that petrol coupons were to be had from the Italian Automobile Club, and there we decided to apply for petrol coupons for our two days in Italy. It was very cold and the water was freezing. We drove out into intensively farmed countryside, with lovely farm houses, like small chateaux, so often built with one side of the roof elongated to cover a farm wagon, or for use as a barn. We passed many fruit trees and many square miles of vineries, with the vines espaliers. Fruit trees were red topped, golden or bare. Walnut, cherry, peach, apricot, apple etc. Also sprouts, cabbage and grain. Hooped wood covered with polythene was in use for the early vegetables, lettuce and the like. Some hoops were covered but mostly they were still bare. Gradually the mountains became higher and nearer. We crossed the Po River this morning near to Ferrara and the Adigo, and followed this river valley North from Verona to Bolzano. A stop at Trento to have more anti-freeze and gear box oil put in at a Fiat garage. The brakes were in need of repair, but would have been too costly in terms of time and money at this juncture.

As we drove into the mountain region North of Trento we came upon frost and snow-capped mountains, and snow lying on the dirt roads. The sun cast a lovely red blush over the little sky we could see and struck and lit the marble face of a mountain top, giving it a golden glow. We saw evidence of white grey and gold reddish marble in great chunks at the factories ready for carving, cutting, polishing and sale. The shops were all agog for Christmas, with much coloured paper and well displayed goods which seemed pretty expensive. Verona, a city of fine gateways and a sturdy

C17/C18 wall, and the promise of grace and style, but sensibly the through road skirts the outside of these walls and leaves Verona in a degree of peace.

We were told that petrol was cheaper here than in Germany. We reached a barrier en route to Innsbruck and were asked for a large toll payment; then we went over the highest road pass in Europe to Innsbruck and up the side of a hill towards Garmische. We were told at Mittenwald to go to Klais, and tried unsuccessfully, as *Peregrine* was too high to go under a railway bridge. We found another road to Klais and Elmau through lovely snowladen fir tree and mountainous country, and found Gasthaus Elmau, a friendly homely spot with everyone enjoying the warmth of a green tiled German heater. Oil for cooking and heating and water heating was being conserved. We were welcomed by tall and grey-haired Ingrid, and Ingrid showed us around her house, prepared for 40 guests for Christmas! Helen and I went off for a walk past snow-laden trees and the dear little chapel, with its Christmas tree that is lighted up at night. We saw the large rectangular schloss that holds 250 guests. We walked through paths with the swept snow piled 2ft or 3ft high at the sides, under a blue sky. This was a veritable fairyland.

We worked out our route homeward and heard that no travelling was permitted on Sundays in Germany, petrol could still be bought at about 10s.6d. a gallon. We then visited the chapel with the C8 ceiling painting of the Virgin being offered a crown by Our Lord, with the Father assisting and the dove of the Spirit in attendance: blue, pink and old gold predominated, along with a brass sanctuary lamp.

We left the comfort of Elmau with the roads covered in about a foot of snow, and with difficulty found the autobahn to Munich. The sky was mostly grey-white, and snow, sleet or rain accompanied us most of the way. By 1800 in a near blizzard we turned off at Mulhausen and found a high wall behind which we sheltered.

Apart from the autobahn we found the roads snowy, icy and slippery, but managed to reach Munchengladbach and there found a good spot sheltered by two walls at the end of a disused car park, near a railway station. We were grounded because of the petrol scare.

We were allowed to drive on Monday but perhaps because of the cold the connections in the battery were loose, giving no juice to the starter. We put that right, and off we went to discover there was no movement on the speedometer and fearsome noises came from the brakes. Each of the two things righted themselves, and off we went to the Dutch border and autobahn to Eindhoven. The rain dispersed the snow and we reached Waalre, and my cousin Charmian and her husband, Nico, soon after 11:00a.m. as arranged!! We were given a great welcome and champagne, before Helen left for her train to Amsterdam where her family was due to meet her.

I stayed with these cousins for Christmas and until 30th December, and returned to my home at midnight on 31st December 1973 to fulfil an undertaking I had given to a very trusting official who, against all the rules, had forwarded to me, the necessary 'tax disc' for *'Peregrine'*, without the required MOT Certificate, on the understanding that I would be back in Saxtead by the end of the year ... ...
I just made it ... !!

7th November 1973—25th November 1973
Mileage: Alexandropolis—Patras Total 760

25th November 1973—31st December 1973
Home via Italy, Germany and Holland, Mileage: 1,251

Greece, Italy & Home—Route Map

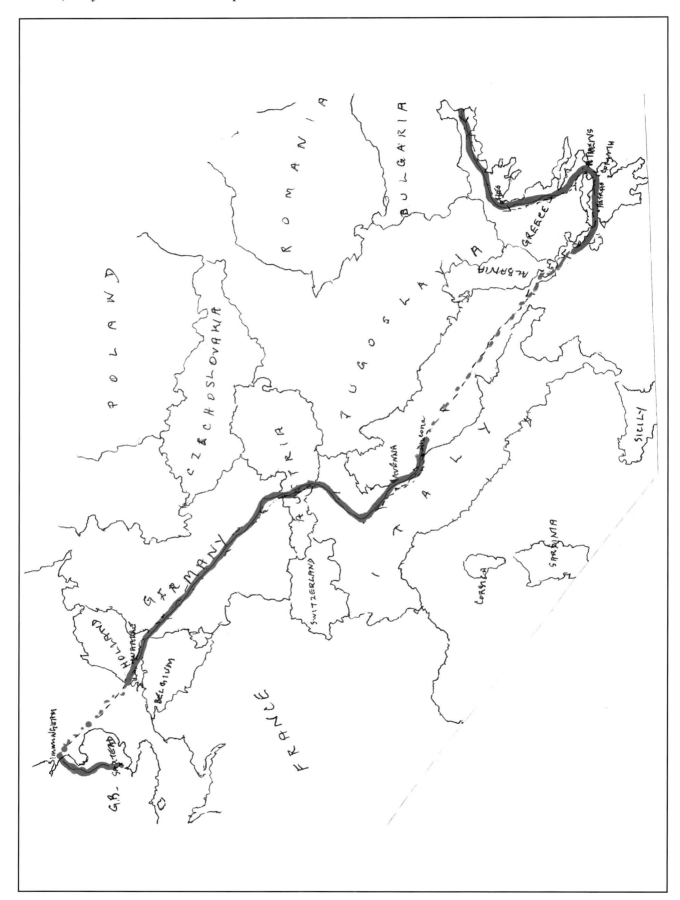